1 · 9 · 9 · 9

STOCK · TRADER'S

ALMANAC

BY YALE HIRSCH

THE HIRSCH ORGANIZATION INC. • 184 CENTRAL AVENUE • OLD TAPPAN NJ 07675
WWW.HIRSCHORGANIZATION.COM

Editor/Publisher: Yale Hirsch
Production Coordinator: Elizabeth Ross
Associate Editor: Jeffrey A. Hirsch
Page Layout and Design: Brendan M. Stewart
Data Coordinator: Scott Barrie
Director of Research: Robert Cardwell

The *Stock Trader's Almanac* is an organizer. It puts investing on a business basis by making things easier.

1. It is a monthly reminder and refresher course.

2. It updates investment knowledge; informs you of new techniques and tools.

3. It alerts you to seasonal opportunities and dangers.

4. It provides an historical viewpoint by providing pertinent statistics on past market behavior.

5. It supplies every form needed for portfolio-planning, record-keeping and tax preparation.

For several years prior to the publication of our first *Stock Trader's Almanac*, we collected items from financial columns, books and articles that pointed to seasonal tendencies in the stock market. It occurred to us that these intriguing phenomena should be thoroughly researched and arranged in calendar order. So we did it! We also examined various investment, record-keeping forms and found some hadn't been updated for 20-30 years. Others were so cumbersome they were beyond anyone's patience. So we designed new and more practical forms.

We are constantly searching for new insights and nuances about the stock market and welcome any suggestions from our readers.

Have a healthy and prosperous 1999!

This symbol signifies THIRD FRIDAY OF THE MONTH on calendar pages and tells you to be alert to extraordinary volatility due to expiration of equity and index options and index future contracts. Triple-witching days appear during March, June, September and December. See "Revelations From New Investment Research" on page 112, item #4.

The bull symbol on calendar pages signifies very favorable trading days (see pages 64, 66, 80, 114, 120 and especially 134) near the ends and beginnings of months, before holidays and around Thanksgiving and Christmas.

This Thirty-Second Edition is respectfully dedicated to

Sheldon Jacobs

A friend and colleague for more than twenty-five years,
Sheldon is also the editor and publisher of the
No-Load Fund Investor in Irvington-on-Hudson NY,
which provides the best single source of information
on no-load funds.

INTRODUCTION TO THE
THIRTY-SECOND EDITION

It is with a great feeling of celebration that I introduce the Thirty-Second Annual Edition of the *Stock Trader's Almanac*. I am pleased and proud to have brought significant and useful information to investors over the years. This edition, I hope, continues in that tradition.

J.P. Morgan's classic retort when questioned about the future course of the stock market was, "Stocks will fluctuate." This remark is often quoted with a wink-of-the-eye implication that the only prediction one can truly make about the market is that it will go up, down, or sideways. Many investors wholeheartedly believe that no one ever really knows which way the market will go. Nothing could be further from the truth—as Almanac readers well know.

During the past thirty two years I have made many exceptionally accurate forecasts in the *Stock Trader's Almanac*. These forecasts were based on thousands of hours of research into recurring patterns. I learned that while stocks do indeed fluctuate, they do so in well-defined, often predictable patterns which recur too frequently to be the result of chance or coincidence. However, giant bull markets can and do alter well-established patterns, as we have seen in recent years.

The Almanac is a practical working tool. Its wealth of information is organized on a calendar basis. It alerts you to those little-known market patterns and tendencies on which shrewd professionals maximize profit potential. You will be able to forecast market trends with accuracy and confidence when you use the Almanac to help you understand:

1. How our quadrennial presidential elections unequivocally affect the economy and the stock market—just as the moon affects the tides. Many investors have made fortunes following the political cycle. You can be certain that money managers who control hundreds of millions of dollars are also political cycle watchers. Sharp people are not likely to ignore a pattern that has been working like a charm this century.

2. How the passage of the Twentieth Amendment to the Constitution fathered the January Barometer which has a super record for predicting the course of the stock market each year and a perfect record in odd-numbered years since 1937.

3. That there is significant market bias at certain times of the day, week, month and year.

Even if you are an investor who pays scant attention to cycles, indicators and patterns, your investment survival could hinge on your interpretation of one of the recurring patterns found within these pages. One of the most intriguing and important patterns is the symbiotic relationship between Washington and Wall Street. Aside from the potential profitability in seasonal patterns, there's the pure joy of seeing the market very often do just what you expected.

> As we approach both a new century and a new Millennium, there are two factors that lead me to believe 1999 could be another major Dow gainer. No pre-presidential election year has lost ground in 60 years. Ninth years of decades also have an excellent track record despite two big losers, 1929 and 1969, which were both post-election years. Prospects are best if the Dow cools somewhat during 1998's last half.

THE 1999 STOCK TRADER'S ALMANAC

CONTENTS

DIRECTORY OF TRADING PATTERNS & DATABANK

STRATEGY PLANNING AND RECORD SECTION

1999 STRATEGY CALENDAR
(Option expiration dates encircled)

	MONDAY	TUESDAY	WEDNESDAY	THURSDAY	FRIDAY	SATURDAY	SUNDAY
JANUARY	28	29	30	31	1 JANUARY New Year's Day	2	3
	4	5	6	7	8	9	10
	11	12	13	14	(15)	16	17
	18 Martin Luther King Day	19	20	21	22	23	24
	25	26	27	28	29	30	31
FEBRUARY	1 FEBRUARY	2	3	4	5	6	7
	8	9	10	11	12	13	14 ♥
	15 Presidents' Day	16	17 Ash Wednesday	18	(19)	20	21
	22	23	24	25	26	27	28
MARCH	1 MARCH	2	3	4	5	6	7
	8	9	10	11	12	13	14
	15	16	17	18 ♣	(19)	20	21
	22	23	24	25	26	27	28
	29	30	31	1 APRIL Passover	2 Good Friday	3	4 Easter
APRIL	5	6	7	8	9	10	11
	12	13	14	15	(16)	17	18
	19	20	21	22	23	24	25
	26	27	28	29	30	1 MAY	2
MAY	3	4	5	6	7	8	9 Mother's Day
	10	11	12	13	14	15	16
	17	18	19	20	(21)	22	23
	24	25	26	27	28	29	30
JUNE	31 Memorial Day	1 JUNE	2	3	4	5	6
	7	8	9	10	11	12	13
	14	15	16	17	(18)	19	20 Father's Day
	21	22	23	24	25	26	27

Market closed on shaded weekdays; closes early when half-shaded.

1999 STRATEGY CALENDAR
(Option expiration dates encircled)

MONDAY	TUESDAY	WEDNESDAY	THURSDAY	FRIDAY	SATURDAY	SUNDAY	
28	29	30	1 JULY	2	3	4 Independence Day	JULY
5	6	7	8	9	10	11	
12	13	14	15	(16)	17	18	
19	20	21	22	23	24	25	
26	27	28	29	30	31	1 AUGUST	
2	3	4	5	6	7	8	AUGUST
9	10	11	12	13	14	15	
16	17	18	19	(20)	21	22	
23	24	25	26	27	28	29	
30	31	1 SEPTEMBER	2	3	4	5	SEPTEMBER
6 Labor Day	7	8	9	10	11 Rosh Hashanah	12	
13	14	15	16	(17)	18	19	
20 Yom Kippur	21	22	23	24	25	26	
27	28	29	30	1 OCTOBER	2	3	
4	5	6	7	8	9	10	OCTOBER
11 Columbus Day	12	13	14	(15)	16	17	
18	19	20	21	22	23	24	
25	26	27	28	29	30	31 Boo!	
1 NOVEMBER	2 Election Day	3	4	5	6	7	NOVEMBER
8	9	10	11 Veteran's Day	12	13	14	
15	16	17	18	(19)	20	21	
22	23	24	25 Thanksgiving	26	27	28	
29	30	1 DECEMBER	2	3	4 Chanukah	5	DECEMBER
6	7	8	9	10	11	12	
13	14	15	16	(17)	18	19	
20	21	22	23	24	25 Christmas	26	
27	28	29	30	31			

PROGNOSTICATING TOOLS AND PATTERNS FOR 1999

Almanac readers in most years have profited from being able to predict the timing of the Political Market Cycle. To help you gain perspective in 1999, a pre-presidential election year, a valuable array of tables, charts and pertinent information are presented on the pages noted:

THE NINTH YEAR OF DECADES

Graphic presentation reveals "nine" years are great years, except post-election 1929 and 1969. All other "nine" years were up during the past twelve decades, though war-torn 1939 was down sharply in the first five months before recovering with a small loss at year-end. *Page 16.*

THE INCREDIBLE JANUARY BAROMETER
ONLY THREE SIGNIFICANT ERRORS IN 48 YEARS

Since 1937 the January Barometer has compiled a perfect record in all odd-numbered years and a very good one in the others. *Page 20 and 28.*

MARKET CHARTS OF PRE-PRESIDENTIAL ELECTION YEARS

Individual charts for the century's last 21 pre-presidential election years. *Page 32.*

PRE-PRESIDENTIAL ELECTION YEARS: NO LOSERS IN 60 YEARS

Graphic presentation of pre-presidential election years along with the pre-presidential election year record since 1915. *Page 36.*

DOW COULD GAIN WELL OVER 3000 POINTS
FROM ITS 1998 LOW TO ITS HIGH IN 1999

An average gain of 50.0% has been recorded since 1914 between the Dow's midterm low and its pre-presidential election year high. *Page 76.*

PRESIDENTIAL ELECTION/STOCK MARKET CYCLE

Stock prices have been impacted by elections for 166 years, gaining the most in the pre-presidential election years. *Page 139.*

1998 NOVEMBER/DECEMBER

MONDAY
 30

*The mind is not a vessel to be filled
but a fire to be kindled.*
— Plutarch

TUESDAY
 1

*If anyone out there has a dream,
I'm living proof that dreams come true.*
— Kim Basinger, on receiving an Academy Award
for her role in *L.A. Confidential*

WEDNESDAY
 2

*From time to time there appear on the face
of the earth men of rare and consummate
experience, who dazzle us by their virtue, and
whose outstanding qualities shed a stupendous light.*
— Jean de La Bruyere, 1688

THURSDAY
3

*The greatest good you can do for another is
not just to share your riches, but to reveal to him his own.*
— Benjamin Disraeli

FRIDAY
4

*We are made to persist.
That's how we find out who we are.*
— Tobias Wolff, *In Pharoah's Army*

SATURDAY
5

SUNDAY
6

BEAT THE DOW WITH ONE ARM TIED BEHIND YOUR BACK

A simple system any investor can use to outperform the market was presented in the book *Beating the Dow*, by Michael O'Higgins and John Downes (available from us at $8.00, 20% off the cover price, plus $4.95 shipping).

TEN HIGHEST YIELDERS

Investing in the ten highest-yielding Dow Jones industrial stocks at the start of each year between 1973 and 1997 produced a cumulative total gain of 6,558%, an 18.3% annual compounded return. The Dow average of 30 industrials during this 25-year period gained 2,042%, or 13.0% annually.

FIVE LOWEST PRICED

Choosing just the five lowest-priced issues among the ten highest yielders each year resulted in a 11,813% total return, equal to 21.1% per year.

SECOND LOWEST-PRICED

Remarkably, picking one Dow stock each year, the second lowest-priced stock of the ten highest yielders, did best of all, a 35,402% return, or 26.5% a year.

Isn't it amazing that you can beat the Dow from within, using a few of its own components? However, to rely on just one stock can be dangerous in some years.

A SIMPLE BEATING-THE-DOW SYSTEM (1973-1997)

	Total Return	Annual Return
30 Dow Jones Industrials	2,042%	13.0%
10 highest-yielding Dow stocks	6,558%	18.3%
5 lowest-priced of 10 high yielders	11,813%	21.1%
2nd lowest-priced of 10 high yielders	35,402%	26.5%

THREE WEEKS EACH YEAR AVERAGE 4.8%
THAT'S A COMPOUNDED ANNUAL RETURN OF 122%

Want an interesting way to average 4.8% for a particular three-week period every year? Investing in the five worst Dow losers in the two weeks prior to the last trading day in December and getting out on the fourth trading day in January has produced the 4.8% return over the past 22 years.

BEATING THE DOW NEWSLETTER

For a FREE copy of the latest monthly *Beating the Dow* newsletter, published by the Hirsch Organization, send a stamped, self-addressed envelope to: Beating the Dow, P O Box 2069, River Vale NJ 07675. Or, if you prefer, fax your address to 201.767.7337 or email it to sample@beatingthedow.com.

DECEMBER

Decembers after congressional elections usually fare well.

MONDAY
7

*Women are expected to do twice as much as men
in half the time and for no credit.
Fortunately, this isn't difficult.*
— Charlotte Whitton (1896–1975)

TUESDAY
8

*If there were only one religion in England there
would be danger of despotism; if there were two,
they would be at each other's throats; but there are
thirty and they live in peace and happiness.*
— Voltaire

WEDNESDAY
9

*Nothing gives one person so much advantage
over another as to remain always cool and
unruffled under all circumstances.*
— Thomas Jefferson

THURSDAY
10

*In this game, the market has to keep pitching,
but you don't have to swing. You can stand there
with the bat on your shoulder for six months
until you get a fat pitch.*
— Warren Buffet

FRIDAY
11

*Ninety-nine percent of what most people see
on television about business is not only
irrelevant, but possibly damaging.*
— George W. Goodman (a.k.a. Adam Smith)

SATURDAY
12

SUNDAY
13

BEING AN EARLY BIRD IN DECEMBER IMPROVES YOUR BEATING-THE-DOW PERFORMANCE

Outperforming the stock market by investing in the ten highest-yielding Dow industrial stocks, known as the "Dogs of the Dow," at the start of each year has produced numerous Dow-beating unit trusts and mutual funds.

An investment stampede occurred in recent years to use this Dow strategy to outperform the stock market. All the major wire houses now have unit trusts that each year enable investors to take advantage of the superior returns garnered by the selection of Dow stocks over the Dow's performance as a whole. In addition, there are several mutual funds that utilize this Dow strategy.

Each year around the last trading day, a number of money managers and brokers and thousands of individual investors religiously purchase a portfolio of the ten Dow stocks. Consequently, billions of dollars in Dow strategy portfolios handled by money managers are reshuffled in tandem near the last trading day of the year.

The table reveals a superior strategy to beat these money managers at their own game, using the five lowest-priced of the ten highest-yielding Dow stocks. December's Dow point and percentage changes for 26 years are shown in the first section of the table. However, the next section shows that December lows usually come far earlier than the year-end close.

It seems wiser to make investment decisions utilizing the Dow strategy earlier in the month—most likely, the first week. Over the last 13 years (1985-1997) the Dow on December's first trading day was 2.4% lower than the last. The strategy of buying earlier obviously has an enormous performance advantage over the long term. Of course, on the occasions a bear market strikes, one's short-term performance could suffer.

DECEMBER DOW INDUSTRIAL CHANGES

	Nov Close	Dec Close	Point Change	% Change	December Low Day	December Low Close	Next Year's % Change Five Stock Strategy	Next Year's % Change What The Dow Did
1972	1018.21	1020.02	1.81	0.2%	21	1000.00	19.6%	—13.1%
1973	822.25	850.86	28.61	3.5	5	788.31	— 3.8	—23.1
1974	618.66	616.24	— 2.42	—0.4	6	577.60	70.1	44.4
1975	860.67	852.41	— 8.26	—1.0	5	818.80	40.8	22.7
1976	947.22	1004.65	57.43	6.1	2	946.64	4.5	—12.7
1977	829.70	831.17	1.47	0.2	20	806.22	1.7	2.7
1978	799.03	805.01	5.98	0.7	18	787.51	9.9	10.5
1979	822.35	838.74	16.39	2.0	3	819.62	40.5	21.4
1980	993.34	963.99	—29.35	—3.0	11	908.45	0.0	— 3.4
1981	888.98	875.00	—13.98	—1.6	29	868.25	37.4	25.8
1982	1039.28	1046.54	7.26	0.7	16	990.25	36.1	25.7
1983	1276.02	1258.64	—17.38	—1.4	15	1236.79	12.6	1.1
1984	1188.94	1211.57	22.63	1.9	7	1163.21	37.8	32.8
1985	1472.13	1546.67	74.54	5.1	2	1457.91	27.9	26.9
1986	1914.23	1895.95	—18.28	—1.0	31	1895.95	11.1	6.1
1987	1833.55	1938.83	105.28	5.7	4	1766.74	18.4	16.0
1988	2114.51	2168.57	54.06	2.6	2	2092.28	10.5	31.7
1989	2706.27	2753.20	46.93	1.7	20	2687.93	—15.2	— 0.4
1990	2559.65	2633.66	74.01	2.9	3	2565.59	61.9	23.9
1991	2894.68	3168.83	274.15	9.5	10	2863.82	23.2	7.4
1992	3305.16	3301.11	— 4.05	—0.1	16	3255.18	34.3	16.8
1993	3683.95	3754.09	70.14	1.9	1	3697.08	8.6	4.9
1994	3739.23	3834.44	95.21	2.5	8	3685.73	30.5	36.4
1995	5074.49	5117.12	42.63	0.8	20	5059.32	26.0	28.9
1996	6521.70	6448.27	—73.43	—1.1	16	6268.35	20.5	24.9
1997	7823.13	7908.25	85.12	1.1	24	7660.13	?	?
						What $1,000 grew to:	**$119,229**	**$21,422**

14

DECEMBER

Chanukah

MONDAY
14

*Follow the course opposite to custom
and you will almost always do well.*
— Jean Jacques Rousseau

TUESDAY
15

*It's amazing what you can achieve when
you don't care who gets the credit.*
— Tubby Smith, Coach
University of Kentucky
Champion basketball team 1998

WEDNESDAY
16

*When talking to company presidents,
a stock analyst's job is to separate the doers
from the bluffers.*
— Anonymous

THURSDAY
17

*The history is clear: when incumbent presidents
avoid a primary, they win. When they don't, they lose.
And nothing scares off a challenger like money.*
— George Stephanopoulos

FRIDAY
 # 18

*Achievement is largely the product of steadily
raising one's levels of aspiration and expectation.*
— Jack Nicklaus, *My Story*

SATURDAY
19

SUNDAY
20

THE NINTH YEAR OF DECADES

Excluding the Crash of 1929, the bear market of 1969 and the small loss in pre-World War II 1939, all other "nine" years were up during the past twelve decades. Being a pre-presidential election year and the year before the Milennium will be bullish for 1999, unless the market runs up too much in 1998.

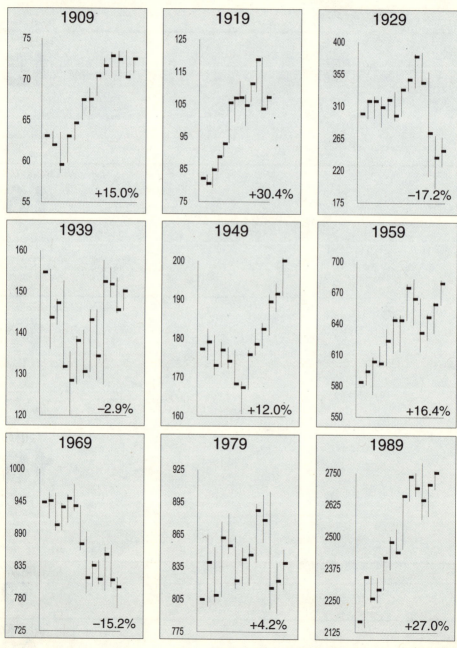

Based on Dow Jones industrial average monthly ranges and closing prices

DECEMBER

MONDAY
21

*Every time you influence another person to do
better you benefit him and increase your own value.*
— Napoleon Hill

TUESDAY
22

*I do not believe in the collective wisdom
of individual ignorance.*
— Thomas Carlyle

WEDNESDAY
 # 23

MURANY & MURANY   4 HRS ✓
PC Law Setup
General Ledger Accounts

*I must convince myself that the CEOs of the
companies in my portfolio are credible and
telling the truth.*
— Fred Kobrick, Kobrick-Cendant Capital

THURSDAY
24

*If you put a small value upon yourself,
rest assured that the world will not raise the price.*
— Anonymous

**Christmas
(Market Closed)**

FRIDAY
25

The sun shines not on us, but within us.
— John Muir

SATURDAY
26

SUNDAY
27

20th Amendment made "Lame Ducks" disappear
Now, "As January goes, so goes the odd-numbered year."

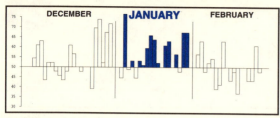

JANUARY ALMANAC

JANUARY						
S	M	T	W	T	F	S
					1	2
3	4	5	6	7	8	9
10	11	12	13	14	15	16
17	18	19	20	21	22	23
24	25	26	27	28	29	30
31						

FEBRUARY						
S	M	T	W	T	F	S
	1	2	3	4	5	6
7	8	9	10	11	12	13
14	15	16	17	18	19	20
21	22	23	24	25	26	27
28						

See Market Probability Chart on page 125.

❑ As January goes, so goes the year (pgs 20-30) ❑ Greatest concentration of turndowns since 1949 occurred in month's first six trading days ❑ January Barometer since 1937 has a perfect record in predicting odd-numbered years ❑ More Dow points gained than any other month ❑ Low-priced stocks beat quality in early weeks of year ❑ Worst five Dow stocks average 4.8% gain in the last two weeks of the year through the fourth trading day of January over the last 22 years.

JANUARY DAILY POINT CHANGES DOW JONES INDUSTRIALS

Previous Months	1989	1990	1991	1992	1993	1994	1995	1996	1997	1998
Close	2168.57	2753.20	2633.66	3168.83	3301.11	3754.09	3834.44	5117.12	6448.27	7908.25
1	H	H	H	H	H	H	H	H	H	H
2	—	56.95	−23.02	3.58	—	—	—	60.33	− 5.78	56.79
3	−23.93	− 0.42	−37.13	29.07	—	2.51	4.04	16.62	101.60	—
4	33.04	−13.65	− 7.42	—	8.11	27.30	19.17	−20.23	—	—
5	12.86	−22.83	—	—	− 1.35	14.92	− 6.73	7.59	—	13.95
6	3.75	—	—	− 1.35	− 2.71	5.06	16.49	—	23.09	− 72.74
7	—	—	−43.32	4.70	−36.20	16.89	—	—	33.48	− 3.98
8	—	21.12	−13.36	− 0.89	−17.29	—	—	16.25	−51.18	− 99.65
9	5.17	−28.37	−39.11	5.59	—	− 6.06	−67.55	76.19	−222.20
10	− 6.25	−15.36	28.46	−10.07	—	44.74	5.39	−97.19	78.12	—
11	13.22	10.03	2.73	—	11.08	−15.20	− 4.71	32.16	—	—
12	15.89	−71.46	—	—	1.89	− 1.68	− 3.03	−3.98	—	66.76
13	3.75	—	—	−13.86	− 1.08	− 6.20	49.46	—	5.39	84.95
14	—	—	−17.58	60.60	4.32	24.77	—	—	53.11	52.56
15	—	−19.84	6.68	12.30	3.24	—	—	−17.34	−35.41	− 92.92
16	− 1.43	23.25	18.32	− 8.95	—	—	23.88	44.44	38.49	61.78
17	−10.00	−33.49	114.60	15.43	—	3.09	− 1.68	−21.32	67.73	—
18	24.11	7.25	23.27	—	3.79	N/C	− 1.68	57.45	—	—
19	0.36	11.52	—	—	−18.92	14.08	−46.77	60.33	—	H
20	− 3.75	—	—	−10.95	−14.04	7.59	−12.78	—	10.77	119.57
21	—	—	−17.57	−30.64	11.07	22.52	—	—	40.03	− 78.72
22	—	−77.45	−25.99	32.42	3.79	—	—	34.68	−33.87	− 63.52
23	−16.97	14.87	15.84	−29.07	—	—	− 2.02	−27.09	−94.28	− 30.14
24	38.04	−10.82	24.01	6.04	—	− 1.69	− 4.71	50.57	−59.27	—
25	9.46	−43.46	16.34	—	35.39	−17.45	8.75	−26.01	—	—
26	25.18	− 1.81	—	—	6.75	12.66	− 1.01	54.92	—	12.20
27	31.79	—	—	7.83	− 7.56	18.30	−12.45	—	−35.79	102.14
28	—	—	− 4.95	31.53	14.86	19.13	—	—	− 4.61	100.39
29	—	− 5.85	8.16	−47.18	4.05	—	—	33.23	84.66	57.55
30	1.25	−10.14	50.50	19.90	—	—	−25.91	76.23	83.12	− 66.52
31	18.21	47.30	23.27	−21.47	—	32.93	11.78	14.09	−10.77	—
Close	2342.32	2590.54	2736.39	3223.39	3310.30	3978.36	3843.86	5395.30	6813.09	7906.50
Change	173.75	−162.66	102.73	54.56	9.19	224.27	9.42	278.18	364.82	−1.75

18

DECEMBER/JANUARY 1999

MONDAY
 28

*Keep away from people who try to belittle
your ambitions. Small people always do that, but the really great
make you feel that you, too, can become great.*
— Mark Twain

TUESDAY
 29

*Two advertisements:
"Free trip to Disneyland.
Driver needed to deliver new car from New York."
(Got 3 responses.)
"Drive free from New York to Disneyland
delivering new air-conditioned Cadillac."
(Got 103 responses.)*

WEDNESDAY
30

*The Edison Company offered me
the general superintendency of the
company but only on the condition that I would
give up my gas engine and devote myself to
something really useful.*
— Henry Ford (1922)

January Barometer perfect record in odd-numbered years.

THURSDAY
 31

*Establish a no-excuses environment
and watch your productivity and earnings soar.*
— Jordan Kimmel, Private Money Manager

**New Year's Day
(Market Closed)**

FRIDAY
1

*To see a World in a grain of sand
and a Heaven in a wild flower
Hold infinity in the palm of your hand
and eternity in an hour.*
— William Blake

SATURDAY
2

SUNDAY
3

THE INCREDIBLE JANUARY BAROMETER
ONLY THREE SIGNIFICANT ERRORS IN 48 YEARS

Since 1950, the January Barometer has predicted the annual course of the stock market with amazing accuracy. Based on whether Standard & Poor's composite index is up or down in January, most years (excluding four flat years 1970, 1978, 1984, and 1994) have, in essence, followed suit—43 out of 48 times—for an 90% batting average. However, there were **no errors in odd years** when new congresses convened.

January performance chronologically and by rank is shown below. The top 28 Januarys (except 1994) had gains of 1% and launched the best market years. Twenty-one Januarys were losers or had miniscule gains. Only one very good year—1982— followed a January loss. Of the three significant errors 1966, 1968, and 1982, Vietnam affected the first two.

AS JANUARY GOES, SO GOES THE YEAR

	Market Performance in January				January Performance by Rank			
	Previous Year's Close	January Close	January Change		Rank		January Change	Year's Change
1950	16.76	17.05	1.7%		1	1987	13.2%	2.0%
1951	20.41	21.66	6.1		2	1975	12.3	31.5
1952	23.77	24.14	1.6		3	1976	11.8	19.1
1953	26.57	26.38	− 0.7		4	1967	7.8	20.1
1954	24.81	26.08	5.1		5	1985	7.4	26.3
1955	35.98	36.63	1.8		6	1989	7.1	27.3
1956	45.48	43.82	− 3.6		7	1980	6.7	25.8
1957	46.67	44.72	− 4.2		8	1961	6.3	23.1
1958	39.99	41.70	4.3		9	1997	6.1	31.0
1959	55.21	55.42	0.4		10	1951	6.1	16.5
1960	59.89	55.61	− 7.1		11	1954	5.1	45.0
1961	58.11	61.78	6.3		12	1963	4.9	18.9
1962	71.55	68.84	− 3.8		13	1958	4.3	38.1
1963	63.10	66.20	4.9		14	1991	4.1	26.3
1964	75.02	77.04	2.7		15	1971	4.0	10.8
1965	84.75	87.56	3.3		16	1988	4.0	12.4
1966	92.43	92.88	0.5		17	1979	4.0	12.3
1967	80.33	86.61	7.8		18	1965	3.3	9.1
1968	96.47	92.24	− 4.4		19	1983	3.3	17.3
1969	103.86	103.01	− 0.8		20	1996	3.3	20.3
1970	92.06	85.02	− 7.6		21	1994	3.3	− 1.5
1971	92.15	95.88	4.0		22	1964	2.7	13.0
1972	102.09	103.94	1.8		23	1995	2.4	34.1
1973	118.05	116.03	− 1.7		24	1972	1.8	15.6
1974	97.55	96.57	− 1.0		25	1955	1.8	26.4
1975	68.56	76.98	12.3		26	1950	1.7	21.8
1976	90.19	100.86	11.8		27	1952	1.6	11.8
1977	107.46	102.03	− 5.1		28	1998	1.0	??
1978	95.10	89.25	− 6.2		29	1993	0.7	7.1
1979	96.11	99.93	4.0		30	1966	0.5	−13.1
1980	107.94	115.12	6.7		31	1959	0.4	8.5
1981	135.76	129.55	− 4.6		32	1986	0.2	14.6
1982	122.55	120.40	− 1.8		33	1953	− 0.7	− 6.6
1983	140.64	145.30	3.3		34	1969	− 0.8	−11.4
1984	164.93	163.42	− 0.9		35	1984	− 0.9	1.4
1985	167.24	179.63	7.4		36	1974	− 1.0	−29.7
1986	211.28	211.78	0.2		37	1973	− 1.7	−17.4
1987	242.16	274.08	13.2		38	1982	− 1.8	14.8
1988	247.09	257.07	4.0		39	1992	− 2.0	4.5
1989	277.72	297.48	7.1		40	1956	− 3.6	2.6
1990	353.40	329.07	− 6.9		41	1962	− 3.8	−11.8
1991	330.23	343.93	4.1		42	1957	− 4.2	−14.3
1992	417.09	408.79	− 2.0		43	1968	− 4.4	7.7
1993	435.71	438.78	0.7		44	1981	− 4.6	− 9.7
1994	466.45	481.61	3.3		45	1977	− 5.1	−11.5
1995	459.27	470.42	2.4		46	1978	− 6.2	1.1
1996	615.93	636.02	3.3		47	1990	− 6.9	− 6.6
1997	740.74	786.16	6.1		48	1960	− 7.1	− 3.0
1998	970.43	980.28	1.0		49	1970	− 7.6	0.1

Based on S&P composite index

JANUARY

MONDAY

4

*In an uptrend, if a higher high
is made but fails to carry through,
and prices dip below the previous high,
the trend is apt to reverse.
The converse is true for downtrends.*
— Victor Sperandeo

Murphy & Murphy – PC Low Setup – 5 HRS✓ **TUESDAY**

Analysis of Accounts 2

1 1/2 /Hr✓

5

*It's a buy when the 10-week moving
average crosses the 30-week moving
average and the slope of both averages is up.*
— Victor Sperandeo

WEDNESDAY

6

*Pullbacks near the 30-week moving
average are often good times to take action.*
— Michael Burke, Chartcraft

THURSDAY

7

*News on stocks is not important.
How the stock reacts to it is important.*
— Michael Burke, Chartcraft

FRIDAY

8

*The first stocks to double in a bull market
will usually double again.*
— Michael Burke, Chartcraft

SATURDAY

9

SUNDAY

10

JANUARY BAROMETER IN GRAPHIC FORM

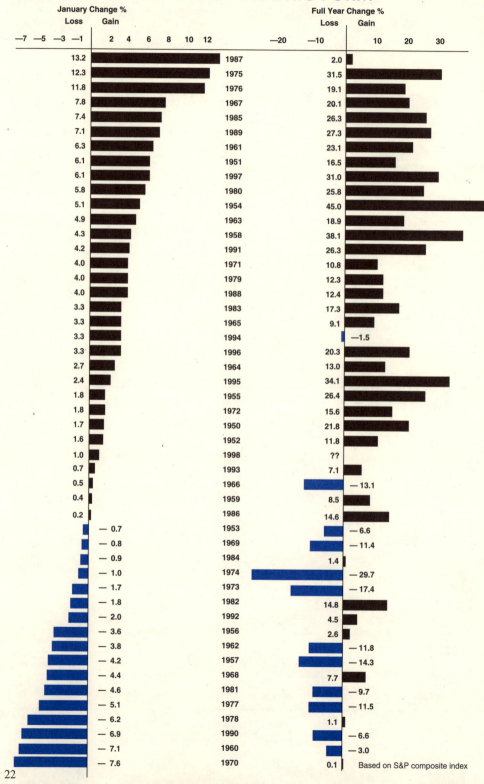

January Change %		Full Year Change %	
Loss — Gain	Year	Loss — Gain	
13.2	1987	2.0	
12.3	1975	31.5	
11.8	1976	19.1	
7.8	1967	20.1	
7.4	1985	26.3	
7.1	1989	27.3	
6.3	1961	23.1	
6.1	1951	16.5	
6.1	1997	31.0	
5.8	1980	25.8	
5.1	1954	45.0	
4.9	1963	18.9	
4.3	1958	38.1	
4.2	1991	26.3	
4.0	1971	10.8	
4.0	1979	12.3	
4.0	1988	12.4	
3.3	1983	17.3	
3.3	1965	9.1	
3.3	1994	—1.5	
3.3	1996	20.3	
2.7	1964	13.0	
2.4	1995	34.1	
1.8	1955	26.4	
1.8	1972	15.6	
1.7	1950	21.8	
1.6	1952	11.8	
1.0	1998	??	
0.7	1993	7.1	
0.5	1966	—13.1	
0.4	1959	8.5	
0.2	1986	14.6	
—0.7	1953	—6.6	
—0.8	1969	—11.4	
—0.9	1984	1.4	
—1.0	1974	—29.7	
—1.7	1973	—17.4	
—1.8	1982	14.8	
—2.0	1992	4.5	
—3.6	1956	2.6	
—3.8	1962	—11.8	
—4.2	1957	—14.3	
—4.4	1968	7.7	
—4.6	1981	—9.7	
—5.1	1977	—11.5	
—6.2	1978	1.1	
—6.9	1990	—6.6	
—7.1	1960	—3.0	
—7.6	1970	0.1	

Based on S&P composite index

22

MONDAY

11

Jones Termite & Pest Control   2 HRS
Depreciation Worksheet

*Mr. Bell, after careful consideration of
your invention, while it is a very interesting
novelty, we have come to the conclusion
that it has no commercial possibilities.*
— J.P. Morgan, after a demonstration of the telephone (1876)

TUESDAY

12

Every crowd has a silver lining.
— P.T. Barnum

WEDNESDAY

13

Jones Termite & Pest Control   6 HRS
Proof of Cash — Jan — Nov.

*Ah, but a man's reach should exceed his grasp
Or what's a heaven for?*
— Robert Browning

THURSDAY

14

*When people are free to do as they please,
they usually imitate each other.*
— Eric Hoffer

FRIDAY

 # 15

Call Loscalzo

*The fireworks begin today
Each diploma is a lighted match.
Each one of you is a fuse.*
— NYC Mayor Edward Koch, Commencement Address, 1983

SATURDAY

16

SUNDAY

17

JANUARY'S FIRST FIVE DAYS
AN "EARLY WARNING" SYSTEM

Market action during the first five trading days of the month often serve as an excellent "early warning" system for the year as a whole.

Early January gains since 1950 (excluding 1994) were matched by whole-year gains with just three war related exceptions: The start of the Vietnam war triggered big military spending which delayed the start of the 1966 bear market; and the imminence of a final ceasefire raised stock prices temporarily in early January 1973; Saddam Hussein's actions in Kuwait brought the market down in 1990. Seventeen Januarys got off to a bad start and eight of those ended on the downside. The nine that didn't follow suit were 1955, 1956, 1978, 1982, 1985, 1986, 1988, 1991, and 1993.

Remember that five days is a brief span and some extraordinary event could sidetrack this indicator as on 1986's fifth day and again on 1990's fifth day.

THE FIRST-FIVE-DAYS-IN-JANUARY INDICATOR

	Chronological Data				Ranked By Performance			
	Previous Year's Close	5th Day In January	Change 1st 5 Days	Rank			Change 1st 5 Days	Change For Year
1950	16.76	17.09	2.0%	1	1987		6.2%	2.0%
1951	20.41	20.88	2.3	2	1976		4.9	19.1
1952	23.77	23.91	0.6	3	1983		3.3	17.3
1953	26.57	26.22	− 1.3	4	1967		3.1	20.1
1954	24.81	24.93	0.5	5	1979		2.8	12.3
1955	35.98	35.33	− 1.8	6	1963		2.6	18.9
1956	45.48	44.51	− 2.1	7	1958		2.5	38.1
1957	46.67	46.25	− 0.9	8	1984		2.4	1.4
1958	39.99	40.99	2.5	9	1951		2.3	16.5
1959	55.21	55.40	0.3	10	1975		2.2	31.5
1960	59.89	59.50	− 0.7	11	1950		2.0	21.8
1961	58.11	58.81	1.2	12	1973		1.5	− 17.4
1962	71.55	69.12	− 3.4	13	1972		1.4	15.6
1963	63.10	64.74	2.6	14	1964		1.3	13.0
1964	75.02	76.00	1.3	15	1961		1.2	23.1
1965	84.75	85.37	0.7	16	1989		1.2	27.3
1966	92.43	93.14	0.8	17	1997		1.0	31.0
1967	80.33	82.81	3.1	18	1980		0.9	25.8
1968	96.47	96.62	0.2	19	1966		0.8	− 13.1
1969	103.86	100.80	− 2.9	20	1994		0.7	− 1.5
1970	92.06	92.68	0.7	21	1965		0.7	9.1
1971	92.15	92.19	0.0	22	1970		0.7	0.1
1972	102.09	103.47	1.4	23	1952		0.6	11.8
1973	118.05	119.85	1.5	24	1954		0.5	45.0
1974	97.55	96.12	− 1.5	25	1996		0.4	20.3
1975	68.56	70.04	2.2	26	1959		0.3	8.5
1976	90.19	94.58	4.9	27	1995		0.3	34.1
1977	107.46	105.01	− 2.3	28	1992		0.2	4.5
1978	95.10	90.64	− 4.7	29	1968		0.2	7.7
1979	96.11	98.80	2.8	30	1990		0.1	− 6.6
1980	107.94	108.95	0.9	31	1971		0.0	10.8
1981	135.76	133.06	− 2.0	32	1960		− 0.7	− 3.0
1982	122.55	119.55	− 2.4	33	1957		− 0.9	− 14.3
1983	140.64	145.23	3.3	34	1953		− 1.3	− 6.6
1984	164.93	168.90	2.4	35	1974		− 1.5	− 29.7
1985	167.24	163.99	− 1.9	36	1998		− 1.5	??
1986	211.28	207.97	− 1.6	37	1988		− 1.5	12.4
1987	242.16	257.28	6.2	38	1993		− 1.5	7.1
1988	247.09	243.40	− 1.5	39	1986		− 1.6	14.6
1989	277.72	280.98	1.2	40	1955		− 1.8	26.4
1990	353.40	353.79	0.1	41	1985		− 1.9	26.3
1991	330.23	314.90	− 4.6	42	1981		− 2.0	− 9.7
1992	417.09	418.10	0.2	43	1956		− 2.1	2.6
1993	435.71	429.05	− 1.5	44	1977		− 2.3	− 11.5
1994	466.45	469.90	0.7	45	1982		− 2.4	14.8
1995	459.27	460.83	0.3	46	1969		− 2.9	− 11.4
1996	615.93	618.46	0.4	47	1962		− 3.4	− 11.8
1997	740.74	748.41	1.0	48	1991		− 4.6	26.3
1998	970.43	956.04	− 1.5	49	1978		− 4.7	1.1

Based on S&P composite index

JANUARY

**Martin Luther King Jr. Day
(Market Closed)**

*The heights by great men reached and kept
Were not attained by sudden flight,
But they, while their companions slept,
Were toiling upward in the night.*
— Henry Wadsworth Longfellow
"The Ladder of Saint Augustine," 1858

TUESDAY
19

Jones Termite & Pest Control   7 HRS
Account Analysis & Cash Proofs

*In democracies, nothing is more great
or brilliant than commerce; it attracts
the attention of the public and fills the
imagination of the multitude; all passions
of energy are directed towards it.*
— Alexis de Tocqueville, *Democracy in America*, 1840

WEDNESDAY
20

Jones Termite & Pest Control   5 HRS
Adjustment and Worksheets

*There are three ingredients in the good life:
learning, earning and yearning.*
— Christopher Morley

THURSDAY
21

*This is the biggest fool thing we have ever done.
The (atom) bomb will never go off, and I
speak as an expert in explosives.*
— Admiral William Leahy to President Truman (1945)

FRIDAY
22

Jones Termite & Pest Control   4 HRS
F1120S Preparation
Worksheets to Tax Return

Eighty percent of success is showing up.
— Woody Allen

SATURDAY
23

SUNDAY
24

Big January moves ebb
When they spill into Feb

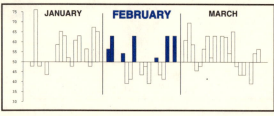

See Market Probability Chart on page 125.

FEBRUARY ALMANAC

FEBRUARY						
S	M	T	W	T	F	S
		1	2	3	4	5	6
7	8	9	10	11	12	13
14	15	16	17	18	19	20
21	22	23	24	25	26	27
28						

MARCH						
S	M	T	W	T	F	S
		1	2	3	4	5	6
7	8	9	10	11	12	13
14	15	16	17	18	19	20
21	22	23	24	25	26	27
28	29	30	31			

❑ Sharp January moves tend to consolidate in February ❑ If January is up, stay in; if down, move to sidelines ❑ RECORD: S&P 28 up, 21 down ❑ February's average change is 0.3% since 1950 (page 50) ❑ Many analysts may revise annual forecasts at the beginning of February, as the rest of the year tends to follow the lead of January's performance, especially in odd years ❑ Tends to follow whatever major market trend we're in, bull or bear. ❑ FLASH: February has been the third best month in the last 13 years as the Dow was gaining about 7500 points (pages 50 and 146).

FEBRUARY DAILY POINT CHANGES DOW JONES INDUSTRIALS

Previous Month Close	1989 2342.32	1990 2590.54	1991 2736.39	1992 3223.39	1993 3310.03	1994 3978.36	1995 3843.86	1996 5395.30	1997 6813.09	1998 7906.50
1	− 4.11	− 4.28	− 5.70	—	22.15	−14.35	3.70	9.76	—	—
2	− 4.46	16.44	—	—	− 3.51	11.53	23.21	−31.07	—	201.28
3	− 2.50	—	—	10.73	45.12	− 7.88	57.87	—	− 6.93	52.57
4	—	—	41.59	38.69	42.95	−96.24	—	—	27.32	−30.64
5	—	19.82	16.09	−15.21	25.40	—	—	33.60	−86.58	−12.46
6	−10.18	−16.21	42.57	− 2.01	—	—	9.09	52.02	26.16	72.24 <
7	26.07	33.78	−20.30	−30.19 <	—	34.90	− 0.34	32.51	82.74 <	—
8	− 3.93 <	4.28 <	20.05 <	—	− 4.60 <	− 0.29 <	− 2.02 <	47.33 <	—	—
9	−20.17	3.83	—	—	−22.96	25.89	− 2.69	2.17	—	−8.97
10	−36.97	—	—	19.68	− 2.16	−36.58	6.39	—	−49.26	115.09
11	—	—	71.54	6.49	10.27	− 0.56	—	—	51.57	18.94
12	—	−29.06	−27.48	25.26	−30.26	—	—	58.53	103.52	55.05
13	− 3.57	4.96	34.41	−30.18	—	—	15.14	1.08	60.81	0.50
14	− 1.25	0.22	−31.93	− 0.68	—	9.28	4.04	−21.68	−33.48	—
15	22.68	25.23	57.42	—	H	24.21	27.92	−28.18	—	—
16	7.50	−13.96	—	—	−82.94	9.00	1.35	−48.05	—	H
17	13.39	—	—	H	2.70	−14.63	−33.98	—	H	28.40
18	—	—	H	−21.24	−10.00	−35.18	—	—	78.50	52.56
19	—	H	− 2.47	5.59	19.99	—	—	H	−47.33	−75.48
20	H	−38.74	−33.17	50.32	—	—	H	−44.79	−92.75	38.36
21	1.61	−13.29	− 7.18	− 0.45	—	H	10.43	57.44	4.24	—
22	−42.50	− 8.79	− 2.47	—	20.81	24.20	9.08	92.49	—	—
23	5.53	−10.58	—	—	−19.72	−19.98	30.28	22.03	—	− 3.74
24	−43.92	—	—	2.23	33.23	−51.78	8.41	—	76.58	−40.10
25	—	—	− 1.49	−24.59	8.64	− 1.12	—	—	30.01	87.68
26	—	38.29	−23.27	25.49	5.67	—	—	−65.39	−55.03	32.89
27	4.82	14.64	24.51	−13.87	—	—	−23.17	−15.89	−58.11	55.05
28	8.03	10.13	− 6.93	− 1.78	—	− 6.76	22.48	−43.00	−47.33	—
29				—				−20.59		
Close	2258.39	2627.25	2882.18	3267.67	3370.81	3832.02	4011.05	5485.62	6877.74	8545.72
Change	−83.93	36.71	145.79	44.28	60.78	−146.34	167.19	90.32	64.65	639.22

JANUARY

MONDAY
25

*Days between the 26th through the 10th
of months outperform middle
11th through 25th days.*
— Yale Hirsch (see page 48)

TUESDAY
 ## 26

*Better to sell "too late" than "too soon"
in a momentum driven market as stocks
often go much, much higher.
Let your stock hit at least two lower
tops and bottoms before you sell.*
— Jordan Kimmel, Private Money Manager

Jones Termite & Pest Control
   PA. Corp. Return   .2 HR
   Closing Books   2 HR
   Quickbooks Setup   3 HR
Murphy & Murphy - Peachtree Setup 1 HR ✓

WEDNESDAY
 ## 27

*I was in search of a one-armed economist so
that the guy could never make a statement
and then say: "on the other hand."*
— Harry S. Truman

Jones Termite & Pest Control - 2 HRS
   Profit Sharing Contribution Worksheet

THURSDAY
 ## 28

*As far as paying off debt is concerned, there
are very few instances in history when any
government has ever paid off debt.*
— Walter Wriston

Murphy & Murphy - 5 HRS ✓
Posting General Ledger Aug thru Dec

FRIDAY
29

*In Boston they ask, "How much does he know?"
In New York, "How much is he worth?"
In Philadelphia, "Who were his parents?"*
— Mark Twain

Murphy & Murphy - 2 HRS ✓
Account Analysis

SATURDAY
30

SUNDAY
31

1933 "LAME DUCK" AMENDMENT
REASON JANUARY BAROMETER WORKS

Between 1901 and 1933 the market's direction in January was similar to that of the whole year 19 times and different 14 times. Comparing January to the 11 subsequent months, 16 were similar and 17 dissimilar.

A dramatic change occurred in 1934—the Twentieth Amendment to the Constitution! Since then it has essentially been "As January goes, so goes the year." January's direction has been correct in most of the subsequent years.

January Barometer (Odd Years)
LAME DUCK AMENDMENT RATIFIED 1933
JANUARY BAROMETER IS BORN

January % Change	12 Month % Change	Same	Opposite
— 4.2%	41.2%		1935
3.8	— 38.6		1937
— 6.9	— 5.4	1939	
— 4.8	— 17.9	1941	
7.2	19.4	1943	
1.4	30.7	1945	
2.4	0.0	1947	
0.1	10.3	1949	
6.1	16.5	1951	
— 0.7	— 6.6	1953	
1.8	26.4	1955	
— 4.2	— 14.3	1957	
0.4	8.5	1959	
6.3	23.1	1961	
4.9	18.9	1963	
3.3	9.1	1965	
7.8	20.1	1967	
— 0.8	— 11.4	1969	
4.0	10.8	1971	
— 1.7	— 17.4	1973	
12.3	31.5	1975	
— 5.1	— 11.5	1977	
4.0	12.3	1979	
— 4.6	— 9.7	1981	
3.3	17.3	1983	
7.4	26.3	1985	
13.2	2.0	1987	
7.1	27.3	1989	
4.2	26.3	1991	
0.7	7.1	1993	
2.4	34.1	1995	
6.1	31.0	1997	

12 month's % change includes January's % change
Based on S&P composite index

Prior to 1934, newly elected Senators and Representatives did not take office until December of the following year, **13 months later** (except when new Presidents were inaugurated). Defeated Congressmen stayed in Congress for all of the following session. They were known as "lame ducks."

Since the Twentieth (Lame Duck) Amendment was ratified in 1933, Congress convenes January 3 and includes those members newly elected the previous November. Inauguration Day was also moved up from March 4 to January 20. As a result several events have been squeezed into January which affect our economy and our stock market and quite possibly those of many nations of the world. During January, Congress convenes, the President gives the State of the Union message, presents the annual budget and sets national goals and priorities. Switch these events to any other month and chances are the January Barometer would become a memory.

The table shows the January Barometer in odd years. In 1935 and 1937, the Democrats already had the most lopsided congressional margins in history, so when these two Congresses convened it was anticlimactic. The January Barometer in all subsequent odd years compiled a **perfect record**. See its predecessors on page 30.

(continued on page 30)

FEBRUARY

MONDAY

1

M&M, LORS, RJK — UC-1 GUCIA
FORM 940

1 1/2 HRS
1/2 HR

*Big Business breeds bureaucracy and
bureacrats exactly as big government does.*
— T.K. Quinn

TUESDAY

2

MUVPHY & Murphy
Year End Adjustments, Etc
Analysis of Accounts

PAYROLL SOFTWARE

6 HRS
1 HR

*All organizations are at least 50 percent
waste— waste people, waste effort, waste
space, and waste time.*
— Robert Townsend

WEDNESDAY

3

*A committee is a cul de sac down which ideas
are lured and then quietly strangled.*
— Barnett Cocks

THURSDAY

4

*A good new chairman of the Federal Reserve
Bank is worth a $10 billion tax cut.*
— Paul H. Douglas

FRIDAY

5

*An entrepreneur tends to lie some
of the time. An entrepreneur in trouble
tends to lie most of the time.*
— Anonymous

SATURDAY

6

SUNDAY

7

(continued from page 28)

Prior to the Twentieth Amendment in this century, we had a "March Barometer" when newly-elected Presidents (Taft, Wilson, Harding, Hoover, and Roosevelt) were inaugurated on March 4. Newly elected Congresses convened in March for the occasion. Score 5 out of 5 for the "March Barometer" prior to the Twentieth Amendment.

Between 1900 and 1933, eight new Congresses convened on the first Monday in December (13 months after the election). But because of annual year-end reinvestment, it would be misleading to use December as a barometer. I used a "November Barometer" instead and the score was almost perfect. In 1903, the only time Congress actually convened in November, the barometer was in error. The Panic of 1903 took the Dow down 37.7% and the new Congress was called in one month earlier, ostensibly to "stem the tide." The Panic ended on November 9, the day Congress convened, but the month remained negative while the market moved up over the next 11 months.

Three other new Congresses were convened in other months for different reasons—April in 1911 and 1917 and May in 1919. The record is a double bulls-eye for the "April Barometer." As for the one-shot "May Barometer" a post-Armisitice 30.9% surge in four months (February to May) took May up 13.6% but the 12-month period (including May) almost lost it all. President Wilson spent six months in Europe trying to win the peace.

New Congress Barometers (Odd Years)

NEWLY ELECTED PRESIDENT INAUGURATED MARCH 4TH

March % Change	12 Month's % Change	Same	Opposite
5.2%	11.6%	1909	
0.7	2.4	1913	
1.0	14.0	1921	
− 2.7	− 14.6	1929	
7.8	101.3	1933	

12 month's % change includes March

NEW CONGRESS CONVENES FIRST WEEK IN DECEMBER 13 MONTHS AFTER ELECTION

November % Change	12 Month's % Change	Same	Opposite
0.9%	2.5%	1901	
− 1.8	39.7		1903*
7.3	10.9	1905	
1.2	4.3	1907	
0.7	8.9	1915	
4.3	17.5	1923	
3.5	3.9	1925	
9.1	38.8	1927	
− 11.0	− 41.3	1931	

*Panic of 1903 ends 11/9 as Congress convenes (off 37.7%)
12 month's % change includes November

NEW CONGRESS CONVENES IN APRIL OR MAY EARLIER THAN USUAL, NO CHANGE IN PRESIDENCY

Month's % Change	12 Month's % Change	Same	Opposite
0.5%	6.0%	1911	
− 2.3	− 19.6	1917	
13.6	0.7	1919**	

**Wilson in Europe 6 months; Post-Armistice surge (up 30.9% Feb to May)
12 month's % change includes applicable month

Based on Dow Jones industrial average (1901-1933)

This "New Congress Barometer" performed rather impressively until the passage of the Twentieth Amendment. Since then, it's successor, the January Barometer has compiled the best record in odd-numbered years of all other known indicators. A perfect record since 1937 is hard to beat.

FEBRUARY

MONDAY
8

There is always plenty of capital for those who can create practical plans for using it.
— Napoleon Hill

TUESDAY
9

In business, the competition will bite you if you keep running; if you stand still, they will swallow you.
— William Knudsen

Murphy & Murphy — 4 HRS ✓
Computer Payroll Problem Solving

WEDNESDAY
10

All the features and achievements of modern civilization are, directly or indirectly, the products of the capitalist process.
— Joseph A. Schumpeter

THURSDAY
11

The political problem of mankind is to combine three things: economic efficiency, social justice, and individual liberty.
— John Maynard Keynes

FRIDAY
12

The only thing that saves us from the bureaucracy is its inefficiency.
— Eugene McCarthy

Jones Termite & Pest Control — Not

SATURDAY
13

St. Valentine's Day

SUNDAY
14

MARKET CHARTS OF PRE-PRESIDENTIAL ELECTION YEARS

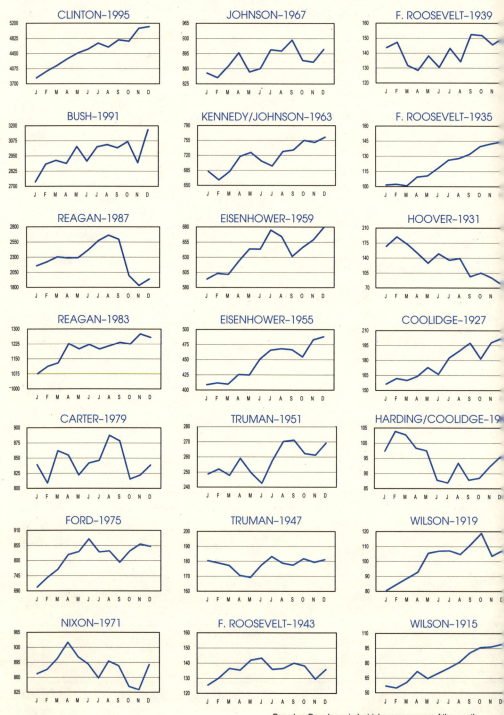

Based on Dow Jones industrial average mean of the month

FEBRUARY

Murphy & Murphy - 4 1/2 Hrs ✓
Post Adjusting Journal Entries
Worksheet for Partner's SE+ IRA
1065 - p 3 & 4 Drafts

*Without development there is no profit,
without profit, no development.*
— Joseph A. Schumpeter

Reyner Vending Service Co - Not

Murphy & Murphy   4 1/2 Hrs ✓

Forms 1065 + Worksheets

*The most valuable executive is one who is
training somebody to be a better man than he is.*
— Robert G. Ingersoll

Ash Wednesday

Murphy & Murphy
Worksheet Changes   2 1/2 Hrs ✓
Posting Simple IRA
Adjustments
Running Trial Balance

*Love of money is either the chief or a
secondary motive at the bottom of everything
the Americans do.*
— Alexis de Tocqueville

---

*Economy is the art of making the most of life.
The love of economy is the root of all virtue.*
— George Bernard Shaw

---

*How can I adopt a creed (socialism) which
exalts the boorish proletariat above the
bourgeois and the intelligentsia who, with
whatever faults, are the quality of life and surely
carry the seeds of all human advancement?*
— John Maynard Keynes

Up, up in March is the Dow's direction
In the year before a Presidential election

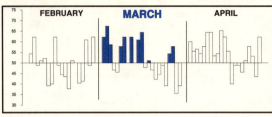

MARCH ALMANAC

See Market Probability Chart on page 125.

❑ "In like a lion, out like a lamb" describes stronger first half than second ❑ Many substantial rallies of at least 5% started here since 1949 ❑ RECORD: S&P 32 up, 17 down ❑ Average S&P gain 1.0%, sixth best ❑ Gain of 495.55 Dow points, eighth best over 49 years (gained 254 points in 1998 but lost 294 points in 1997) ❑ March fares much better when the market takes a hit in February (1994 was an exception). ❑ March 19th will be a triple expiration day and potentially volatile.

MARCH DAILY POINT CHANGES DOW JONES INDUSTRIALS

	1989	1990	1991	1992	1993	1994	1995	1996	1997	1998
Previous Month Close	2258.39	2627.25	2882.18	3267.67	3370.81	3832.02	4011.05	5485.62	6877.74	8545.72
1	−15.35	8.34	27.72	—	−15.40	−22.79	−16.25	50.94	—	—
2	22.67	24.77	—	7.60	45.12	22.51	−14.87	—	—	4.73
3	8.58	—	—	14.98	3.51	− 7.32	9.68	—	41.18	34.38
4	—	—	4.21	−21.69	− 5.13	7.88	—	63.59	− 66.20	−45.59
5	—	−10.81	58.41	−27.06	5.67	—	—	42.27	93.13	−94.91
6	20.53	27.25	0.75	−19.90	—	—	7.95	− 12.65	− 1.15	125.06
7	− 4.11	− 7.21	− 9.90	—	—	23.92	−34.93	11.92	56.19	—
8	4.83	26.58	− 8.17	—	64.84	− 4.50	16.60	−171.24	—	—
9	− 4.11	−12.84	—	− 6.48	2.70	1.69	4.16	—	—	− 2.25
10	− 9.29	—	—	15.87	6.22	−22.79	52.22	—	78.50	75.98
11	—	—	−15.84	−22.36	−21.34	32.08	—	110.55	5.77	32.63
12	—	3.38	−16.84	N/C	−29.18	—	—	2.89	− 45.79	−16.19
13	24.11	−12.16	32.68	27.28	—	—	−10.38	− 15.17	−160.48	−57.04
14	N/C	13.29	− 2.97	—	—	0.28	23.52	17.34	56.57	—
15	14.29	7.88	− 3.96	—	14.59	−13.39	−10.38	− 1.09	—	—
16	20.17	45.50	—	0.45	0.54	− 1.44	30.78		—	116.33
17	−48.57	—	—	19.68	−16.21	16.99	4.50	—	20.02	31.14
18	—	—	−18.32	− 1.79	38.90	30.51		98.63	− 58.92	25.41
19	—	14.41	−62.13	7.15	5.94	—	—	− 14.09	− 18.88	27.65
20	−29.64	−16.89	4.21	14.99	—	—	10.03	− 14.09	− 57.40	103.38
21	3.75	−10.81	−16.58	—	—	−30.80	−11.07	− 28.54	− 15.49	—
22	− 3.04	−32.21	3.46	—	− 8.10	− 2.30	10.38	9.76	—	—
23	−20.17	8.56	—	− 4.25	− 1.62	6.91	4.84	—	—	−90.18
24	H	—	—	−11.18	−16.48	−48.37	50.84	—	100.46	88.19
25	—	—	6.93	− 1.57	15.94	−46.36	—	7.22	− 29.08	−31.64
26	—	3.38	49.01	8.28	−21.34	—	—	26.74	4.53	−25.91
27	14.82	29.28	2.72	−36.23	—	—	18.67	− 43.72	−140.11	−50.81
28	17.68	6.75	− 3.71	—	—	−12.38	− 5.53	3.97	H	—
29	5.98	−15.99	H	—	15.12	−63.33	8.99	− 43.71	—	—
30	− 0.18	−20.49	—	3.80	2.17	−72.27	11.76	—	—	−13.96
31	12.28	—	—	0.23	−22.16	9.21	−14.87	—	−157.11	17.69
Close	2293.62	2707.21	2913.86	3235.47	3435.11	3635.96	4157.69	5587.14	6583.48	8799.81
Change	35.23	79.96	31.68	−32.20	64.30	−196.06	146.64	101.52	−294.26	254.09

FEBRUARY

MONDAY
22

TUESDAY
 ## 23

Pennsylvania Probate
Rayner Vending — 1½ H
Letter to LuNrell
Form 8594
Aggravation
Fax

WEDNESDAY
 ## 24

James Termite ePest Control
Cell Quick Books   2 HRS
Review Corrections Items

THURSDAY
 ## 25

FRIDAY
 ## 26

SATURDAY
27

SUNDAY
28

PRE-PRESIDENTIAL ELECTION YEARS
NO LOSERS IN 60 YEARS

Investors should have it very easy in 1999. There hasn't been a down year in the third year of a presidential term since war-torn 1939, Dow off 2.9%. The only severe loss in a pre-presidential election year going back 84 years occurred in 1931 during the Depression.

Electing a president every four years has set in motion a political stock market cycle. Most bear markets take place in the first or second years after elections (see page 139). Then, the market improves. What happens is that each administration usually does everything in its power to juice up the economy so that voters are in a positive mood at election time.

Quite an impressive record. Chances are the winning streak will continue and that the market in pre-presidential election 1999 will gain ground. Prospects improve considerably if the market has experienced a correction, or has spent many months going sideways in the last half of 1998.

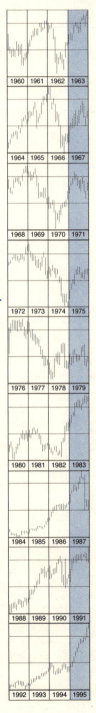

PRE-PRESIDENTIAL ELECTION YEAR RECORD SINCE 1915

1915	Wilson (D)	World War I in Europe, but U.S. stocks up 81.7%.
1919	Wilson (D)	Post-Armistice 45.5% gain through November 3rd top.
1923	Harding / Coolidge (R)	Teapot Dome scandal a depressant. Dow loses 3.3%.
1927	Coolidge (R)	Bull market rolls on, up 28.8%.
1931	Hoover (R)	Depression, stocks slashed in half.
1935	Roosevelt (D)	Almost a straight up year, S&P 500 up 41.2%.
1939	Roosevelt (D)	War clouds, Dow off 2.9% but 23.7% April/December gain.
1943	Roosevelt (D)	U.S. at war, prospects brighter, S&P up 19.4%
1947	Truman (D)	S&P unchanged, Dow up a few percent.
1951	Truman (D)	S&P up 16.5%.
1955	Eisenhower (R)	S&P up 26.4%.
1959	Eisenhower (R)	S&P up 8.5%.
1963	Kennedy/Johnson (D)	S&P up 18.9%.
1967	Johnson (D)	S&P up 20.1%.
1971	Nixon (R)	S&P up 10.8%.
1975	Ford (R)	S&P up 31.5%.
1979	Carter (D)	S&P up 12.3%.
1983	Reagan (R)	S&P up 17.3%.
1987	Reagan (R)	S&P up 2.0% despite the meltdown in October.
1991	Bush (R)	S&P up 26.3%.
1995	Clinton (D)	S&P up 34.1%.

MONDAY

1

File Form 7004 for Murphy & Slota

Jones Termite & Pest Control   6 HRS

Quickbooks Setup

TUESDAY

2

Jo.

WEDNESDAY

3

11:00 AM - F Shea   215-517-7402

1:00 AM - TRACZ

THURSDAY

4

FRIDAY

5

SATURDAY

6

BOZZELLI - 10:00 AM

1-215-643-5692

SUNDAY

7

PROFITING PRE-ST. PATRICK'S DAY—MORE THAN LUCK!

Most savvy traders know that the day before a major holiday strongly tends to be bullish. Dan Turov, editor of *Turov On Timing* (published by the Hirsch Organization), has investigated the seasonality of market trading around St. Patrick's Day. Results appear in the table below.

Note the stellar performance of the market on the day before St. Patrick's Day. The average gain of 0.28% on the S&P is equivalent to more than 25 Dow points (at current levels for the Dow). That's equal to an annualized rate of return of over 100%! So the day before St. Patrick's Day outperforms the days before more conventional holidays.

In 1999 St. Patrick's Day falls on Wednesday, March 17th. Therefore, it's more than likely that Tuesday, March 16th will provide you with an added edge to make a little extra profit in the market.

During the past 46 years St. Patrick's Day itself has posted an average gain of 0.02%. The record for this day would be improved quite a bit if we could discount the 3% loss in 1980 during the Hunt Silver Crisis. The average gain then would be 0.09%.

ST. PATRICK'S DAY TRADING RECORD (DAYS BEFORE AND AFTER)

Year	% Change 2 Days Prior	% Change 1 Day Prior	% Change St. Patrick's Day	S&P Day After St. Patrick's Day	% Change Day After
1953	0.19%	0.15%	0.42%	26.24	−0.34%
1954	−0.45	−0.04	0.23	26.73	0.41
1955	2.15	0.76	0.39	36.18	0.17
1956	0.97	0.31	0.93	48.87	0.58
1957	0.07	−0.05	−0.45	44.04	0.43
1958	0.12	−0.31	−0.69	41.89	−0.36
1959	0.12	−1.08	0.82	56.39	−0.23
1960	0.77	0.55	−0.15	55.01	0.09
1961	0.30	1.01	0.61	64.86	0.40
1962	0.21	−0.17	−0.13	70.66	−0.27
1963	−0.47	0.50	−0.49	65.47	−0.21
1964	0.08	0.00	0.23	79.38	0.08
1965	0.03	−0.13	−0.13	86.81	−0.24
1966	−0.57	0.58	0.35	88.53	0.41
1967	0.95	1.01	0.18	90.20	−0.06
1968	−1.90	0.88	0.55	88.99	−0.67
1969	−0.67	−0.40	0.26	98.49	0.24
1970	−0.53	−1.08	0.44	87.54	0.29
1971	1.14	0.50	−0.09	101.19	0.07
1972	0.13	−0.23	0.39	107.59	−0.31
1973	−0.75	−0.51	−1.21	111.95	−0.20
1974	−0.09	−0.37	−1.24	97.23	−0.84
1975	0.18	1.22	1.47	85.13	−1.02
1976	−1.05	1.12	−0.06	100.45	−0.41
1977	0.55	0.19	−0.09	101.86	−0.22
1978	−0.26	0.44	0.77	90.82	0.69
1979	0.15	0.83	0.37	100.50	−0.55
1980	−1.17	−0.18	−3.01	104.10	1.80
1981	−0.06	1.18	−0.56	134.22	0.22
1982	0.77	−0.16	−0.18	110.30	1.12
1983	0.35	−1.03	−0.14	149.90	0.21
1984	0.41	1.18	−0.94	158.86	0.68
1985	−0.20	−0.74	0.20	179.54	1.50
1986	0.28	1.44	−0.79	235.78	0.47
1987	−0.46	−0.57	1.47	292.78	0.11
1988	−0.09	0.95	0.96	271.12	−0.04
1989	0.52	0.93	−2.25	289.92	−0.95
1990	0.36	1.14	0.47	341.57	−0.57
1991	−0.29	0.02	−0.40	366.59	−1.48
1992	0.48	0.14	0.78	409.15	−0.10
1993	0.36	−0.01	−0.68	451.88	0.80
1994	−0.08	0.52	0.31	471.06	0.04
1995	−0.20	0.72	0.02	496.14	0.13
1996	0.37	0.09	1.75	651.69	−0.15
1997	−1.83	0.46	0.32	789.66	−0.76
1998	−0.12	1.00	0.11	1085.52	0.47
Average	**0.02%**	**0.28%**	**0.02%**		**0.03%**

MARCH

MONDAY
8

In the realm of ideas, everything depends on enthusiasm; in the real world, all rests on perseverance.
— Goethe

TUESDAY
9

For a country, everything will be lost when the jobs of an economist and a banker become highly respected professions.
— Montesquieu

WEDNESDAY
10

M. SKITAKEVIC   11:00 AM

J. MC BONLOGUE   1:00 PM

Those heroes of finance are like beads on a string, when one slips off, the rest follow.
— Henrik Ibsen

THURSDAY
11

Every man is the architect of his own fortune.
— Appius Claudius

FRIDAY
12

All a parent can give a child is roots and wings.
— Chinese proverb

SATURDAY
13

SUNDAY
14

SPRING PORTFOLIO REVIEW

NO. OF SHARES	SECURITY	A ORIGINAL COST	B CURRENT VALUE	C GAIN (B – A) OR LOSS (A – B)	D % CHANGE (C ÷ A)	E MONTHS HELD	F CHANGE PER MO. (D ÷ E)	G ANNUAL RETURN (F × 12)
200	Sample Corp.	$10,000	$10,400	$400	4.0%	8	0.5%	6.0%
TOTALS								

Stocks which have achieved their potential
1
2
3

Candidates for addition to portfolio
1
2
3

Stocks which have been disappointments
1
2
3

Investment decisions
1
2
3

MARCH

MONDAY
15

DEAL   1145

*The worse a situation becomes the less
it takes to turn it around, the bigger
the upside.*
— George Soros

Market much luckier day before St. Patrick's Day.

TUESDAY
 ## 16

:00   LAPLANTE

4:30 E. KRAUSS

*Poor Mexico, so far from God, but so
close to the United States.*
— Quoted on CNBC May 1993

St. Patrick's Day

WEDNESDAY
♣ ## 17

*There is only one side of the market
and it is not the bull side or the bear side,
but the right side.*
— Jesse Livermore

6:00 URBAIN

THURSDAY
18

*Drawing on my fine command of
language, I said nothing.*
— Robert Benchley

3:00PM :- KRAUSS

FRIDAY
 ## 19

*Markets are constantly in a state of
uncertainty and flux and money is made
by discounting the obvious and betting on
the unexpected.*
— George Soros

SATURDAY
20

SUNDAY
21

FIRST HALF OF APRIL OUTPERFORMS SECOND HALF

On balance the first half of April prior to the April 15th income tax deadline has far outperformed the second half ever since the deadline was changed from March 15th back in 1955. One would suppose that people writing checks to the IRS would have a dampening effect on the stock market. However, the obvious is seldom true in investing. From 1955 through 1998, the first half of April outperformed the second half 28 out of 44 times. Note: the last four out of five second halves have been superior.

MARKET PERFORMANCE IN APRIL

	End of March	Mid-April Tax Deadline	End of April	April 1-15	April 16-30
1955	36.58	37.96	37.96	3.8%	0.0%
1956	48.48	47.96	48.38	—1.1	0.9
1957	44.11	44.95	45.74	1.9	1.8
1958	42.10	42.43	43.44	0.8	2.4
1959	55.44	56.96	57.59	2.7	1.1
1960	55.34	56.59	54.37	2.3	—3.9
1961	65.06	66.68	65.31	2.5	—2.1
1962	69.55	67.60	65.24	—2.8	—3.5
1963	66.57	69.09	69.80	3.8	1.0
1964	78.98	80.09	79.46	1.4	—0.8
1965	86.16	88.15	89.11	2.3	1.1
1966	89.23	91.99	91.06	3.1	—1.0
1967	90.20	91.07	94.01	1.0	3.2
1968	90.20	96.59	97.46	7.1	0.9
1969	101.51	101.53	103.69	0.0	2.1
1970	89.63	86.73	81.52	—3.2	—6.0
1971	100.31	103.52	103.95	3.2	0.4
1972	107.20	109.51	107.67	2.2	—1.7
1973	111.52	111.44	106.97	—0.1	—4.0
1974	93.98	92.05	90.31	—2.1	—1.9
1975	83.36	86.30	87.30	3.5	1.2
1976	102.77	100.67	101.64	—2.0	1.0
1977	98.42	101.04	98.44	2.7	—2.6
1978	89.21	94.45	96.83	5.9	2.5
1979	101.59	101.12	101.76	—0.5	0.6
1980	102.09	102.83	106.29	0.7	3.4
1981	136.00	134.17	132.87	—1.3	—1.0
1982	111.96	116.35	116.44	3.9	0.1
1983	152.96	158.75	164.43	3.8	3.6
1984	159.18	158.32	160.04	—0.5	1.1
1985	180.66	180.92	179.83	0.1	—0.6
1986	238.90	237.73	235.52	—0.5	—0.9
1987	291.70	284.43	288.35	—2.5	1.4
1988	258.89	259.77	261.33	0.3	0.6
1989	294.87	301.72	309.64	2.3	2.6
1990	339.94	344.74	330.80	1.4	—4.0
1991	375.22	381.19	375.35	1.6	—1.5
1992	403.69	416.27	414.95	3.1	—0.3
1993	451.67	448.40	440.19	—0.7	—1.8
1994	445.76	446.18	450.99	0.1	1.1
1995	500.71	506.13	514.71	1.1	1.7
1996	645.50	642.49	654.18	—0.5	1.8
1997	757.12	754.72	801.34	—0.3	6.2
1998	1101.75	1119.32	1111.75	1.6	—0.7
Based on S&P composite index				Average 1.2%	0.1%

Five of the thirteen Aprils with losses in the first half of the month were in bear market years. These declining years had more of an adverse effect on the last two weeks of the month. When April 15 falls on the weekend and the IRS extends its deadline, the following Monday's market close is used. (See page 46 for market performance of first half of all months vs. second half.)

MARCH

MONDAY
22

TUESDAY
23

WEDNESDAY
24

11:00 Cleaver

THURSDAY
25

1 HR ✓

FRIDAY
26

Murphy & Murphy
Review Form 1065 with MTM

SATURDAY
27

SUNDAY
28

Murphy & Murphy — 6 HRS ✓
Review PA Form 65 — Need Booklet
Prepare Philadelphia Forms
Assemble Form 1065 — Prepare Worksheet

Market does better, two weeks before taxes
Remainder of April, Dow often relaxes

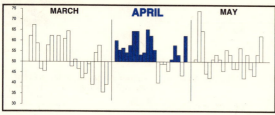

See Market Probability Chart on page 125.

APRIL ALMANAC

APRIL						
S	M	T	W	T	F	S
				1	2	3
4	5	6	7	8	9	10
11	12	13	14	15	16	17
18	19	20	21	22	23	24
25	26	27	28	29	30	

MAY						
S	M	T	W	T	F	S
						1
2	3	4	5	6	7	8
9	10	11	12	13	14	15
16	17	18	19	20	21	22
23	24	25	26	27	28	29
30	31					

❏ More ground gained in the two weeks prior to federal tax deadline than in the last two ❏ Superbull temporarily altering pattern (See page 42) ❏ When a company's first quarter earnings double, its stock tends to score a 25.2% gain the previous 30 days and only 5.0% more in the next 30 ❏ RECORD: S&P 34 up, 15 down ❏ Fourth best S&P gain of 1.3% (page 50) ❏ Not usually dangerous except in certain sharp bear markets (1962, 1970, 1973, 1974) ❏ Best Aprils often follow great Januarys ❏ Expect a down month during a bear market.

APRIL DAILY POINT CHANGES DOW JONES INDUSTRIALS

Previous Month Close	1989 2293.62	1990 2707.21	1991 2913.86	1992 3235.47	1993 3435.11	1994 3635.96	1995 4157.69	1996 5587.14	1997 6583.48	1998 8799.81
1	—	—	−32.67	13.86	4.33	H	—	50.58	27.57	68.51
2	—	−6.76	63.86	−15.21	−68.63	—	—	33.96	−94.04	118.32
3	11.18	36.26	−18.32	14.99	—	—	10.72	18.06	−39.66	−3.23
4	−6.60	−17.34	−2.23	—	—	−42.61	33.20	−6.86	48.72	—
5	6.60	1.80	−27.72	—	8.38	82.06	−1.04	H	—	—
6	−12.83	−4.05	—	26.38	−1.62	4.32	4.84	—	—	49.82
7	12.83	—	—	−61.94	19.45	13.53	−12.79	—	29.84	−76.73
8	—	—	21.78	−32.20	−0.54	−19.00	—	−88.51	53.25	−65.02
9	—	4.95	−45.54	43.61	H	—	—	−33.96	−45.32	103.38
10	−2.93	9.01	1.48	30.41	—	—	5.53	−74.43	−23.79	H
11	9.71	−1.35	30.95	—	—	14.57	−11.07	1.09	−148.36	—
12	8.07	22.07	15.34	—	31.61	−7.14	10.73	45.52	—	—
13	−23.65	H	—	14.53	15.94	−20.22	10.37	—	—	17.44
14	41.06	—	—	36.23	11.61	1.78	H	—	60.21	97.90
15	—	—	12.38	47.63	0.28	−1.78	—	60.33	135.26	52.07
16	—	11.26	53.71	12.74	22.69	—	—	27.10	92.71	−85.70
17	0.73	2.71	17.58	H	—	—	−12.80	−70.09	−21.27	90.93
18	41.61	−32.89	−5.20	—	—	−41.05	−16.25	1.81	44.95	—
19	7.51	−20.94	−33.67	—	−11.62	−0.60	28.36	−16.26	—	—
20	−9.53	−15.99	—	−30.19	−23.50	−21.11	23.17	—	—	−25.66
21	32.08	—	—	6.94	−4.05	53.83	39.43	—	−43.34	43.10
22	—	—	−37.87	−4.48	−10.27	−3.86	—	29.26	173.38	−8.22
23	—	−29.28	2.73	9.84	−15.40	—	—	23.85	−20.87	−33.39
24	−6.78	−12.17	19.05	−24.15	—	—	33.89	−34.69	−20.47	−78.71
25	−15.77	11.94	−28.46	—	—	57.10	−3.81	13.01	−53.38	—
26	2.20	10.14	−8.66	—	−15.40	−6.24	−0.34	1.08	—	—
27	29.88	−31.53	—	−19.90	17.56	H*	14.87	—	—	−146.98
28	−0.19	—	—	3.36	−2.43	−31.23	6.57	—	44.15	−18.68
29	—	—	−35.40	25.26	11.62	13.38	—	5.42	179.01	52.56
30	—	11.71	10.89	25.94	2.43	—	—	−4.33	46.96	111.85
Close	2418.80	2656.76	2887.87	3359.12	3427.55	3681.69	4321.27	5569.08	7008.99	9063.37
Change	125.18	−50.45	−25.99	123.65	−7.56	45.73	163.58	−18.06	425.51	263.56

* Nixon Memorial

MARCH/APRIL

Last three days of March have been terrible (page 34).

MONDAY

29

From listening comes wisdom, and from speaking repentance.
— Italian proverb

TUESDAY

30

He who knows nothing is confident of everything.
— Anonymous

WEDNESDAY

31

I must create a system or be enslaved by another man's.
— William Blake

Passover

THURSDAY

 # 1

I just wait until the fourth year, when the business cycle bottoms, and buy whatever I think will have the biggest bounce.
— Larry Tisch's investment style

Good Friday
(Market Closed)

FRIDAY

2

*How a minority
Reaching majority
Seizing authority
Hates a minority.*
— Leonard H. Robbins

SATURDAY

3

Easter Sunday

SUNDAY

4

FIRST HALVES OF ALL MONTHS OUTPERFORM SECOND HALVES

In the hunt for stock market seasonality, it often pays to compare different time periods. In this regard, I thought it would be interesting to divide the months into two parts and compare one to another. This was done for the past 35 years and the results are presented in the table below.

AVERAGE GAINS FIRST HALVES OF ALL MONTHS VS. SECOND HALVES

| | 1963–1973 | | 1974–1984 | | 1985–1998 | | Avg All Months 1963–Apr 1998 | |
	1st Half	2nd Half	1st Half	2nd Half	1st Half	2nd Half	1st Half	2nd Half
Jan	1.2%	—0.3%	0.6%	1.0%	0.8%	2.5%	0.9%	1.2%
Feb	0.4	—1.0	—1.0	0.0	1.8	0.3	0.5	—0.2
Mar	0.7	0.6	0.8	—0.2	0.8	—0.2	0.8	0.1
Apr	1.9	—0.4	1.1	0.9	0.5	0.4	1.1	0.3
May	—0.8	—0.8	0.4	—1.4	1.1	2.3	0.3	0.1
June	—0.6	—1.1	1.6	0.1	0.8	—0.2	0.6	—0.4
July	1.0	—0.5	0.1	—1.1	0.8	1.0	0.6	—0.1
Aug	0.2	0.7	1.0	0.1	—0.3	0.4	0.2	0.4
Sep	1.1	0.3	—0.6	—0.8	—0.6	0.1	—0.1	—0.1
Oct	0.4	0.3	2.8	—1.3	0.1	—0.8	1.0	—0.6
Nov	—0.4	0.2	1.2	0.9	0.5	0.6	0.4	0.5
Dec	0.4	1.1	—1.7	2.0	1.1	1.3	0.0	1.5
Total	**5.5%**	**—0.9%**	**6.3%**	**0.2%**	**7.4%**	**7.7%**	**6.3%**	**2.7%**
Avg.	**0.46%**	**—0.08%**	**0.53%**	**0.02%**	**0.62%**	**0.64%**	**0.53%**	**0.23%**

Based on S&P composite index

The gain for the first half of all the months averaged 0.53%. This is two and a half times the 0.23% average gain for the second half of all months.

I separated the entire period into three sections because the 8000-point gain in the Dow in the 1985-1998 years altered previous patterns.

In the 1963-1973 and the 1974-1984 periods, the first half of the month outperformed the second half by an extremely wide margin. However, during the latest period, which contained the greatest bull market ever, second halves are slightly ahead of first halves.

The first halves of January, March, April, July and October were gainers in all periods. The best second half for the entire period was December. January was next best on average.

The biggest surprise was May's spectacular showing in the latest period, especially its average 2.3% gain during the second half of the month. January held top honors while December ran third with 1.3%.

When we separated the months into different segments the results were quite dramatic. We divided them into the 26th through the 10th days vs. the 11th through the 25th days. Please turn to page 48 and see how the better half of the month has outperformed the other half so impressively.

APRIL

MONDAY

5

Day after Easter down sharply six of last eight years.

*Spend at least as much time
researching a stock as you would
choosing a refrigerator.*
— Peter Lynch

TUESDAY

6

Buy Puts

Check on CISCO Puts
Down before April 15

*The world will not see another such talent
for a hundred years.*
— Franz Joseph Haydn, after Mozart's death at 35

WEDNESDAY

7

*The mass of men lead lives
of quiet desperation.*
— Henry David Thoreau (a favorite Ross Perot quote)

THURSDAY

8

*The first rule is not to lose. The second
rule is not to forget the first rule.*
— Warren Buffet

FRIDAY

9

Murphy & Murphy — PAGE
Worksheets & Prep   3 HRS ✓

*Press on. Nothing in the world can take the place of persistence.
Talent will not: nothing is more common than unrewarded talent.
Education alone will not: the world is full of educated failures.
Persistence alone is omnipotent.*
— Calvin Coolidge

SATURDAY

10

SUNDAY

11

MUSSER — CONTRIBUTION — 8283 — 2 HRS

DAYS BETWEEN 26TH THROUGH 10TH OF MONTHS OUTPERFORM MIDDLE 11TH THROUGH 25TH DAYS

It is evident that the first half of all months outperforms the second half (see page 46). What would happen if months were divided into two different segments? Since the greatest gains come at the ends and beginnings of months I contrasted the days between the twenty-sixth of one month and the tenth of the following month with those days between the eleventh and the twenty-fifth. An interesting pattern develops.

The timespan is separated into three periods because the 8000-point gain in the Dow during 1985-1998 altered previous patterns.

HALF OF MONTHS INCLUDING ENDS AND BEGINNINGS VS. REST OF DAYS BETWEEN 11TH AND 25TH

	1963–1973		1974–1984		1985–April 1998		Avg All Months 1963–Apr 1998	
	26 to 10	11 to 25	26 to 10	11 to 25	26 to 10	11 to 25	26 to 10	11 to 25
Jan	1.5%	0.4%	1.6%	0.1%	—0.1%	2.0%	1.0%	0.8%
Feb	—0.1	—0.4	0.1	—0.1	2.8	0.7	1.1	0.1
Mar	0.3	0.1	0.4	0.3	0.9	0.4	0.6	0.3
Apr	1.9	0.1	0.2	1.5	—0.1	0.5	0.6	0.7
May	—0.2	—1.6	0.7	—0.9	1.1	1.3	0.6	—0.3
Jun	—0.1	—1.0	1.1	0.9	1.2	0.6	0.7	0.2
Jul	1.1	—0.6	—1.3	0.5	0.5	0.0	0.1	0.0
Aug	—0.2	0.6	0.4	—0.3	0.7	0.2	0.3	0.2
Sep	1.0	0.9	0.0	—0.1	0.1	—0.7	0.3	0.0
Oct	0.2	0.8	1.5	—1.7	0.3	—0.9	0.7	—0.6
Nov	—0.2	—1.1	1.5	0.7	0.6	0.7	0.6	0.1
Dec	1.7	—0.5	—0.8	0.6	1.0	1.1	0.7	0.5
Total	**6.9%**	**—2.3%**	**5.4%**	**1.5%**	**9.0%**	**5.9%**	**7.3%**	**2.0%**
Avg	**0.58%**	**—0.19%**	**0.45%**	**0.13%**	**0.75%**	**0.49%**	**0.60%**	**0.17%**

Based on S&P composite index

During the 1963-1998 period, the first 11 whole years averaged puny annual gains of 4.6% (6.9% *minus* 2.3%). The next 11 years gained 6.9% per year while the third and current period had an average annual gain of 14.9%.

The table shows the prime halves of the month during 1963-1973 averaged annual gains of 6.9% while the other halves lost 2.3% per year. During 1974-1984 the results were 5.4% versus 1.5%. A vast improvement occurs during 1985-1998 with the prime days gaining 9.0% on average annually and the remaining days also improving considerably to 5.9% per year.

All months from 1963 through April 1998 show an annual gain of 7.3% for the prime days, compared to only 2.0% for the remaining days. The average month gained 0.60% during the twenty-sixth through the tenth day of the following month. A gain of 0.17% was registered for days eleven through twenty-five. The 3.5 to one advantage is far higher than the 2.3 to one ratio when the months are split in half right down the middle as on page 46.

MUSSER EXTENSIONS 1 HR

MUSSER ENTER ADDL INFO
K-1 Contributions 1½ HRS
Extension Letters

MUSSER / STARWOOD 2 HRS
DRIP SUMMARY
CALLS - ITT/CCH

MUSSER - FIGURE OUT STOCK - ITT
1 HR

BEST MONTHS IN PAST 48⅓ YEARS

Seasonality for different months of the year is usually based on the number of times the month has closed higher in either the Dow industrials or the S&P 500.

December ranks Number One with an average monthly gain of 1.7% since 1950 based on the S&P 500. Next comes January 1.7%, November 1.6%, and April 1.3%. Using Dow points as a measuring stick is misleading as the Dow was mostly under 1000 prior to 1982. The worst month has been September, the only negative month on the S&P in 48 years. While October was the biggest loser on the Dow, losing 602.75 in 1987 and 502.46 in 1997, it was seventh on S&P percent changes. See the graphic presentation on page 135.

MONTHLY % AND POINT CHANGES (JANUARY 1950-APRIL 1998)

Standard & Poor's 500

Month	Total % Change	Avg. % Change	# Up	# Down
Jan	81.0%	1.7	32	17
Feb	13.3	0.3	28	21
Mar	47.1	1.0	32	17
Apr	65.2	1.3	34	15
May	15.0	0.3	28	20
June	7.5	0.2	24	24
July	63.4	1.3	28	20
Aug	14.1	0.3	26	22
Sep	—16.7	—0.3	21	27
Oct	18.8	0.4	27	21
Nov	77.4	1.6	31	17
Dec	81.9	1.7	36	12

% Rank	Total % Change	Avg. % Change	# Up	# Down
Dec	81.9%	1.7%	36	12
Jan	81.0	1.7	32	17
Nov	77.4	1.6	31	17
Apr	65.2	1.3	34	15
July	63.4	1.3	28	20
Mar	47.1	1.0	32	17
Oct	18.8	0.4	27	21
May	15.0	0.3	28	20
Aug	14.1	0.3	26	22
Feb	13.3	0.3	28	21
June	7.5	0.2	24	24
Sep	—16.7	—0.3	21	27

Dow Jones Industrials

Month	Total Points Change	Avg. Points Change	# Up	# Down
Jan	1617.19	33.00	34	15
Feb	1178.33	24.05	29	20
Mar	495.55	10.11	31	18
Apr	1500.46	30.62	31	18
May	944.22	19.67	26	22
Jun	263.32	5.49	24	24
Jul	1309.77	27.29	30	18
Aug	—425.25	— 8.86	27	21
Sep	105.45	2.20	18	30
Oct	—604.54	—12.59	26	22
Nov	1338.55	27.89	32	16
Dec	1140.19	23.75	34	14

Points Rank	Total Points Change	Avg. Points Change	# Up	# Down
Jan	1617.19	33.00	34	15
Apr	1500.46	30.62	31	18
Nov	1338.55	27.89	32	16
Jul	1309.77	27.29	30	18
Feb	1178.33	24.05	29	20
Dec	1140.19	23.75	34	14
May	944.22	19.67	26	22
Mar	495.55	10.11	31	18
Jun	263.32	5.49	24	24
Sep	105.45	2.20	18	30
Aug	—425.25	— 8.86	27	21
Oct	—604.54	—12.59	26	22

One must always be diligent when analyzing long periods of seasonal data as market seasonality can change just like the weather. While the Dow was gaining almost 7500 points since the October 19, 1987 bottom of 1738.74, the total S&P percent changes between 1985 and 1997 for each month in ranking order were: May 43.3%, January 36.6%, December 30.6%, February 30.6%, July 23.6%, November 15.1%, April 13.0%, March 10.6%, June 7.5%, August 0.7%, September *minus* 6.2% and October *minus* 8.5%.

APRIL

MONDAY
19

MUSSER - ITT ~ FAX ~ WORKSHEET
TAX RETURN   1 HR

*The greatest discovery of my generation
is that human beings can alter their
lives by altering their attitudes.*
— William James

TUESDAY
20

*If all the economists in the world
were laid end to end, they still
wouldn't reach a conclusion.*
— George Bernard Shaw

WEDNESDAY
21

*The best minds are not in government. If
any were, business would hire them away.*
— Ronald Reagan

THURSDAY
22

*The quality of a person's life is in direct
proportion to their commitment to
excellence, regardless of their chosen
field of endeavor.*
— Vince Lombardi

FRIDAY
23

*Quality is never an accident; it is always
the result of high intention, genuine
effort, intelligent direction,
and skillful execution.*
— Willa A. Foster

SATURDAY
24

SUNDAY
25

*In the very merry month of May
Bulls have lately romped away*

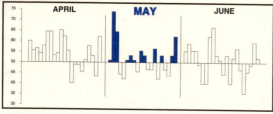

See Market Probability Chart on page 125.

MAY ALMANAC

❑ Between 1964 and 1984 May was the "disaster month" with the S&P 500 down 15 out of 20 times ❑ S&P then moved higher thirteen straight years till 1998 (page 140) ❑ May ranks fifth from last on the S&P since 1950 ❑ However, between 1985 and 1997, May beat all other months, gaining a spectacular 43.3% (page 50) ❑ Why the turnabout? Short (3-month) bear markets in 1987 and 1990 ending in October and almost 10% drops ending March 1994 and April 1997 left May unscathed.

MAY DAILY POINT CHANGES DOW JONES INDUSTRIALS

Previous Month Close	1988 2032.33	1989 2418.80	1990 2656.76	1991 2887.87	1992 3359.12	1993 3427.55	1994 3681.69	1995 4321.27	1996 5569.08	1997 7008.99
1	—	– 3.84	12.16	42.33	–23.03	—	—	– 5.19	6.14	– 32.51
2	10.94	–12.10	20.72	8.41	—	—	19.33	12.80	–76.95	94.72
3	15.09	– 9.16	6.53	0.25	—	18.91	13.39	44.27	–20.24	—
4	–22.05	– 8.80	14.19	—	42.04	– 0.27	–16.66	–13.49	—	—
5	–16.08	– 2.94	—	—	–18.78	2.91	– 1.78	–16.26	—	143.29
6	–12.77	—	—	2.78	10.06	– 7.20	–26.47	—	–13.72	10.83
7	—	—	11.26	–24.15	– 6.04	– 4.71	—	—	–43.36	–139.67
8	—	– 5.49	11.94	13.41	6.04	—	—	40.47	53.11	50.97
9	–10.11	– 5.14	– 0.68	40.25	—	—	–40.46	6.91	1.08	32.91
10	6.30	3.12	5.63	–50.98	—	6.09	27.37	13.84	43.00	—
11	–37.80	8.43	63.07	—	28.17	25.47	–27.37	6.57	—	—
12	2.15	56.82	—	—	–12.46	13.56	23.80	19.37	—	123.22
13	22.55	—	—	4.25	6.86	–34.32	6.84	—	64.46	– 18.54
14	—	—	19.95	–37.57	–23.10	– 4.98	—	—	42.11	11.95
15	—	24.19	0.92	–21.47	–15.79	—	—	6.91	0.73	47.39
16	17.08	–10.44	– 2.77	28.63	—	—	11.82	– 2.42	9.61	–138.88
17	–21.22	8.98	12.03	– 7.38	—	6.92	49.11	–12.45	52.45	—
18	–35.32	7.69	–11.80	—	22.94	– 5.54	12.28	–81.96	—	—
19	7.63	30.98	—	—	21.96	55.64	26.09	0.69	—	34.21
20	– 6.13	—	—	5.59	– 4.15	23.25	7.37	—	61.32	74.58
21	—	—	24.77	13.86	–15.13	–30.45	—	—	–12.56	– 12.77
22	—	0.92	7.55	4.25	8.06	—	—	54.30	41.74	– 32.56
23	–11.11	–24.01	4.03	–10.29	—	—	–23.94	40.81	–15.88	87.78
24	21.05	5.86	– 0.71	13.87	—	14.95	2.76	1.72	0.74	—
25	– 1.16	– 1.28	–34.63	—	H	8.85	10.13	–25.93	—	H
26	5.38	11.18	—	—	–22.56	23.53	– 1.84	–43.23	—	H
27	–10.31	—	—	H	6.23	14.67	3.68	—	H	37.50
28	—	—	H	44.95	27.99	–27.40	—	—	–53.19	– 26.18
29	—	H	49.57	10.73	– 1.55	—	—	H	–35.84	– 27.05
30	H	–18.22	8.07	30.86	—	—	H	9.68	19.58	0.86
31	74.68	4.60	– 1.90	27.05	—	H	1.23	86.46	–50.23	—
Close	2031.12	2480.15	2876.66	3027.50	3396.88	3527.43	3758.37	4465.14	5643.18	7331.04
Change	– 1.21	61.35	219.90	139.63	37.76	99.88	76.68	143.87	74.10	322.05

APRIL/MAY

MONDAY
26

*It is a funny thing about life; if you refuse
to accept anything but the best, you
very often get it.*
— W. Somerset Maugham

TUESDAY
 ## 27

*Capitalism without bankruptcy is like
Christianity without hell.*
— Frank Borman, CEO, Eastern Airlines, April 1986

WEDNESDAY
 ## 28

*Management is always going to be biased,
either they're too close to the company
to see what's really going on, or
they're not totally upfront.*
— D.H. Blair, Morton Davis, Chairman

THURSDAY
 ## 29

*I'm always turned off by an overly
optimistic letter from the president in the
annual report. If his letter is mildly
pessimistic to me that's a good sign.*
— Philip Carret

FRIDAY
 ## 30

*When I talk to a company that tells me the
last analyst showed up three years ago,
I can hardly contain my enthusiasm.*
— Peter Lynch

SATURDAY
1

SUNDAY
2

MAY

MONDAY 3

Analysts are supposed to be critics of corporations. They often end up being public relations spokesmen for them.
— Ralph Wanger

TUESDAY 4

It's a lot of fun finding a country nobody knows about. The only thing better is finding a country everybody's bullish on and shorting it.
— Jim Rogers

WEDNESDAY 5

Short-term volatility is greatest at turning points and diminishes as a trend becomes established.
— George Soros

THURSDAY 6

Patriotism is when love of your own people comes first; nationalism, when hate for people other than your own comes first.
— Charles DeGaulle, *Life* May 9, 1969

FRIDAY 7

The bigger a man's head gets, the easier it is to fill his shoes.
— Anonymous

SATURDAY 8

Mother's Day   ## SUNDAY 9

MONDAY AND TUESDAY NOW BEST DOW DAYS OF WEEK

Since the giant bull began in 1990, Mondays have never had a losing year, in contrast to its miserable record in the previous 37 years. Can you believe Tuesdays point gain in 1997? See pages 132 and 133.

ANNUAL DOW POINT CHANGES FOR DAYS OF THE WEEK SINCE 1953

	Monday	Tuesday	Wednesday	Thursday	Friday	Closing D.J.I.	Point Change
1953	− 37.39	− 6.70	19.63	7.25	6.21	280.90	− 11.00
1954	9.80	9.15	24.31	36.05	44.18	404.39	123.49
1955	− 56.09	34.31	45.83	0.78	59.18	488.40	84.01
1956	− 30.15	− 16.36	− 15.30	9.86	63.02	499.47	11.07
1957	−111.28	− 5.93	64.12	4.26	− 14.95	435.69	− 63.78
1958	14.36	26.73	29.10	24.25	53.52	583.65	147.96
1959	− 35.69	20.25	4.11	20.49	86.55	679.36	95.71
1960	−104.89	− 9.90	− 5.62	10.35	46.59	615.89	− 63.47
1961	− 17.66	4.29	87.51	− 5.74	46.85	731.14	115.25
1962	− 88.44	13.03	9.97	− 4.46	− 9.14	652.10	− 79.04
1963	− 43.61	81.85	16.23	26.07	30.31	762.95	110.85
1964	− 3.89	− 14.34	39.84	21.96	67.61	874.13	111.18
1965	− 70.23	36.65	57.03	2.75	68.93	969.26	95.13
1966	−126.73	− 54.24	56.13	− 45.69	− 13.04	785.69	−183.57
1967	− 73.17	35.94	25.50	98.37	32.78	905.11	119.42
1968*	3.28	37.97	25.16	− 59.00	31.23	943.75	38.64
1969	−152.05	− 48.82	18.33	17.79	21.36	800.36	−143.39
1970	− 99.00	− 47.14	116.07	1.81	66.82	838.92	38.56
1971	− 15.89	22.44	13.70	6.23	24.80	890.20	51.28
1972	− 85.08	− 3.55	65.24	6.14	147.07	1020.02	129.82
1973	−192.68	29.09	− 5.94	41.56	− 41.19	850.86	−169.16
1974	−130.99	29.13	− 20.31	− 12.60	− 99.85	616.24	−234.62
1975	59.80	−129.96	56.93	129.48	119.92	852.41	236.17
1976	81.16	61.32	50.88	− 26.79	− 14.33	1004.65	152.24
1977	− 66.38	− 43.66	− 79.61	8.53	7.64	831.17	−173.48
1978	− 31.79	− 70.34	71.33	− 65.71	70.35	805.01	− 26.16
1979	− 27.72	4.72	− 18.84	73.97	1.60	838.74	33.73
1980	− 89.40	137.92	137.77	−112.98	51.74	963.99	125.25
1981	− 55.47	− 39.72	− 13.95	− 13.66	33.81	875.00	− 88.99
1982	21.69	70.22	28.37	14.65	36.61	1046.54	171.54
1983	39.34	− 39.75	149.28	48.30	14.93	1258.64	212.10
1984	− 40.48	44.70	−129.24	84.36	− 6.41	1211.57	− 47.07
1985	86.96	43.97	56.19	49.45	98.53	1546.67	335.10
1986	− 56.03	113.72	178.65	32.17	80.77	1895.95	349.28
1987	−651.77	338.45	382.03	142.47	−168.30	1938.83	42.88
1988	139.28	295.28	− 60.48	−220.90	76.56	2168.57	229.74
1989	− 3.23	93.25	233.25	70.08	191.28	2753.20	584.63
Sub Total	**−2041.51**	**1053.97**	**1713.20**	**422.10**	**1313.54**		**2461.30**
1990	153.11	41.57	47.96	−330.48	− 31.70	2633.66	−119.54
1991	174.58	64.52	174.53	251.08	−129.54	3168.83	535.17
1992	302.94	−114.81	3.12	90.38	−149.35	3301.11	132.28
1993	441.72	−155.93	243.87	− 0.04	− 76.64	3754.09	452.98
1994	133.77	− 22.69	29.98	−159.66	98.95	3834.44	80.35
1995	203.99	269.04	357.02	150.44	302.19	5117.12	1282.68
1996	631.88	150.08	− 34.24	261.66	321.77	6448.27	1331.15
1997	762.68	2362.53	−590.17	−989.48	− 85.58	7908.25	1459.98
Sub Total	**2804.67**	**2594.31**	**232.07**	**−726.10**	**250.10**		**5155.05**
Totals	**763.16**	**3648.28**	**1945.27**	**−304.00**	**1563.64**		**7616.35**

* Most Wednesdays closed last 7 months of 1968

56

MAY

MONDAY
10

The test of success is not what you do when you are on top. Success is how high you bounce when you hit bottom.
— General George S. Patton

TUESDAY
11

When an old man dies, a library burns down.
— African proverb

WEDNESDAY
12

Do your work with your whole heart and you will succeed — there is so little competition.
— Elbert Hubbard

THURSDAY
13

The usual bull market successfully weathers a number of tests until it is considered invulnerable, whereupon it is ripe for a bust.
— George Soros

FRIDAY
14

The people who sustain the worst losses are usually those who overreach. And it's not necessary: Steady, moderate gains will get you where you want to go.
— John Train

SATURDAY
15

SUNDAY
16

1997 DAILY DOW POINT CHANGES
(Dow Jones Industrial Average)

WEEK #		MONDAY	TUESDAY	WEDNESDAY	THURSDAY	FRIDAY	WEEKLY DOW CLOSE	NET POINT CHANGE
						1996 Close	6448.27	
1				H	— 5.78	101.60	6544.09	95.82†
2	J	23.09	33.48	— 51.18	76.19	78.12	6703.79	159.70
3	A	5.39	53.11	— 35.41	38.49	67.73	6833.10	129.31
4	N	10.77	40.03	— 33.87	— 94.28	— 59.27	6696.48	—136.62
5		— 35.79	— 4.61	84.66	83.12	— 10.77	6813.09	116.61
6	F	— 6.93	27.32	— 86.58	26.16	82.74	6855.80	42.71
7	E	— 49.26	51.57	103.52	60.81	— 33.48	6988.96	133.16
8	B	H	78.50	— 47.33	— 92.75	4.24	6931.62	— 57.34
9		76.58	30.01	— 55.03	— 58.11	— 47.33	6877.74	— 53.88
10	M	41.18	— 66.20	93.13	— 1.15	56.19	7000.89	123.15
11	A	78.50	5.77	— 45.79	—160.48	56.57	6935.46	— 65.43
12	R	20.02	— 58.92	— 18.88	— 57.40	— 15.49	6804.79	—130.67
13		100.46	— 29.08	4.53	—140.11	H	6740.59	— 64.20
14		—157.11	27.57	— 94.04	— 39.66	48.72	6526.07	—214.52
15	A	29.84	53.25	— 45.32	— 23.79	—148.36	6391.69	—134.38
16	P	60.21	135.26	92.71	— 21.27	44.95	6703.55	311.86
17	R	— 43.34	173.38	— 20.87	— 20.47	— 53.38	6738.87	35.32
18		44.15	179.01	46.96	— 32.51	94.72	7071.20	332.33
19	M	143.29	10.83	—139.67	50.97	32.91	7169.53	98.33
20	A	123.22	— 18.54	11.95	47.39	—138.88	7194.67	25.14
21	Y	34.21	74.58	— 12.77	— 32.56	87.78	7345.91	151.24
22		H	37.50	— 26.18	— 27.05	0.86	7331.04	— 14.87
23		— 41.64	22.75	— 42.49	35.63	130.49	7435.78	104.74
24	J	42.72	60.77	36.56	135.64	70.57	7782.04	346.26
25	U	— 9.95	— 11.31	— 42.07	58.35	19.45	7796.51	14.47
26	N	—192.25	153.80	— 68.08	— 35.73	33.47	7687.72	—108.79
27		— 14.93	49.54	73.05	100.43	H	7895.81	208.09
28	J	— 37.32	103.82	—119.88	44.33	35.06	7921.82	26.01
29	U	1.16	52.73	63.17	— 18.11	—130.31	7890.46	— 31.36
30	L	16.26	154.93	26.71	28.57	— 3.49	8113.44	222.98
31		7.67	53.42	80.35	— 32.28	— 28.57	8194.04	80.60
32	A	4.41	— 10.91	71.77	— 71.31	—156.78	8031.22	—162.82
33	U	30.89	—101.27	— 32.52	13.71	—247.37	7694.66	—336.56
34	G	108.70	114.74	103.13	—127.28	6.04	7887.91	193.25
35		— 28.34	— 77.35	5.11	— 92.90	— 72.01	7622.42	—265.49
36	S	H	257.36	14.86	— 27.40	— 44.83	7822.41	199.99
37	E	12.77	16.73	—132.63	— 58.30	81.99	7742.97	— 79.44
38	P	— 21.83	174.78	— 9.48	36.28	— 5.45	7917.27	174.30
39		79.56	— 26.77	— 63.35	— 58.70	74.17	7922.18	4.91
40		69.25	— 46.17	70.24	12.03	11.05	8038.58	116.40
41	O	61.64	78.09	— 83.25	— 33.64	— 16.21	8045.21	6.63
42	C	27.01	24.07	— 38.31	—119.10	— 91.85	7847.03	—198.18
43	T	74.41	139.00	— 25.79	—186.88	—132.36	7715.41	—131.62
44		—554.26	337.17	8.35	—125.00	60.41	7442.08	—273.33
45	N	232.31	14.74	3.44	— 9.33	—101.92	7581.32	139.24
46	O	— 28.73	6.14	—157.41	86.44	84.72	7572.48	— 8.84
47	V	125.74	— 47.40	73.92	101.87	54.46	7881.07	308.59
48		—113.15	41.03	— 14.17	H	28.35*	7823.13	— 57.94
49	D	189.98	5.72	13.18	18.15	98.97	8149.13	326.00
50	E	— 38.29	— 61.18	— 70.87	—129.80	— 10.69	7838.30	—310.83
51	C	84.29	53.72	— 18.90	—110.91	— 90.21	7756.29	— 82.01
52		63.02	—127.54	— 31.64*	H	19.18*	7679.31	— 76.98
53		113.10†	123.56	— 7.72		Year's Close	7908.25	228.94†
TOTALS		762.68	2362.53	—590.17	—989.48	—85.58		1459.98

*Shortened trading day †Partial week

58

MONDAY
17

*The best time to buy long-term bonds is
when short-term rates are higher than
long-term rates.*
— George Soros

TUESDAY
18

*Most periodicals and trade journals are
deadly dull, and indeed full of fluff
provided by public relations agents.*
— Jim Rogers

WEDNESDAY
19

*A poor stock market will discourage both
consumer and business outlays. Also a
decline in the value of stocks reduces their
value as collateral, a further depressant.*
— George Soros

THURSDAY
20

*You try to be greedy when others are fearful,
and fearful when others are greedy.*
—Warren Buffet

FRIDAY
 # 21

*I never hired anybody who wasn't smarter
than me.*
— Don Hewett, Producer, *60 Minutes*

SATURDAY
22

SUNDAY
23

MEMORIAL DAY WEEK, 12-YEAR WINNING STREAK BOMBED THRICE IN A ROW, OUT THE DOOR YOU GO!

We used to call this time of year the "May-June Disaster Area." Over the years we cautioned investors, "If one month doesn't get you, the other one will!"

Then came the turnabout. For twelve years in a row the four-day Memorial Day Week became a bastion of bullishness. We attributed the phenomenon to the giant bull market cycle we experienced since the 776.92 bottom on August 12, 1982. During the last ten years, May became the best performing month of the year and was up 13 years in a row until 1998.

It's always dangerous to publicize a favorable seasonal pattern lest a multitude of traders rush in to take advantage of a "sure thing." But this time, I seriously doubt that we had anything to do with it.

DOW POINT CHANGES DURING MEMORIAL DAY WEEK

	Memorial Day	Tuesday	Wednesday	Thursday	Friday	Points Change	Percent Change	Week's Close
1984		— 5.86	1.35	2.26	19.50	**17.25**	1.6%	1124.35
1985		— 0.45	1.46	2.80	9.63	**13.44**	1.0	1315.41
1986	C	29.74	25.25	4.07	— 5.64	**53.42**	2.9	1876.71
1987		54.74	— 2.13	14.87	—19.11	**48.37**	2.2	2291.57
1988	L	74.68	32.89	—11.56	18.85	**114.86**	5.8	2081.30
1989		— 18.22	4.60	10.48	27.20	**24.06**	1.0	2517.83
1990	O	49.57	8.07	— 1.90	24.31	**80.05**	2.8	2900.97
1991		44.95	10.73	30.86	27.05	**113.59**	3.9	3027.50
1992	S	— 22.56	6.23	27.99	— 1.55	**10.11**	0.3	3396.88
1993		24.91	1.11	— 8.58	0.27	**17.71**	0.5	3545.14
1994	E	1.23	2.46	1.84	13.23	**18.76**	0.5	3772.22
1995		9.68	88.46	7.61	—28.36	**75.39**	1.7	4444.39
1996	D	— 53.19	—35.84	19.58	—50.23	**—119.68**	—2.1	5643.18
1997		37.50	—26.18	—27.05	0.86	**— 14.87**	—0.2	7331.04
1998		—150.71	—27.16	33.63	—70.25	**—214.49**	—2.4	8899.95

A threat of rising interest rates and a 30% gain in the previous 12 months killed the pattern in 1996. The 1000-point move over the preceding six weeks in 1997 paused during the holiday week. A Russian Ruble crisis and nuclear testing in both India and Pakistan hammered the market during Memorial Day Week 1998.

May 1998 suffered its first loss in 14 years, off 1.9% on the S&P composite index and 1.8% on the 30 Dow Jones industrials. To paraphrase an old ditty, "And it's one, two, three strikes you're out at the old bull game!"

MONDAY
24

With its circular flows of purchasing power, its invisible-handed markets, its intricate interplays of goods and money, all modern economics resembles a vast mathematical drama, on an elaborate stage of theory, without a protagonist to animate the play.
—George Gilder

TUESDAY
 # 25

I've never been poor, only broke. Being poor is a frame of mind. Being broke is only a temporary situation.
—Mike Todd, 1958

WEDNESDAY
 # 26

There are now more than a million U.S. dollar-based millionaires in China.
—John Naisbitt, *Megatrends Asia*

THURSDAY
 # 27

There is nothing good or bad, only thinking makes it so.
— William Shakespeare

FRIDAY
 # 28

Chance favors the informed mind.
—Louis Pasteur

SATURDAY
29

SUNDAY
30

O "Summer Rally" start in June
Lift my portfolio to the moon!

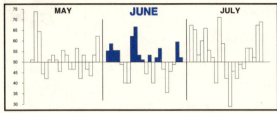

JUNE ALMANAC

See Market Probability Chart on page 125.

❑ After rising just three times between 1965 and 1974, the S&P rose in eleven of the following fourteen Junes ❑ From 1989 through 1997, June was up four times and down five ❑ RECORD: very little ground gained in 48 Junes ❑ 1997 was biggest June point gain ever, Dow was up 341 points ❑ Many sharp spring corrections accelerate into June ❑ June is the leading rallying point after October during both bull and bear markets ❑ June tends to be a down month during bear markets.

JUNE DAILY POINT CHANGES DOW JONES INDUSTRIALS

Previous Month Close	1988 2031.12	1989 2480.15	1990 2876.66	1991 3027.50	1992 3396.88	1993 3527.43	1994 3758.37	1995 4465.14	1996 5643.18	1997 7331.04
1	32.89	10.48	24.31	—	16.33	24.91	2.46	7.61	—	—
2	−11.56	27.20	—	—	−17.11	1.11	− 1.84	−28.36	—	− 41.64
3	18.85	—	—	7.83	10.89	− 8.58	13.23	—	−18.47	22.75
4	—	—	34.22	− 7.38	− 7.26	0.27	—	—	41.00	− 42.49
5	—	−37.13	−10.19	−22.58	− 1.04	—	—	32.16	31.77	35.63
6	3.91	15.62	−13.35	−10.51	—	—	− 3.70	8.65	−30.29	130.49
7	−20.62	16.00	−14.32	−18.12	—	−13.01	−12.61	−23.17	29.92	—
8	48.36	4.59	−34.95	—	5.44	−21.59	− 6.46	− 3.46	—	—
9	− 9.60	− 3.49	—	—	−34.21	1.39	3.69	−34.58	—	42.72
10	8.36	—	—	− 1.34	−26.70	−20.21	20.31	—	− 9.24	60.77
11	—	—	30.19	10.51	8.29	13.29	—	—	−19.21	36.56
12	—	5.42	40.85	−23.92	2.85	—	—	22.47	− 0.37	135.64
13	− 2.31	−15.30	− 3.72	3.13	—	—	9.67	38.05	−10.34	70.57
14	25.07	− 0.18	− 1.48	35.33	—	9.68	31.71	6.57	− 8.50	—
15	6.93	−28.36	7.67	—	0.54	−22.69	−24.42	5.19	—	—
16	−37.16	11.38	—	—	−25.41	19.65	20.93	14.52	—	− 9.95
17	9.78	—	—	− 6.49	−41.73	10.24	−34.56	—	3.33	− 11.31
18	—	—	−53.71	− 7.15	−13.64	−27.12	—	—	−24.75	− 42.07
19	—	− 6.49	11.38	−31.31	11.23	—	—	42.89	20.32	58.35
20	−20.09	− 7.01	1.74	− 1.56	—	—	−34.88	− 3.12	11.08	19.45
21	25.24	− 7.97	6.43	11.62	—	16.05	−33.93	− 3.46	45.80	—
22	43.03	17.26	−44.55	—	− 4.55	−13.29	16.80	42.54	—	—
23	− 3.91	49.70	—	—	4.82	−30.72	−25.68	− 3.80	—	−192.25
24	− 5.33	—	—	−52.55	5.08	23.80	−62.15	—	12.56	153.80
25	—	—	−12.13	− 2.90	− 6.69	0.28	—	—	1.48	− 68.08
26	—	−20.49	− 2.72	2.90	− 1.60	—	—	−34.59	−36.57	− 35.73
27	−34.50	14.99	19.80	21.92	—	—	48.56	− 8.64	− 5.17	33.47
28	22.41	−21.63	16.58	−28.18	—	39.31	−15.86	14.18	−22.90	—
29	− 8.89	−46.47	1.98	—	37.45	−11.35	− 2.59	− 6.23	—	—
30	19.73	−18.21	—	—	− 1.34	− 2.77	−42.09	5.54	—	− 14.93
Close	2141.71	2440.06	2880.69	2906.75	3318.52	3516.08	3624.96	4556.10	5654.63	7672.79
Change	110.59	−40.09	4.03	−120.75	−78.36	−11.35	−133.41	90.96	11.45	341.75

MONDAY

31

The man who masters himself,
masters the universe.
— Robert Krausz

KRAMER — MUTUAL FUND TRANSFER
BULAND IOWA REFUND

TUESDAY

 1

The measure of success is not whether
you have a tough problem to deal with,
but whether its the same problem
you had last year.
— John Foster Dulles

WEDNESDAY

 2

Don't be scared to take big steps—you
can't cross a chasm in two small jumps.
— David Lloyd George

THURSDAY

3

Choose a job you love, and you will never
have to work a day in your life.
— Confucius

FRIDAY

4

I cannot give you a formula for success
but I can give you a formula for failure:
Try to please everybody.
— Herbert Swope

SATURDAY

5

SUNDAY

6

LAST 4 + FIRST 2 DAYS VS. REST OF MONTH 1990-98

The "best days" are no longer the last plus the first four. So many investors trying to take advantage of this lucrative seasonality pattern have caused a change. Now, the last four days of the month and the first two of the following month perform much better. (Also, see page 66.)

NET DOW POINT CHANGES SHOWING MONTHLY BIAS

	Super 6 Days	Rest of Month	Super 6 Days	Rest of Month	Super 6 Days	Rest of Month
	1990		**1991**		**1992**	
Jan	98.34	—248.69	— 47.78	85.90	150.50	39.13
Feb	41.66	— 27.93	112.87	117.08	32.20	9.61
Mar	85.59	47.30	24.75	— 55.20	7.83	— 30.86
Apr	29.05	— 82.21	86.14	4.45	— 25.27	90.34
May	35.14	165.91	— 10.89	— 24.70	53.67	8.64
June	79.64	— 90.14	114.04	—114.94	9.33	—105.40
July	66.58	19.31	59.71	7.38	39.59	— 48.09
Aug	— 66.34	—252.97	26.16	33.10	102.12	—152.10
Sep	16.59	—175.25	— 30.86	20.57	58.09	— 2.44
Oct	52.23	— 21.04	— 16.55	— 7.60	— 87.26	43.50
Nov	6.68	42.33	40.70	—142.89	8.37	— 29.44
Dec	46.53	41.59	26.83	121.42	63.21	39.99
Totals	**491.69**	**—581.79**	**385.12**	**44.57**	**412.38**	**—137.12**
Average	**40.97**	**— 48.48**	**32.09**	**3.71**	**34.37**	**— 11.43**
	1993		**1994**		**1995**	
Jan	— 18.37	— 15.67	— 9.03	111.44	24.22	13.80
Feb	36.47	14.32	80.20	— 63.88	— 0.68	102.28
Mar	57.54	60.79	— 79.92	— 57.01	6.88	177.41
Apr	— 90.51	27.56	— 99.32	— 26.73	44.27	102.37
May	47.82	61.59	65.73	30.76	24.90	109.28
June	45.67	— 62.84	13.82	—122.05	6.23	106.86
July	— 6.64	83.73	15.54	89.36	63.98	99.22
Aug	— 6.43	90.82	54.38	33.67	— 24.30	— 88.75
Sep	— 25.99	— 82.99	55.69	— 36.34	68.68	99.85
Oct	34.65	95.85	— 48.11	49.46	— 20.23	3.98
Nov	24.03	— 23.47	— 13.46	—162.50	54.91	240.25
Dec	27.94	90.82	70.99	87.81	90.68	— 41.55
Totals	**126.18**	**340.51**	**106.51**	**— 66.01**	**339.54**	**925.00**
Average	**10.52**	**28.38**	**8.88**	**— 5.50**	**28.30**	**77.08**
	1996		**1997**		**1998**	
Jan	96.10	22.76	21.24	116.60	318.86	—266.05
Feb	157.16	256.50	172.79	174.72	447.41	249.85
Mar	— 30.34	43.71	—155.48	52.53	174.63	287.97
Apr	27.82	—117.78	—388.24	275.24	113.84	77.98
May	— 55.63	264.59	278.95	274.71		
June	— 97.15	52.08	— 33.76	445.91		
July	2.59	—298.37	37.32	318.06		
Aug	257.82	14.06	85.01	—338.88		
Sep	— 36.99	217.13	35.07	12.07		
Oct	59.94	73.05	120.82	—866.37		
Nov	34.66	430.08	527.98	191.94		
Dec	— 29.07	80.16	137.76	—358.70		
Totals	**386.91**	**1037.97**	**839.46**	**297.82**	**1054.74**	**349.75**
Average	**32.24**	**86.50**	**69.96**	**24.82**	**263.69**	**87.44**

Note: Average day of Super Six nearly five times better than the average day in the rest of the month. (See box below)

		Super Six Days		Rest of Month (15 Days)	
100	Net Change	4171.60		Net Change	2210.70
MONTH	Average Period	41.72		Average Period	22.11
TOTALS	Average Day	6.95		Average Day	1.47

JUNE

MONDAY 7

Narberth Tax Return   6/30/99
Penn State Register   6/17/99

*Under capitalism, the seller chases after
the buyer, and that makes both of them
work better; under socialism, the buyer
chases the seller, and neither has
time to work.*
— Andrei Sakharov's Uncle Ivan

TUESDAY 8

*Get inside information from the president and you
will probably lose half your money. If you get it from the
chairman of the board, you will lose all your money.*
—Jim Rogers

WEDNESDAY 9

Murphy & Murphy — 5 Hours ✓
Review PC Law — Change January
Payroll Mistakes
Norristown Tax Return — Business Privelege — 1999
               1 HR ✓

*Things may come to those who wait, but
only the things left by those who hustle.*
— Abraham Lincoln

THURSDAY 10

*There is one thing stonger than all the armies in the world,
and this is an idea whose time has come.*
—Victor Hugo

FRIDAY 11

*He who wants to persuade should put his
trust not in the right argument, but in the
right word. The power of sound
has always been greater than
the power of sense.*
— Joseph Conrad

SATURDAY 12

SUNDAY 13

MARKET GAINS MORE ON SIX DAYS OF MONTH THAN ON ALL 15 REMAINING DAYS COMBINED

See the monthly Dow % change in the first table for the last trading day of the previous month plus the first four of the current month between 1967 and 1983. During this 17-year period, spent mostly in the Dow 750-1000 range, these prime five days gained 793.27 points while the rest of the month's 16 (on average) trading days *lost* 319.46. So many investors taking advantage of this seasonality by switching between no-load equity and money market funds, along with the start of the biggest bull cycle in history, altered the pattern (see page 134).

NET DOW PERCENT CHANGE OF PRIME FIVE DAYS (1967-1983)

	JAN	FEB	MAR	APR	MAY	JUN	JUL	AUG	SEP	OCT	NOV	DEC
1967	2.85	0.83	0.66	—1.00	0.80	—0.26	0.82	2.47	1.62	—0.24	—3.53	1.03
1968	0.38	0.20	—0.89	4.48	0.68	1.67	1.54	—0.73	3.01	2.45	—0.05	0.20
1969	—2.05	0.48	1.16	—1.30	2.99	—0.66	1.55	2.78	—1.08	—1.06	0.55	—1.73
1970	0.90	0.26	3.02	0.83	—2.58	3.27	—1.98	—1.62	0.70	2.83	2.39	4.44
1971	—0.41	1.12	1.06	1.03	—1.13	1.81	1.54	—1.39	1.67	1.89	0.66	3.13
1972	2.18	0.03	2.80	2.83	—0.92	—2.03	1.28	2.70	0.48	—1.45	4.06	0.86
1973	3.95	—1.31	3.28	—3.72	3.44	—1.18	—2.74	—2.25	1.82	0.28	—5.73	—2.51
1974	3.40	—4.37	1.90	0.53	1.13	5.20	—1.48	1.07	3.20	—6.01	—0.58	—5.20
1975	6.29	2.55	4.19	—2.99	3.95	3.33	—1.38	—2.16	0.78	1.79	0.18	—3.43
1976	5.43	—0.41	—0.84	0.96	—1.26	—0.17	—0.95	0.75	2.86	—3.18	—1.00	1.23
1977	—1.92	—1.01	2.15	—0.70	1.74	0.47	—0.42	—0.20	2.04	0.24	—1.55	—2.46
1978	—4.44	—0.49	—0.75	0.57	—0.30	3.87	—1.12	3.75	1.47	1.76	0.37	4.02
1979	3.07	—3.40	2.43	1.25	—1.06	1.62	0.37	1.17	—1.08	0.30	—2.10	0.40
1980	—0.82	—0.01	—3.09	—1.20	0.61	1.47	1.86	0.22	1.14	4.75	1.60	—1.94
1981	1.96	—0.22	—0.23	0.21	—3.08	—0.76	—3.09	0.83	—3.42	0.99	3.14	0.76
1982	—1.30	—1.99	—2.21	1.80	2.16	—2.42	—1.55	—2.01	2.35	4.19	5.98	5.26
1983	2.25	1.24	1.79	—2.24	0.02	—0.16	—0.28	—2.73	4.02	2.31	—0.42	—1.39
Totals	21.71%	—6.52%	16.44%	1.34%	7.18%	15.07%	—6.03%	2.64%	21.58%	11.84%	3.96%	2.68%
Up	11	8	11	10	10	9	7	9	14	12	9	10
Down	6	9	6	7	7	8	10	8	3	5	8	7

The second table shows the new seasonality which has shifted to the last four trading days of the previous month and the first two of the current month in the 1984-1998 period. These *super six* days did 75% better than the *prime five* did in these years. In the earlier period the *prime five* outperformed the *super six* by three to one. Complete figures are available at **www.stocktradersalmanac.com**. Total Dow points gained in 1984-1998 period were 7736.13. *Super six* (1032 days) gained 5343.85, other 15 (2565 days) gained 2392.28. Each *super-six* day gained 5½ points, for every 1 point gained by any other trading day of the month.

NET DOW PERCENT CHANGE OF SUPER SIX DAYS (1984-1998)

	JAN	FEB	MAR	APR	MAY	JUN	JUL	AUG	SEP	OCT	NOV	DEC
1984	1.48	—1.46	3.25	—0.36	2.03	2.55	0.33	6.30	—1.54	—1.14	0.46	—2.25
1985	—1.68	1.10	1.07	0.46	—2.83	0.86	1.02	—0.04	0.69	1.32	2.44	—0.36
1986	1.98	3.62	—0.70	0.69	—3.11	2.59	1.79	—2.21	0.51	—1.22	2.75	3.27
1987	2.31	2.90	0.45	—1.82	2.27	1.56	0.34	2.12	—4.42	2.91	9.45	—3.85
1988	1.59	0.33	1.58	0.94	1.10	4.58	0.73	2.87	2.18	0.81	—0.76	0.00
1989	0.40	2.99	—0.80	1.79	0.01	1.37	—2.18	2.88	0.45	3.59	—0.82	2.92
1990	3.63	1.63	3.32	1.07	1.32	2.79	2.34	—2.26	0.64	2.13	0.27	1.84
1991	—1.82	4.24	0.86	3.01	—0.37	3.91	2.05	0.88	—1.02	—0.55	1.35	0.92
1992	4.93	0.99	0.24	—0.78	1.61	0.28	1.20	3.11	1.80	—2.65	0.26	1.96
1993	—0.55	1.11	2.06	—2.61	1.41	1.30	—0.19	—0.18	—0.71	0.98	0.65	0.76
1994	—0.24	2.06	—2.04	—2.63	1.80	0.37	0.43	1.45	1.45	—1.25	—0.35	1.93
1995	0.63	—0.02	0.17	1.06	0.58	0.14	1.41	—0.52	1.49	—0.42	1.16	1.80
1996	1.89	3.01	—0.54	0.49	—1.00	—1.69	0.05	4.76	—0.65	1.02	0.58	—0.45
1997	0.33	2.59	—2.22	—5.62	4.11	—0.46	0.48	1.05	0.45	1.53	7.37	1.75
1998	4.16	5.80	2.08	1.28								
Totals	19.03%	30.91%	8.44%	—3.03%	8.93%	20.15%	9.79%	20.19%	1.31%	7.04%	24.82%	10.24%
Up	11	13	10	9	10	12	12	9	9	8	11	10
Down	4	2	5	6	4	2	2	5	5	6	3	4

Incidentally, between September 1997 and July 1st 1998 all first trading days were up eleven months in a row and gained a spectacular 1283.97 points on the Dow Jones industrial average. Meanwhile, all the rest of the 199 trading days through July 1, 1998 gained just 142.28 points. Amazing!

MONDAY
14

I have brought myself, by long meditation, to the conviction that a human being with a settled purpose must accomplish it, and that nothing can resist a will which will stake even existence upon its fulfillment.
— Benjamin Disraeli

TUESDAY
15

Great works are performed not by strength, but perseverance.
— Samuel Johnson

WEDNESDAY
16

You've got to think about "big things" while you're doing small things, so that all the small things go in the right direction.
— Alvin Toffler

Penn State Course

THURSDAY
17

Obstacles are those frightful things you see when you take your eyes off the goal.
— Hannah More

FRIDAY
 # 18

There have been three great inventions since the beginning of time. The fire, the wheel, and central banking.
— Will Rogers

SATURDAY
19

Father's Day

SUNDAY
20

SUMMER PORTFOLIO REVIEW

NO. OF SHARES	SECURITY	A ORIGINAL COST	B CURRENT VALUE	C GAIN (B – A) OR LOSS (A – B)	D % CHANGE (C ÷ A)	E MONTHS HELD	F CHANGE PER MO. (D ÷ E)	G ANNUAL RETURN (F × 12)
200	Sample Corp.	$10,000	$10,400	$400	4.0%	8	0.5%	6.0%
TOTALS								

Stocks which have achieved their potential
1
2
3

Candidates for addition to portfolio
1
2
3

Stocks which have been disappointments
1
2
3

Investment decisions
1
2
3

JUNE

MONDAY
21

I measure what's going on, and I adapt to it. I try to get my ego out of the way. The market is smarter than I am so I bend.
— Martin Zweig

TUESDAY
22

Financial genius is a rising stock market.
—John Kenneth Galbraith

WEDNESDAY
23

We go to the movies to be entertained, not see rape, ransacking, pillage and looting. We can get all that in the stock market.
— Kennedy Gammage

THURSDAY
24

Murphy & Murphy — 4 Hours ✓
Computer — PCLzw Problems

Liberals have practiced tax and tax, spend and spend, elect and elect but conservatives have perfected borrow and borrow, spend and spend, elect and elect.
— George Will, *Newsweek*, 1989

FRIDAY
25

The worst mistake investors make is taking their profits too soon, and their losses too long.
— Michael Price, Mutual Shares Fund

SATURDAY
26

SUNDAY
27

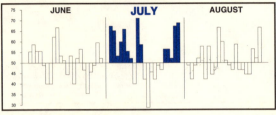

Stocks like to rocket in July, and how!
Best summer month, Dow take a bow

JULY ALMANAC

See Market Probability Chart on page 125.

JULY						
S	M	T	W	T	F	S
				1	2	3
4	5	6	7	8	9	10
11	12	13	14	15	16	17
18	19	20	21	22	23	24
25	26	27	28	29	30	31

AUGUST						
S	M	T	W	T	F	S
1	2	3	4	5	6	7
8	9	10	11	12	13	14
15	16	17	18	19	20	21
22	23	24	25	26	27	28
29	30	31				

❑ Last 48 years July was up 14 times on the Dow in first 17 years, down 14 in next 22, and up 7 straight until 1996's loss ❑ July fifth best in S&P 500, up 1.3% on average since 1950 ❑ Best Julys were 1989 (Dow up 220.60, S&P up 9.0%) and 1997 (Dow up 549.82, S&P up 7.8%) ❑ Great Julys (up 3% or more) during bull markets invariably precede better buying opportunities sometime in the fall ❑ Four big losers 1969, 1974, 1975, and 1986: down 6.0%, 7.8%, 6.8%, and 5.9%.

JULY DAILY POINT CHANGES DOW JONES INDUSTRIALS

	1988	1989	1990	1991	1992	1993	1994	1995	1996	1997
Previous Month Close	2141.71	2440.06	2880.69	2906.75	3318.52	3516.08	3624.96	4556.10	5654.63	7672.79
1	−10.13	—	—	51.66	35.58	− 5.54	21.69	—	75.35	49.54
2	—	—	18.57	14.31	−23.81	−26.57	—	— −	9.60	73.05
3	—	12.71	12.37	−38.02	—	—	—	29.05	− 17.36	100.43*
4	H	H	H	H	H	H	H	H	H	H
5	27.03	3.79	−32.42	− 2.23	—	—	5.83	30.08	−114.88*	—
6	−28.45	5.88	25.74 '	—	8.91	−34.04	22.02	48.77	—	—
7	− 7.47	25.42 '	—	—	−44.03	25.74	13.92	38.73 '	—	− 37.32
8	−16.54 '	—	—	29.52 '	− 1.89 '	38.75 '	20.72 '	—	− 37.31 '	103.82 '
9	—	—	9.16	−14.76	30.80	6.64	—	—	31.03	−119.88
10	—	14.80	−23.27	− 2.46	6.48	—	—	− 0.34	21.79	44.33
11	5.16	11.95	41.83	14.98	—	—	− 6.15	−21.79	− 83.11	35.06
12	−18.67	18.02	37.13	21.02	—	3.32	− 0.33	46.69	− 9.98	—
13	11.73	5.69	10.40	—	6.75	− 8.94	1.62	0.19	—	—
14	9.25	16.50	—	—	21.08	27.11	34.97	−18.66 '	—	1.16
15	15.83	—	—	9.84	−12.97	8.38	14.56 '	—	−161.05	52.73
16	—	—	19.55	− 6.71	16.21	−22.64	—	—	9.25	63.17
17	—	− 1.33	N/C	− 5.14	−29.99	—	—	27.47	18.12	− 18.11
18	−11.56	− 8.73	−18.07	37.56	—	—	1.62 '	−50.01	87.30	−130.31 '
19	−20.63	39.65	12.13	N/C	—	6.99	− 7.12	−57.41	− 37.36 '	—
20	13.34	− 8.92	−32.67	—	−28.64	9.50	−21.04	12.68	—	—
21	−24.01	31.87	—	—	5.41	10.62	5.18 '	N/C	—	16.26
22	−25.60	—	—	− 3.35	−30.80	−30.18	2.59	—	− 35.88	154.93
23	—	—	−56.44	−29.74	12.43	21.52	—	—	− 44.39	26.71
24	—	−22.38	17.82	−17.00	− 4.33	—	—	27.12	8.14	28.57
25	10.84	− 1.90	8.42	13.87	—	—	6.80	45.78	67.32	− 3.49
26	2.14	29.97	−10.15	− 7.60	—	20.96	− 6.16	− 7.39	51.05	—
27	−20.27	22.38	−22.28	—	− 3.51	− 2.24	−15.21	25.71	—	—
28	28.63	− 0.19	—	—	51.87	−12.01	10.36	−17.26	—	7.67
29	46.40	—	—	12.74	45.12	13.97	33.67	—	− 38.47	53.42
30	—	—	18.82	31.08	12.70	−27.95	—	—	47.34	80.36
31	—	25.42	−12.13	8.50	1.89	—	—	− 7.04	46.98	− 32.28
Close	2128.73	2660.66	2905.20	3024.82	3393.78	3539.47	3764.50	4708.47	5528.91	8222.61
Change	−12.98	220.60	24.51	118.07	75.26	23.39	139.54	152.37	−125.72	549.82

* Shortened trading day

MONDAY

28

*People's spending habits depend more on how
wealthy they feel than with the actual amount of their
current income.*
—A.S. Pigou

TUESDAY

29

*Stock prices tend to discount what
has been unanimously reported
by the mass media.*
— Louis Ehrenkrantz

WEDNESDAY

30

*When prices are high
They want to buy;
When prices are low
They let them go.*
— Ian Notley

First trading day up nine of ten times (1989–1998).

THURSDAY

 # 1

*It is the growth of total government
spending as a percentage of gross national
product— not the way it is financed—
that crowds out the private sector.*
— Paul Craig Roberts, *Business Week*, 1984

FRIDAY

  # 2

*Governments last as long as the
under-taxed can defend themselves
against the over-taxed.*
— Bernard Berenson

SATURDAY

3

Independence Day

SUNDAY

4

A RALLY FOR ALL SEASONS

In any year when the market is a disappointment, you hear talk of a summer rally. Parameters for this "rally" were defined by the late Ralph Rotnem as the lowest close in the Dow industrial average in May or June to the highest close in July, August, or September. Such a big deal is made of the "summer rally" that one might get the impression the market puts on its best razzle-dazzle performance in the summertime. Nothing could be further from the truth! Not only does the market "rally" in every season of the year, but it does so with more gusto in the winter, spring, and fall than in the summer.

Winters in 35 years averaged a 13.9% gain as measured from the low in November or December to the first quarter closing high. Spring was up 10.2% followed by fall with 10.0%. Last and least was the average 9.7% "summer rally." Nevertheless, no matter how thick the gloom or grim the outlook, don't despair! There's always a rally for all seasons, statistically.

SEASONAL GAINS IN DOW JONES INDUSTRIALS

	WINTER RALLY Nov/Dec Low to 1 Q. High	SPRING RALLY Feb/Mar Low to 2 Q. High	SUMMER RALLY May/Jun Low to 3 Q. High	FALL RALLY Aug/Sep Low to 4 Q. High
1964	15.3%	6.2%	9.4%	8.3%
1965	5.7	6.6	11.6	10.3
1966	5.9	4.8	3.5	7.0
1967	11.6	8.7	11.2	4.4
1968	7.0	11.5	5.2	13.3
1969	0.9	7.7	1.9	6.7
1970	5.4	6.2	22.5	19.0
1971	21.6	9.4	5.5	7.4
1972	19.1	7.7	5.2	11.4
1973	8.6	4.8	9.7	15.9
1974	13.1	8.2	1.4	11.0
1975	36.2	24.2	8.2	8.7
1976	23.3	6.4	5.9	4.6
1977	8.2	3.1	2.8	2.1
1978	2.1	16.8	11.8	5.2
1979	11.0	8.9	8.9	6.1
1980	13.5	16.8	21.0	8.5
1981	11.8	9.9	0.4	8.3
1982	4.6	9.3	18.5	37.8
1983	15.7	17.8	6.3	10.7
1984	5.9	4.6	14.1	9.7
1985	11.7	7.1	9.5	19.7
1986	31.1	18.8	9.2	11.4
1987	30.6	13.6	22.9	5.9
1988	18.1	13.5	11.2	9.8
1989	15.1	12.9	16.1	5.7
1990	8.8	14.5	12.4	8.6
1991	21.8	11.2	6.6	9.3
1992	14.9	6.4	3.7	3.3
1993	8.9	7.7	6.3	7.3
1994	9.7	5.2	9.1	5.0
1995	13.6	19.3	11.3	13.9
1996	19.2	7.5	8.7	17.3
1997	17.6	6.5	18.4	7.3
1998	20.3	13.6		
Totals	**487.7%**	**357.2%**	**330.1%**	**340.7%**
Average	**13.9%**	**10.2%**	**9.7%**	**10.0%**

(Market Closed)

MONDAY
5

Marketing is our No. 1 priority...
A marketing campaign isn't worth doing
unless it serves three purposes. It must
grow the business, create news, and
enhance our image.
— James Robinson III, American Express

Day after took a big hit in 1996 and 1997.

TUESDAY
6

Average earnings of an English worker in 1900 came to
half an ounce of gold a week and in 1979 after world wars,
a world slump, and a world inflation, the British worker
has average earnings of half an ounce of gold a week.
—William Rees Mogg

WEDNESDAY
7

Never lend money to someone who must
borrow money to pay interest [on other
money owed].
— A Swiss Banker's First Rule quoted by Lester Thurow

THURSDAY
8

If you don't keep your employees happy,
they won't keep the customers happy.
— Red Lobster V.P., New York Times 4/23/89

FRIDAY
9

Murphy & Murphy - 5 hours / 2000 ✓
Correct Computer Payroll Problems
Correct Previous G/L postings
Post January Journals

A man isn't a man until he has
to meet a payroll.
— Ivan Shaffer

SATURDAY
10

SUNDAY
11

FIRST MONTH OF FIRST THREE QUARTERS IS THE MOST BULLISH

The average month-to-month change since 1950 based on the S&P composite, shows that "the investment calendar reflects the annual, semi-annual and quarterly operations of institutions during January, April and July." The fourth quarter behaves differently since it is affected by year-end portfolio adjustments and presidential and congressional elections in even-numbered years.

This year I grouped all the first months of the first three quarters together and also separated the second and third months. Since 1950 the average first months of the first three quarters have gained 1.43% on average. In contrast, the average second month gained only 0.23% and the average third month, 0.17%.

Since we are in one of the most powerful bull markets of all time, I also separated all the figures for the Dow Industrial average beginning with 1991 and you can see the difference. Average gains were much higher for the first months, 2.57%. Results for the second and third months were 1.63% and 0.27%, respectfully.

What's an investor to do? Long-term investors can not make use of this seasonal tendency. However, if you put money into the market on a quarterly basis, it would be more advantageous to do it before the crowd lumbers in and pushes up your favorite stocks.

AVERAGE S&P 500 % CHANGE
FIRST THREE QUARTERS SINCE 1950

	1st month	2nd month	3rd month
First Q	1.7%	0.1%	0.9%
Second Q	1.4	0.2	0.1
Third Q	1.2	0.4	−0.5
Total	**4.3%**	**0.7%**	**0.5%**
Average	**1.43%**	**0.23%**	**0.17%**

DJI % CHANGES FOR MOST RECENT YEARS

First Quarter

	Jan	Feb	Mar
1991	3.9%	5.3%	1.1%
1992	1.7	1.4	−1.0
1993	0.3	1.8	1.9
1994	6.0	−3.7	−5.1
1995	0.2	4.3	3.7
1996	5.4	1.7	1.9
1997	5.7	0.9	−4.3
1998	−0.02	8.1	3.0

Second Quarter

	Apr	May	Jun
1991	−0.9%	4.8%	−4.0%
1992	3.8	1.1	−2.3
1993	−0.2	2.9	−0.3
1994	1.3	2.1	−3.5
1995	3.9	3.3	2.0
1996	−0.3	1.3	0.2
1997	6.5	4.6	4.7

Third Quarter

	Jul	Aug	Sep
1991	4.1%	0.6%	−0.9%
1992	2.3	−4.0	0.4
1993	0.7	3.2	−2.6
1994	3.8	4.0	−1.8
1995	3.3	−2.1	3.9
1996	−2.2	1.6	4.7
1997	7.2	−7.3	4.2
Total	**56.5%**	**36.9%**	**5.9%**
Average	**2.57%**	**1.63%**	**0.27%**

JULY

MONDAY
12

*Wall Street has a uniquely hysterical way of thinking
the world will end tomorrow but be fully recovered in
the long run, then a few years later believing the
immediate future is rosy but that the long term stinks.*
— Kenneth L. Fisher, *Wall Street Waltz*

TUESDAY
13

*Early in March (1960), Dr. Arthur F. Burns called on me…Burns'
conclusion was that unless some decisive action was taken, and
taken soon, we were heading for another economic dip which
would hit its low point in October, just before the elections.*
— Richard M. Nixon, *Six Crises*

WEDNESDAY
14

*If you can buy all you want of a new issue,
you do not want any;
if you cannot obtain any,
you want all you can buy.*
— Rod Fadem, Oppenheimer & Co.

THURSDAY
15

*Make money and the whole nation
will conspire to call you a gentleman.*
— George Bernard Shaw

FRIDAY
 ## 16

*Central Bankers are brought up
pulling the legs off ants.*
— Paul Volker, quoted by William Grieder, *Secrets of the Temple*

SATURDAY
17

SUNDAY
18

DOW COULD GAIN WELL OVER 3000 POINTS
FROM ITS 1998 LOW TO ITS HIGH IN 1999

Normally, major corrections occur sometime in the first or second years following presidential elections. In the last nine midterm election years, bear markets began or were in progress six times in a row before the onset in 1982 of our current biggest bull cycle in Wall Street history. Since then, we experienced a bull year in 1986, a Saddam Hussein-induced bear in 1990 and a flat year in 1994. Absent an economic collapse, the 7580.42 close on January 9, 1998 seems likely to be the low for the year.

The puniest advance from a midterm bottom, 14.5% from the 1946 low, was during the industrial contraction after World War II. The next four smallest advances with the major depressant in parentheses were: 1978 (OPEC–Iran) 20.9%, 1930 (economic collapse) 23.4%, 1966 (Vietnam) 26.7%, and 1990 (Persian Gulf War) 34.0%.

% CHANGE IN DOW JONES INDUSTRIALS BETWEEN THE
MIDTERM YEAR LOW AND THE HIGH IN THE FOLLOWING YEAR

Midterm Year Low		Pre-Election Year High		
Date of Low	Dow	Date of High	Dow	% Gain
Jul 30 1914	71.42	Dec 8 1915	134.00	87.6%
Jan 15 1918	73.38	Nov 3 1919	119.62	63.0
Jan 10 1922	78.59	Mar 20 1923	105.38	34.1
Mar 30 1926	135.20	Dec 31 1927	202.40	49.7
Dec 31 1930	157.51	Feb 24 1931	194.36	23.4
Jul 26 1934	85.51	Nov 19 1935	148.44	73.6
Mar 31 1938	98.95	Sep 12 1939	155.92	57.6
Apr 28 1942	92.92	Jul 14 1943	145.82	56.9
Oct 9 1946	163.12	Jul 24 1947	186.85	14.5
Jan 13 1950	196.81	Sep 13 1951	276.37	40.4
Jan 11 1954	279.87	Dec 30 1955	488.40	74.5
Feb 25 1958	436.89	Dec 31 1959	679.36	55.5
Jun 26 1962	535.74	Dec 18 1963	767.21	43.2
Oct 7 1966	744.32	Sep 25 1967	943.08	26.7
May 26 1970	631.16	Apr 28 1971	950.82	50.6
Dec 6 1974	577.60	Jul 16 1975	881.81	52.7
Feb 28 1978	742.12	Oct 5 1979	897.61	20.9
Aug 12 1982	776.92	Nov 29 1983	1287.20	65.7
Jan 22 1986	1502.29	Aug 25 1987	2722.42	81.2
Oct 11 1990	2365.10	Dec 31 1991	3168.84	34.0
Apr 4 1994	3593.35	Dec 13 1995	5216.47	45.2
Jan 9 1998?	7580.42			
			Average Gain	**50.0%**

A hypothetical portfolio of stocks bought at midterm election-year lows since 1914 has gained 50.0% on average when the stock market reached its subsequent highs in the following pre-election years. A swing of such magnitude is equivalent to a move from 7580 to 11,370. With an advance of nearly 7000 Dow points since the 2365.10 bottom on October 11, 1990, I would gladly settle for a 3000-point move between 1998's low and the high of 1999.

MONDAY

19

The power to tax involves the power to destroy.
— John Marshall, U. S. Supreme Court, 1819

TUESDAY

20

The fear of capitalism has compelled socialism to widen freedom, and the fear of socialism has compelled capitalism to increase equality.
— Will and Ariel Durant

WEDNESDAY

21

Nothing contributes so much to the prosperity and happiness of a country as high profits.
— David Ricardo, *On Protection to Agriculture*, 1820

THURSDAY

22

One machine can do the work of fifty ordinary men. No machine can do the work of one extraordinary man.
— Elbert Hubbard

FRIDAY

23

Speed is God and time is the devil.
—David Hancock, Hitachi
(on launching new technical products)

SATURDAY

24

SUNDAY

25

August 25th peaked ere the '87 Crash
Smart the investor who snuck into cash

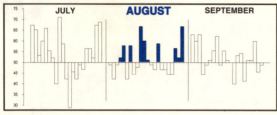

AUGUST ALMANAC

See Market Probability Chart on page 125.

❑ August was up 80% of the time prior to 1950 but barely half the time thereafter ❑ Biggest S&P gains in 1982 (11.6%) and 1984 (10.6%) start of bull market ❑ Last 3 days before Labor Day up 26 times in 37 years (page 86), first three days of week now better ❑ Dow drops 600.19 in 1997 in Southeast Asia crisis ❑ RECORD: S&P 26 up, 22 down. Average gain 0.3% ❑ Tends to get clobbered during bear markets, except when July is hammered earlier.

AUGUST DAILY POINT CHANGES DOW JONES INDUSTRIALS

	1988	1989	1990	1991	1992	1993	1994	1995	1996	1997
Previous Month Close	2128.73	2660.66	2905.20	3024.82	3393.78	3539.47	3764.50	4708.47	5528.91	8222.61
1	1.78	−19.54	− 5.94	− 7.15	—	—	33.67	− 8.10	65.84	− 28.57
2	0.71	16.32	−34.66	−11.41	—	21.52	− 1.95	−10.22	85.08	—
3	2.85	4.17	−54.95	—	1.62	0.28	− 3.56	11.27	—	—
4	− 7.47	− 8.16	—	—	−11.08	− 9.22	−26.87	−17.96	—	4.41
5	− 7.47	—	—	−17.22	−19.18	− 3.08	−18.77	—	− 5.55	− 10.91
6	—	—	−93.31	38.24	−24.58	11.46	—	—	21.83	71.77
7	—	41.54	− 5.70	− 0.67	− 8.38	—	—	9.86	22.56	− 71.31
8	−11.73	4.18	24.26	−12.75	—	—	6.79	N/C	− 5.18	−156.78
9	−28.27	−13.09	24.01	−17.66	—	15.65	1.95	−21.83	−32.18	—
10	−44.99	26.55	−42.33	—	5.40	− 3.35	11.00	−27.83	—	—
11	5.16	−28.64	—	—	− 6.48	10.62	−15.86	−25.36	—	30.89
12	− 1.78	—	—	5.14	−10.27	−14.26	17.81	—	23.67	−101.27
13	—	—	30.20	7.38	− 7.56	0.56	—	—	−57.70	− 32.52
14	—	− 6.07	0.99	− 3.35	15.67	—	—	41.56	19.60	13.71
15	−33.25	9.86	0.50	− 6.94	—	—	− 8.42	−19.02	− 1.10	−247.37
16	17.24	5.51	−66.83	−30.41	—	9.50	24.28	− 1.76	23.67	—
17	4.45	−13.66	−36.64	—	− 4.05	7.83	− 8.09	− 8.45	—	—
18	1.07	8.34	—	—	4.59	7.88	−21.05	−13.03	—	108.70
19	−11.03	—	—	−69.99	−22.42	7.27	0.32	—	9.99	114.74
20	—	—	11.64	15.66	− 2.17	3.35	—	—	21.82	103.13
21	—	−40.97	−52.48	88.10	−50.79	—	—	− 2.82	−31.44	−127.28
22	−25.78	3.99	−43.81	5.59	—	—	− 3.89	5.64	43.65	− 6.04
23	− 0.89	27.12	−76.73	32.87	—	− 9.50	24.61	−35.57	−10.73	—
24	37.34	56.53	49.50	—	−25.93	32.98	70.90	− 4.23	—	—
25	−15.82	− 2.28	—	—	4.05	13.13	−16.84	20.78	—	− 28.34
26	6.58	—	—	− 0.89	14.59	− 3.91	51.16	—	−28.85	− 77.35
27	—	—	78.71	−13.20	7.83	− 7.55	—	—	17.38	5.11
28	—	11.00	3.22	29.07	12.97	—	—	− 7.40	1.11	− 92.90
29	24.00	−16.73	17.58	− 5.59	—	—	17.80	14.44	−64.73	− 72.01
30	− 3.20	1.52	−39.11	− 6.04	—	3.36	18.45	− 3.87	−31.44	—
31	− 6.58	9.12	21.04	—	− 10.26	7.26	− 3.88	5.99	—	—
Close	2031.65	2737.27	2614.36	3043.60	3257.35	3651.25	3913.42	4610.56	5616.21	7622.42
Change	−97.08	76.61	−290.84	18.78	−136.43	111.78	148.92	−97.91	87.30	−600.19

End of July closes well lately (page 70).

(page 70)

MONDAY

26

*I am first and foremost a catalyst. I bring
people and situations together.*
— Armand Hammer

TUESDAY

 # 27

*The average man... is always waiting for
something to happen to him instead of
setting to work to make things happen.*
— A.A. Milne

WEDNESDAY

 # 28

*It is impossible to please all the world
and one's father.*
— Jean de La Fontaine

THURSDAY

 # 29

*Good judgment is usually the result of
experience and experience frequently
is the result of bad judgment.*
— Robert Lovell, quoted by Robert Sobel, *Panic on Wall Street*

FRIDAY

 # 30

*Every human being, no matter how
beaten down, dreams of a better life
and will work like a champion for
it given the opportunity.*
— Mildred & Glen Leet, Founders of "Trickle Up"

SATURDAY

31

SUNDAY

1

MARKET BEHAVIOR ON DAYS BEFORE AND AFTER HOLIDAYS AND END-OF-MONTH BUYING STRATEGIES

Throughout this year's calendar pages little "happy bulls" appear signifying a string of very favorable market days. These mostly include the best days of the month (see pages 64, 66, 134) and days around certain holidays.

Holiday market behavior shows the average basis point change (%) since 1980 for both the S&P 500 and the Zweig Unweighted Price Index (ZUPI). The January Effect for small stocks is dramatically visible in ZUPI starting in the day before New Year's Day. This would even be true going back over the years to 1928. Bullishness the day before other holidays and bearishness for a few days after is also evident except after one holiday: Memorial Day Week has now been hammered three years in a row. Third days after holidays are super.

HOLIDAYS: 3 DAYS BEFORE, 3 DAYS AFTER (Avg. Basis Point Change 1980–1998)

	−3	−2	−1		+1	+2	+3
S&P	−0.17	0.28	−0.10	**New Year's**	0.03	0.43	−0.06
ZUPI	−0.05	0.23	0.56	**Day**	0.42	0.55	0.28
S&P	0.32	−0.15	−0.15	**Presidents'**	−0.22	−0.03	0.06
ZUPI	0.25	−0.03	0.05	**Day**	−0.30	−0.08	0.01
S&P	0.01	0.12	0.09	**Good**	−0.64	0.48	−0.04
ZUPI	−0.05	0.13	0.12	**Friday**	−0.49	0.27	0.07
S&P	0.00	−0.04	0.13	**Memorial**	0.45	0.34	0.14
ZUPI	−0.09	0.06	0.21	**Day**	0.17	0.24	0.19
S&P	0.05	0.08	0.04	**Independence**	−0.42	0.09	0.19
ZUPI	0.07	0.14	0.09	**Day**	−0.24	−0.03	0.11
S&P	0.06	−0.34	0.22	**Labor**	0.07	0.14	0.13
ZUPI	0.12	−0.01	0.24	**Day**	−0.06	0.11	0.29
S&P	−0.30	0.24	0.21	**Thanksgiving**	0.17	−0.13	0.44
ZUPI	−0.26	−0.08	0.19		0.33	−0.24	0.26
S&P	0.30	0.02	0.14	**Christmas**	0.23	−0.07	0.42
ZUPI	0.13	0.10	0.33		0.10	0.00	0.31
S&P	**0.03**	**0.03**	**0.07**	**Average of**	**−0.04**	**0.16**	**0.16**
ZUPI	**0.02**	**0.07**	**0.22**	**All Listings**	**−0.01**	**0.10**	**0.19**

Being invested in small company stocks or no-load funds for five or seven days each month then switching to money market funds the rest of the month has produced annual returns of 15% or more for a good number of years.

END-OF-MONTH BUY STRATEGIES (Average Basis Point Change Over 4 Time Spans)

Strategy I
Last Plus First 4 Days

	Since	1928	1980	1985	1990
S&P		0.54	0.49	0.41	0.32
ZUPI		0.62	0.62	0.55	0.54

Strategy II
Same, Plus Additional Day Before and Day After (if not first day of week)

	Since	1928	1980	1985	1990
S&P		0.75	0.65	0.72	0.59
ZUPI		0.85	0.87	0.91	0.84

Data and ZUPI (Zweig Unweighted Price Index) courtesy of Martin Zweig/Catherine Nolan

AUGUST

August opens poorly in recent years, except 1996 (page 78).

MONDAY
2

*Only buy stocks when the market declines
10% from that date a year ago, which
happens once or twice a decade.*
— Eugene D. Brody, Oppenheimer Capital

TUESDAY
3

*Sell stocks whenever the market
is 30% higher over a year ago.*
— Eugene D. Brody, Oppenheimer Capital

WEDNESDAY
4

*You have to figure out how the consensus
is wrong to be valuable to the client.*
— Edward Yardeni, Prudential Bache

THURSDAY
5

*Never will a man penetrate deeper into
error than when he is continuing on a road
that has led him to great success.*
— Friedrich von Hayek, *Counterrevolution of Science*

FRIDAY
6

*Never overpay for a stock. More money
is lost than in any other way by projecting
above-average growth and paying
an extra multiple for it.*
— Charles Neuhauser, Bear, Stearns

SATURDAY
7

SUNDAY
8

100% ANNUAL RETURNS POSSIBLE
SELLING CALL OPTIONS ON YOUR STOCKS

Most investors fail to realize that selling (writing) options on their stocks can produce up to a 100% annual rate of return.

In 1997 option exchanges experienced a 37% increase in trading to 273 million contracts. There has also been a surge in attendance at options seminars. Participants, after being shown the possibility of enormous gains by the purchase of a few hundred dollars worth of options, may leave seminars believing that options are a sure way to financial freedom.

These new option players have high hopes of using the inherent leverage in option contracts to propel their investment returns into the stratosphere. These "sugar-plum" calculations can be quite seductive. Very simply: An investor with $4,000 buys 100 shares of XYZ Corp. at $40 per share. An option speculator can control the same number of shares by buying one contract of an out-of-the-money option (below current stock price) for $100 or $1 per share. If XYZ goes up 10 points, both parties have made $1,000 but the option purchaser did it on 40 to 1 leverage. Of course he could also have put $4,000 into options by buying 40 contracts controlling 4,000 shares of XYZ. This would have increased by $40,000 while the investor made only $1,000.

But history tells us that few option speculators strike it rich. The ones who naturally profit the most from option speculators are those who SELL THE OPTIONS, the covered call writers. To illustrate: YOU buy 100 shares of ABC Technology at $23 per share. You then write (sell) a call option to an option buyer at $25 (strike price) prior to an expiration, say three months from now, for which you receive $2.00. This reduces your price to $21 a share. Though your potential is limited to just 4 points upside, this would result in a 17.4% gain for you, or 89.9% annualized. And that's not bad! Buy your stock on 50% margin and you've just doubled your annual return!

Sounds like easy money? There is a risk! What if you are not a good stock picker and XYZ or ABC starts to decline? That does happen, especially in a bear market. At least selling the call would have reduced your loss, if the stock is pummeled. Ultimately, your degree of success in writing calls will depend significantly on the performance of your underlying stocks.

There are countless option opportunities out there. If this strategy appeals to you, take a look at **www.coveredcall.com** on the Internet. Their specialty is "7/11 options" on volatile stocks. These are out-of-the-money calls with 4-8 weeks until expiration, which would return 7% if your stock isn't called and about 11% if it does get called. A variation is "Nine is Fine" dealing with stocks above the strike price, "in-the-money." These options will likely be called, producing around a 9% return in 4-8 weeks.

AUGUST

MONDAY
9

*I invest in people, not ideas; I want to see
fire in the belly and intellect.*
— Arthur Rock

TUESDAY
10

*Unless you've interpreted changes
before they've occurred, you'll be
decimated trying to follow them.*
— Robert J. Nurock

WEDNESDAY
11

*There's nothing wrong with cash.
It gives you time to think.*
— Robert Prechter, Jr., *Elliott Wave Theorist*

THURSDAY
12

*The big guys are the status quo,
not the innovators.*
— Kenneth L. Fisher

FRIDAY
13

Down Day

*A bull market tends to bail you out of all
your mistakes. Conversely, bear markets
make you PAY for your mistakes.*
— Richard Russell

SATURDAY
14

SUNDAY
15

BEST STOCK MARKET SEASONAL TRADES
LAST 15 YEARS (1983-1998) USING S&P FUTURES

Trades that exhibit a high degree of accuracy are shown below. Though last year's trades were 100% winners, patterns do change; and when everybody knows about a seasonal trade that "always" works, it often stops working. These trades are for experienced S&P futures traders only. The rationale for each seasonal trade follows:

- **Long December 10/27 to 11/03**
  November's performance as third best month coupled with month end (page 134).

- **Long March 11/20 to 02/07**
  December is the strongest month of the year on average. Government's first fiscal quarter, when most new government funds are spent, ends in December.

- **Long March 12/15 to 12/30**
  Holiday cheer coupled with "thin" markets provide a strong tendency to rally the S&P.

- **Long March 01/12 to 01/19**
  January is the second strongest month of the year.

- **Long March 01/25 to 02/15**
  February's tendency is often to correct January's excesses. Mid-February is a time for quick profit taking by traders and short-term investors.

- **Long March 01/27 to 02/03**
  Same reasons as above, but shortened to take advantage of month end (page 134).

- **Long June 04/28 to 06/03**
  In the last 10 years May has tended to be a very strong month. A bust in 1998.

- **Long June 05/18 to 06/03**
  The last half of May since 1985 has gained 2.2% on average. A bust in 1998.

- **Short December 10/18 to 10/27**
  Last four days of period in 1997 Dow dropped 900 points, even larger than the loss during the Crash of 1987.

15 Years Seasonal S&P Futures Trades (1983-1998)

IN POINTS

Contract	Entry Date	Exit Date	Gains	Losses	Gain Percent	Total Gain	Average Gain	Worst Trade
Dec Long	27 Oct	3 Nov	13	2	87%	129.55	10.41	–3.70
Mar Long	20 Nov	7 Feb	13	2	87%	343.50	27.82	–9.55
Mar Long	15 Dec	30 Dec	13	2	87%	79.25	6.90	–6.20
Mar Long	12 Jan	19 Jan	13	2	87%	98.05	7.58	–0.45
Mar Long	25 Jan	15 Feb	13	2	87%	224.05	18.26	–9.80
Mar Long	27 Jan	3 Feb	13	2	87%	110.90	9.32	–6.00
Jun Long	28 Apr	3 Jun	14	1	93%	201.35	14.93	–7.60
Jun Long	18 May	3 Jun	13	2	87%	106.70	8.59	–2.90
Dec Short	18 Oct	27 Oct	12	3	80%	170.60	14.95	–6.95

IN DOLLARS (1 point equals $250)

Contract	Entry Date	Exit Date	Gains	Losses	Gain Percent	Total Gain	Average Gain	Worst Trade
Dec Long	27 Oct	3 Nov	13	2	87%	$32,388	$2,603	$(925)
Mar Long	20 Nov	7 Feb	13	2	87%	85,875	6,954	(2,388)
Mar Long	15 Dec	30 Dec	13	2	87%	19,813	1,726	(1,550)
Mar Long	12 Jan	19 Jan	13	2	87%	24,513	1,895	(112)
Mar Long	25 Jan	15 Feb	13	2	87%	56,013	4,564	(2,450)
Mar Long	27 Jan	3 Feb	13	2	87%	27,725	2,330	(1,500)
Jun Long	28 Apr	3 Jun	14	1	93%	50,338	3,731	(1,900)
Jun Long	18 May	3 Jun	13	2	87%	26,675	2,147	(725)
Dec Short	18 Oct	27 Oct	12	3	80%	42,650	3,736	(1,738)

Research and data courtesy of Scott Barrie of Great Pacific Trading Company. Past performance is no guarantee of future results.

MONDAY
16

10:00 AM
Buy Calls
@ 1:30

> To turn $100 into $110 is work. To turn
> $100 million into $110 million
> ‑ is inevitable.
> — Edgar Bronfman, Seagrams, in *Newsweek*, 1985

TUESDAY
17

> Almost any insider purchase is worth
> investigating for a possible lead to a
> superior speculation. But very few
> insider sales justify concern.
> — William Chidester

WEDNESDAY
18

Sell Oracle Corp.
Buy Oracle Puts - Sept.
Hold until Monday - After Sell Calls
@ 2:50

> If the models are telling you to sell,
> sell, sell, but only buyers are out
> there, don't be a jerk. Buy!
> — William Silber, Ph.D. (N.Y.U.), in *Newsweek*, 1986

THURSDAY
19

> The higher a people's intelligence and
> moral strength, the lower will be
> the prevailing rate of interest.
> — Eugen von Bohm-Bawerk, 1910

FRIDAY
20

> When everybody starts looking really
> smart, and not realizing that a lot of it
> was luck, I get scared.
> — Raphael Yavneh, *Forbes*

SATURDAY
21

SUNDAY
22

LAST THREE DAYS BEFORE LABOR DAY UP 17 IN A ROW NOW FIRST THREE DAYS OF WEEK ARE BETTER

Summer is drawing to a close. A new business season and school year are about to begin. The air is filled with a sense of anticipation, optimism, and even euphoria. A happy setting indeed, and likely the reason for seventeen straight years of rising markets during the three-day period prior to Labor Day, until 1978.

These three "bullish" days wound up in the minus column in eleven of the next twenty years. However, to spotlight a brief three-day bullish bias is to doom it to subsequent failure. How could traders on stock and index future exchange floors have resisted more than a 1 percent gain on average for just three trading days? That's a return of 7 percent a month and over 100 percent a year compounded. The first three days of Labor Day week now appear to be better. Starting in 1982, of sixteen years, only five were losers: 1984, 1987, 1989, 1996 and 1997. Severe 1987 and 1997 losses were due to bearish climate change.

WEEK BEFORE LABOR DAY DAILY DOW POINT CHANGES

	MONDAY	TUESDAY	WEDNESDAY	THURSDAY	FRIDAY	WEEK'S CLOSE	CHANGE LAST 3 DAYS
1961	— 0.69	— 1.86	2.75	3.04	1.25	721.19	7.04
1962	— 1.17	— 7.32	— 2.01	— 0.92	6.86	609.18	3.93
1963	1.03	— 4.29	5.19	1.33	2.92	729.32	9.44
1964	— 0.61	5.52	1.08	0.94	2.29	848.31	4.31
1965	— 0.33	— 2.53	0.50	6.80	7.57	907.97	14.87
1966	—13.53	8.69	12.69	3.68	— 4.40	787.69	11.97
1967	0.64	0.05	— 1.04	7.57	— 0.11	901.18	6.42
1968	3.79	— 2.48	Closed	0.68	1.68	896.01	3.67
1969	— 5.81	— 7.92	1.26	3.63	8.31	836.72	13.20
1970	— 1.23	— 6.43	— 1.51	8.63	5.88	771.15	13.00
1971	— 6.72	— 3.36	0.95	1.61	12.12	912.75	14.68
1972	— 2.41	— 2.25	3.16	5.87	6.32	970.05	15.35
1973	7.22	1.36	11.36	— 0.90	5.04	887.57	15.50
1974	1.33	—16.59	— 4.93	— 9.77	21.74	678.58	7.04
1975	7.58	— 9.23	4.09	22.27	5.87	835.34	32.23
1976	4.99	4.82	12.21	— 1.16	4.32	989.11	15.37
1977	8.67	— 5.20	2.60	3.37	7.45	872.31	13.42
UP	8	5	12	13	15		17
DOWN	9	12	4	4	2		0
1978	—10.65	— 4.68	0.52	— 3.90	2.51	879.33	
1979	5.21	— 0.77	0.26	— 1.20	3.93	887.63	CHANGE
1980	— 1.96	— 2.82	—10.32	—12.71	2.21	932.59	FIRST 3
1981	—10.75	1.24	1.52	—17.22	— 5.33	861.68	DAYS
1982	9.83	8.01	— 6.26	14.35	15.73	925.13	11.58
1983	2.04	1.93	20.12	— 9.35	8.64	1215.45	24.09
1984	— 8.61	4.19	— 5.19	— 3.64	1.10	1224.38	— 9.61
1985	— 0.67	4.82	8.62	4.04	— 1.12	1334.01	12.77
1986	—16.03	32.48	0.28	— 4.36	— 1.83	1898.34	16.73
1987	23.60	—51.98	— 8.93	— 2.55	—38.11	2561.38	— 37.31
1988	24.00	— 3.20	— 6.58	—29.34	52.28	2054.59	14.22
1989	11.00	—16.73	1.52	9.12	14.82	2752.09	— 4.21
1990	78.71	3.22	17.58	—39.11	21.04	2614.36	99.51
1991	— 0.89	—13.20	29.07	— 5.59	— 6.04	3043.60	14.98
1992	—10.26	8.91	24.05	1.89	—10.27	3281.93	22.70
1993	3.36	7.26	— 6.15	—19.00	7.83	3633.93	4.47
1994	17.80	18.45	— 3.88	—11.98	—15.86	3885.58	32.37
1995	— 7.40	14.44	— 3.87	5.99	36.98	4647.54	3.17
1996	—28.85	17.38	1.11	—64.73	—31.44	5616.21	— 10.36
1997	—28.34	—77.35	5.11	—92.90	—72.01	7622.42	—100.58
UP	8	11	9	5	8		11
DOWN	8	5	7	11	8		5

AUGUST

MONDAY
23

*Methodology is the last refuge
of a sterile mind.*
— Marianne L. Simmel

BUY ORACLE

TUESDAY
24

Don't put all your eggs in one basket.
— Market maxim

WEDNESDAY
25

*Put your eggs in one basket
and watch the basket.*
— An alternate strategy

THURSDAY
26

*Brazil is the country of the future
and always will be.*
— Brazilian joke

FRIDAY
27

*Don't give up on yourself!
There's nothing you can't do!*
—Jacques D'Amboise

SATURDAY
28

SUNDAY
29

Worst month September, shame, shame
Up thrice in a row—'tis a new bull game

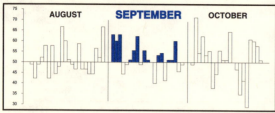

SEPTEMBER ALMANAC

SEPTEMBER						
S	M	T	W	T	F	S
				1	2	3	4
5	6	7	8	9	10	11
12	13	14	15	16	17	18
19	20	21	22	23	24	25
26	27	28	29	30		

OCTOBER						
S	M	T	W	T	F	S
					1	2
3	4	5	6	7	8	9
10	11	12	13	14	15	16
17	18	19	20	21	22	23
24	25	26	27	28	29	30
31						

See Market Probability Chart on page 125.

❑ First half tends to be stronger than second half ❑ September tends to be a "reverse" barometer of the following year (page 90) ❑ RECORD: S&P up 20, down 27, flat 1 ❑ Average September loses 0.3% ❑ Dow was up only 5 times in 26 years, then three great Septembers in a row ❑ Worst month of the year on S&P ❑ Midterm election year Septembers down nine times in a row ❑ Presidential years only two losses in nine years.

SEPTEMBER DAILY POINT CHANGES DOW JONES INDUSTRIALS

Previous Month Close	1988 2031.65	1989 2737.27	1990 2614.36	1991 3043.60	1992 3257.35	1993 3651.25	1994 3913.42	1995 4610.56	1996 5616.21	1997 7622.42
1	−29.34	14.82	—	—	8.91	− 6.15	−11.98	36.98	—	H
2	52.28	—	—	H	24.05	−19.00	−15.86	—	H	257.36
3	—	—	H	−25.93	1.89	7.83	—	—	32.18	14.86
4	—	H	− 0.99	− 9.17	−10.27	—	—	H	8.51	− 27.40
5	H	− 7.41	14.85	N/C	—	—	H	22.54	−49.94	− 44.83
6	10.67	−24.89	−31.93	3.13	—	H	13.12	13.73	52.90	—
7	0.53	−12.91	23.26	—	H	−26.83	−12.45	−14.09	—	—
8	− 2.67	2.66	—	—	−21.34	−18.17	22.21	31.00	—	12.77
9	5.69	—	—	− 4.47	10.80	0.56	−33.65	—	73.98	16.73
10	—	—	− 3.96	−24.60	33.77	32.14	—	—	− 6.66	−132.63
11	—	− 5.13	− 2.97	4.47	0.54	—	—	4.22	27.74	− 58.30
12	3.56	2.85	13.12	20.80	—	—	−14.47	42.27	17.02	81.99
13	10.67	−27.74	−43.07	−22.14	—	12.58	19.52	18.31	66.58	—
14	17.60	−14.63	−18.56	—	70.52	−18.45	15.47	36.28	—	—
15	− 8.36	9.69	—	—	−48.90	17.89	58.55	− 4.23	—	− 21.83
16	5.87	—	—	29.52	− 8.11	− 2.80	−20.53	—	50.68	174.78
17	—	—	3.22	− 2.02	− 3.51	−17.60	—	—	− 0.37	− 9.48
18	—	12.92	3.96	4.70	11.35	—	—	−17.16	−11.47	36.28
19	−17.07	− 0.19	−13.86	6.48	—	—	3.37	−13.37	− 9.62	− 5.45
20	6.40	− 3.42	−39.11	− 5.14	—	−37.45	−67.63	25.65	20.72	—
21	3.02	− 3.61	− 5.94	—	− 6.22	−38.56	−17.49	−25.29	—	—
22	−10.49	1.33	—	—	−39.98	9.78	−14.47	− 3.25	—	79.56
23	10.67	—	—	− 8.72	− 2.16	− 7.27	− 5.38	—	6.28	− 26.77
24	—	—	−59.41	18.56	9.18	3.36	—	—	−20.71	− 63.35
25	—	−22.42	32.67	− 8.05	−37.55	—	—	5.78	3.33	− 58.70
26	− 5.51	4.75	−25.99	− 3.80	—	—	17.49	− 4.33	− 8.51	74.17
27	− 2.84	9.12	−32.17	−11.18	—	24.59	13.80	− 3.25	4.07	—
28	3.20	21.85	25.00	—	25.94	− 1.68	15.14	25.29	—	—
29	33.78	− 2.09	—	—	− 9.46	0.28	−23.55	1.44	—	69.25
30	− 6.40	—	—	10.73	4.86	−11.18	−11.44	—	9.25	− 46.17
Close	**2112.91**	**2692.82**	**2452.48**	**3016.77**	**3271.66**	**3555.12**	**3843.19**	**4789.08**	**5882.17**	**7945.26**
Change	**81.26**	**−44.45**	**−161.88**	**−26.83**	**14.31**	**−96.13**	**−70.23**	**178.52**	**265.96**	**322.84**

MONDAY

 30

In a rising market, the tendency to look beyond the simple fact of increasing value to the reasons on which it depends greatly diminishes.
— John Kenneth Galbraith

TUESDAY

  31

Man's mind, once stretched by a new idea, never regains its original dimensions.
—Oliver Wendell Holmes

WEDNESDAY

 1

To pull off a great investment coup it is best to be the only buyer of a stock that you're building a position in.
— Warren Buffet

THURSDAY

  2

Buy a stock the way you would buy a house. Understand and like it such that you'd be content to own it in the absence of any market.
— Warren Buffet

FRIDAY

3

The market is a voting machine, whereon countless individuals register choices which are the product partly of reason and partly of emotion.
— Graham & Dodd

SATURDAY

4

SUNDAY

5

THE SEPTEMBER REVERSE BAROMETER

During the first sixty years of this century, the stock market in the final quarter of the year often took its cue from its own behavior in September, the start of a new business year and followed a similar course two-thirds of the time.

However, starting with 1960, an incredible transformation occurred. September became a **reverse barometer**. Bearish Septembers tended to be followed by bullish fourth quarters, and vice versa. In the last 38 years, 25 Septembers were losers or gained less than 1.0%. They preceded average fourth quarter gains of 3.8%. The other thirteen Septembers were up and preceded fourth quarters gaining 2.4% on average.

AS SEPTEMBER GOES, BE CONTRARY!

	September % Change	4th Quarter % Change	Next Year's % Change
1960	− 6.0%	8.6%	23.1%
1961	− 2.0	7.2	−11.8
1962	− 4.8	12.1	18.9
1963	− 1.1	4.6	13.0
1964	2.9	0.7	9.1
1965	3.2	2.7	−13.1
1966	− 0.7	4.9	20.1
1967	3.3	− 0.2	7.7
1968	3.9	1.2	−11.4
1969	− 2.5	− 1.1	0.1
1970	3.4	9.3	10.8
1971	− 0.7	3.8	15.6
1972	− 0.5	6.8	−17.4
1973	4.0	−10.0	−29.7
1974	−11.9	7.9	31.5
1975	− 3.5	7.5	19.1
1976	2.3	2.1	−11.5
1977	− 0.2	− 1.5	1.1
1978	− 0.7	− 6.3	12.3
1979	0.0	− 1.3	25.8
1980	2.5	8.2	− 9.7
1981	− 5.4	5.5	14.8
1982	0.8	16.8	17.3
1983	1.0	− 0.7	1.4
1984	− 0.3	0.7	26.3
1985	− 3.5	16.0	14.6
1986	− 8.5	4.7	2.0
1987	− 2.4	−23.2	12.4
1988	4.0	2.1	27.3
1989	− 0.7	1.2	− 6.6
1990	− 5.1	7.9	26.3
1991	− 1.9	7.5	4.5
1992	0.9	4.3	7.1
1993	− 1.0	1.6	− 1.5
1994	− 2.7	− 0.7	34.1
1995	4.0	5.4	20.3
1996	5.4	7.8	31.0
1997	5.3	2.4	??

Based on S&P composite index

Previous Bullish Septembers Ranked			
	September % Change	4th Quarter % Change	Next Year's % Change
1996	5.4%	7.8%	31.0%
1997	5.3	2.4	??
1995	4.0	5.4	20.3
1973	4.0	−10.0	−29.7
1988	4.0	2.1	27.3
1968	3.9	1.2	−11.4
1970	3.4	9.3	10.8
1967	3.3	− 0.2	7.7
1965	3.2	2.7	−13.1
1964	2.9	0.7	9.1
1980	2.5	8.2	− 9.7
1976	2.3	2.1	−11.5
1983	1.0	− 0.7	1.4
Averages		**2.4%**	**2.7%**
Previous Bearish Septembers Ranked			
1992	0.9	4.3	7.1
1982	0.8	16.8	17.3
1979	0.0	− 1.3	25.8
1977	− 0.2	− 1.5	1.1
1984	− 0.3	0.7	26.3
1972	− 0.5	6.8	−17.4
1989	− 0.7	1.2	− 6.6
1971	− 0.7	3.8	15.6
1966	− 0.7	4.9	20.1
1978	− 0.7	− 6.3	12.3
1993	− 1.0	1.6	− 1.5
1963	− 1.1	4.6	13.0
1991	− 1.9	7.5	4.5
1961	− 2.0	7.2	−11.8
1987	− 2.4	−23.2	12.4
1969	− 2.5	− 1.1	0.1
1994	− 2.7	− 0.7	34.1
1975	− 3.5	7.5	19.1
1985	− 3.5	16.0	14.6
1962	− 4.8	12.1	18.9
1990	− 5.1	7.9	26.3
1981	− 5.4	5.5	14.8
1960	− 6.0	8.6	23.1
1986	− 8.5	4.7	2.0
1974	−11.9	7.9	31.5
Averages		**3.8%**	**12.1%**

Even more incredible is September's record as a reverse barometer giving us advance notice of what the market will do in the following year. Six of the thirteen Septembers with gains of 1.0% or more, were followed by bear market years (1966, 1969, 1974, 1977, 1981, and 1984 through August). Twenty-five other Septembers were down, flat or slightly up and their following years gained 12.1% on average. Four losing years were not induced by recessions: 1962 (Kennedy stare-down with Big Steel and Cuban Missile Crisis), 1973 (OPEC oil embargo), 1990 (Persian Gulf Crisis) and 1994 (rising interest rates). A super bull market in recent years may be affecting the pattern.

SEPTEMBER

MONDAY
6

*Your emotions are often a reverse
indicator of what you ought to be doing.*
— John F. Hindelong, Dillon, Reed

Day after Labor Day up four straight years, after five losses in a row.

TUESDAY
7

*When the S&P Index Future premium
over "Cash" gets too high, I sell the
future and buy the stocks. If the
premium disappears, well, buy the future
and sell the stocks.*
— Neil Elliott, Fahnestock

WEDNESDAY
8

*To me, the "tape" is the final arbiter
of any investment decision. I have
a cardinal rule: Never fight the tape!*
— Martin Zweig

THURSDAY
9

*Stocks are super attractive when the Fed
is loosening and interest rates are falling.
In sum: Don't fight the Fed!*
— Martin Zweig

FRIDAY
10

*Every successful enterprise requires
three people— a dreamer, a businessman,
and a son-of-a-bitch.*
— Peter McArthur, 1904

Rosh Hashanah

SATURDAY
11

SUNDAY
12

THE GORILLA GAME
BEST INVESTMENT BOOK OF THE YEAR

Forget everything you know about investing—at least when it comes to technology. That's the lesson from *The Gorilla Game*, an astute new book that shows what's behind the sometimes-puzzling performance of the technology group. Most investors know that tech stocks offer the best growth available. But they also know that these stocks can be dangerous, and many investors have been burned.

That's at least partly because they were investing the wrong way. Trying to buy technology on the cheap, for example, is a good way to wind up with the losers. Looking at P/Es, or even slightly more sophisticated selection screens like price-to-sales or cash flow, is not the way to go.

The winners are always going to look expensive as the market is discounting cash flow years ahead. How do you know which companies are going to be the giant winners with multi-year growth trends? That's the subject of *The Gorilla Game*, by Geoffrey Moore, Paul Johnson and Tom Kippola. The authors have an unusual combination of credentials—practical and successful investing, academic experience and consulting work with some of the largest tech firms. So they have been able to summarize and explain the essence of technology investing better than any other attempt I have seen.

Understanding the concepts will be easier if you know a little about technology, particularly computers and networking. That's the focus. (There's nothing about biotechnology, though many of the same lessons would apply in that area and even in non-technology industries.) Even if you don't know how to turn on a PC, this book should prove useful.

Like the gorilla of the old joke, gorilla companies sit wherever they want to, often on their competition. They achieve a dominant position that allows them to grow faster, longer and more profitably than their competitors. For that matter, they sometimes eliminate all significant competition, giving them even richer profits and a longer life.

An All-Time Gorilla

The classic example is Microsoft, which achieved dominance in the most far-reaching new technology of our time, software for personal computers. How did Microsoft get where it is today? Being in the right place at just the right time—with good (not necessarily the best) technology. The huge piece of luck was getting chosen by IBM to provide the operating system for its new personal computer. IBM's entry into that market legitimized it and set off the huge growth that is still in evidence.

The irony is that Microsoft has benefited far more than IBM, but that's the nature of the gorilla game. Once the gorilla (a dominant company in an exploding industry) is born, there is almost no stopping it. IBM is the former gorilla of computing. But gorillas eventually decline unless they are very astute at adapting. Even if they are, the law of averages tends to catch up with them sooner or later.

Decline of a Gorilla

IBM adapted very well for some 40 years but made a crucial mistake in the

(continued on page 94)

SEPTEMBER

MONDAY
13

The public may boo me, but when I go home and think of my money, I clap.
— Horace, *Epistles*, c. 20 B.C.

TUESDAY
14

Quality is never an accident; it is always the result of intelligent efforts.
— John Ruskin

WEDNESDAY
15

Edison has done more toward abolishing poverty than all the reformers and statesmen.
— Henry Ford

THURSDAY
16

I always keep these seasonal patterns in the back of my mind. My antennae start to purr at certain times of the year.
— Kenneth Ward

FRIDAY

17

Don't compete. Create. Find out what everyone else is doing and then don't do it.
— Joel Weldon

SATURDAY
18

SUNDAY
19

(continued from page 92)

early 1980s, not realizing that software suddenly was more important than hardware. Once Microsoft, with IBM's inadvertent help, became the leading purveyor of PC operating systems, Microsoft was able rather quickly to become the dominant supplier and eventually the only supplier that mattered.

IBM woke up and developed its own operating system, which independent experts generally thought was superior. That didn't matter—by then it was already too late to displace Microsoft. Apple's fate was even worse. It was a pioneer and early leader—and its operating system was also better than Microsoft's. But Apple made a series of mistakes, most notably in keeping prices up to show better earnings in the short run.

Today Microsoft has a total market value more than 50% higher than IBM's, though its sales are less than a seventh of those of the giant. This is what the gorilla game is all about: not current sales, nor current earnings, but the future—and the huge rewards the market will bestow on companies that seem to have the brightest futures.

Gorillas flourish because of industry's (and eventually the public's) need to standardize technology. It quickly became important to have one operating system for PCs. Companies want all their computers to be using the same language—and to be able to talk to their customers' and suppliers' computers as well. Individuals want to learn computer skills they can use wherever they go. Writers of application software, from games to the most sophisticated business programs, are going to concentrate their efforts on the most widely used systems.

This process goes on until the gorilla has pretty much monopolized its niche (as with Microsoft) or at least achieved dominance. Then the gorilla can use that position to move into adjacent areas.

Gorilla businesses become gorilla stocks simply because of the outsize returns expected by the market. "Expected" is the key word. We all know that monopolies, if unregulated, generate "excess" returns. The companies we are talking about have, at least in part, some monopoly power. But since we are talking about growth stocks, and since the stock market is a discounting mechanism, current returns are not very important. The issue is future returns, and the current price of a stock theoretically is the net present value of all future returns.

The future returns from a gorilla will be vastly greater than from an ordinary company. The market recognizes this, yet, even so, it seldom discerns in the early years just how powerful a gorilla can be. So stocks that look expensive keep getting more expensive as their earning power becomes clearer, and as success in one area enables the company to gobble up adjacent territory.

The Tornado

The game does not require you to recognize the gorilla right away, but you need to know when you are in gorilla territory. "The transformation from niche to mass market creates the tornado, when the true gorilla game begins. Tornado is a metaphor for the hypergrowth stage in technology markets caused when the buying resistance of the pragmatist herd finally caves in, and they rush to adopt the new technology en masse. This action creates a mass market overnight, a severe

(continued on page 95)

inversion of supply and demand. This inversion, in turn, stimulates a tornado, or hypergrowth, not atypically 300% per year in the very early going, slowing down to 100% over the longer period."

How can you tell which company will emerge as the gorilla? You can't—and this is a key point. The authors advise buying the leading candidates. If the market is as good as you've calculated, you'll make money with all of them. But eventually you'll start making more money on just one. That's the likely winner. Buy more of it and sell the rest. This breaks the diversification rule, but in gorilla territory there is safety in strength rather than in numbers.

How long should you hold a gorilla? Probably much longer than you expected to. Even when past their prime, they usually offer superior returns. Unless it's exceptionally badly managed, a gorilla lasts until the next technological revolution disrupts its markets. At that point it takes exceptional management to bridge the gap.

Major new technologies, the kind that spawn the largest gorillas, come along only about once a decade. So it should not be surprising that the authors come up with nothing very startling in the way of stock suggestions. There are plenty of stock ideas in the book, but the model portfolio relies in part on some rather old names, including Cisco, Intel and Microsoft. The greatest gorillas don't die easily.

The Essence of the Gorilla Game

Find markets transitioning into hypergrowth. (Hypergrowth makes for a huge competitive advantage through standardization on the products from a single vendor. High-tech hypergrowth markets result in long-standing institutions. The big winners in these markets not only profit from immediate spikes of demand, but even as the initial demand gets fulfilled, they create dominant market shares that will support them for years to come.) This is not as hard as it sounds. The good news about the gorilla game is you can miss the start by three or four quarters, still get into the game and profit.

Buy a basket of stocks that represent all the companies that have a clear shot at being the gorilla. This is the hardest part of the game because it takes industry knowledge. But this knowledge is virtually everywhere, and there is typically a cluster of companies that show up on every list, and the gorilla is virtually always on that short list. Again if you miss the buy by a quarter or two, the game still plays out in your favor.

As the gorilla emerges, sell off the rest of the basket and consolidate your holdings in the gorilla.

Plan to hold the gorilla for the long term.

Sell the gorilla only when a new category, based on an alternative technology, threatens to eradicate its power.

FALL PORTFOLIO REVIEW

NO. OF SHARES	SECURITY	A ORIGINAL COST	B CURRENT VALUE	C GAIN (B − A) OR LOSS (A − B)	D % CHANGE (C ÷ A)	E MONTHS HELD	F CHANGE PER MO. (D ÷ E)	G ANNUAL RETURN (F × 12)
200	Sample Corp.	$10,000	$10,400	$400	4.0%	8	0.5%	6.0%
TOTALS								

Stocks which have achieved their potential
1
2
3

Candidates for addition to portfolio
1
2
3

Stocks which have been disappointments
1
2
3

Investment decisions
1
2
3

BEST INVESTMENT BOOK 1999

As a special service to Almanac readers, we offer the opportunity to purchase THE GORILLA GAME, the 1999 Best Investment Book (see page 92). To place an order or receive any information, call The Hirsch Organization at 201-767-4100, fax 201-767-7337, or email service@HirschOrganization.com.

RESERVE YOUR 2000 STOCK TRADER'S ALMANAC NOW!

❑ Please reserve_____ copies of the Special Year 2000 Edition, The 2000 STOCK TRADER'S ALMANAC. $29.95 for single copies plus $4.95 shipping and handling. *($15.00 shipping and handling for all foreign countries including Canada and Mexico.)* Quantity prices available on request.

❑ $_____ payment enclosed *(US funds only)*

Charge Credit Card (check one)

❑ VISA ❑ MasterCard ❑ AmEx

Name

Address

City

State   Zip

Account #

Expiration Date

Signature

❑ Please rush a copy of THE GORILLA GAME, $20.80 (20% off the cover price), plus $4.95 shipping and handling. *($15.00 shipping and handling for all foreign countries including Canada and Mexico).*

❑ Send_____additional copies of the 1999 STOCK TRADER'S ALMANAC $29.95 for single copies plus $4.95 shipping and handling. *($15.00 shipping and handling for all foreign countries including Canada and Mexico.)* Quantity prices available on request.

❑ $_____payment enclosed *(US funds only)*

Charge Credit Card (check one)

❑ VISA ❑ MasterCard ❑ AmEx

Name

Address

City

State   Zip

Account #

Expiration Date

Signature

THIRTY-THIRDANNUAL**EDITION**
of the 2000 Stock Trader's Almanac will be published in the Fall of 1999. Mail the postpaid card below to reserve your copy of this Special Year 2000 Edition.

NO POSTAGE
NECESSARY
IF MAILED
IN THE
UNITED STATES

BUSINESS   REPLY   MAIL
FIRST CLASS   PERMIT NO. 239   WESTWOOD, NJ

POSTAGE WILL BE PAID BY ADDRESSEE:

The Hirsch Organization Inc.
PO Box 2069
River Vale, NJ 07675-9988

NO POSTAGE
NECESSARY
IF MAILED
IN THE
UNITED STATES

BUSINESS   REPLY   MAIL
FIRST CLASS   PERMIT NO. 239   WESTWOOD, NJ

POSTAGE WILL BE PAID BY ADDRESSEE:

The Hirsch Organization Inc.
PO Box 2069
River Vale, NJ 07675-9988

SEPTEMBER

Yom Kippur

MONDAY
20

Averaging down in a bear market is tantamount to taking a seat on the down escalator at Macy's.
— Richard Russell, *Dow Theory Letters*, 1984

TUESDAY
21

Big money is made in the stock market by being on the right side of major moves. I don't believe in swimming against the tide.
— Martin Zweig

WEDNESDAY
22

The possession of gold has ruined fewer men than the lack of it.
— Thomas Bailey Aldridge, 1903

THURSDAY
23

A man will fight harder for his interests than his rights.
— Napoleon Bonaparte, 1815

FRIDAY
24

In all recorded history, there has not been one economist who has had to worry about where the next meal would come from.
— Peter Drucker

SATURDAY
25

SUNDAY
26

October, October don't show your face
'29, '87, '97—you're a disgrace

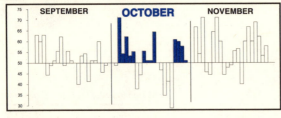

OCTOBER ALMANAC

OCTOBER								NOVEMBER					
S	M	T	W	T	F	S		S	M	T	W	T	F	S
					1	2			1	2	3	4	5	6
3	4	5	6	7	8	9		7	8	9	10	11	12	13
10	11	12	13	14	15	16		14	15	16	17	18	19	20
17	18	19	20	21	22	23		21	22	23	24	25	26	27
24	25	26	27	28	29	30		28	29	30				
31													

See Market Probability Chart on page 125.

❑ Poor October, crashes in 1929 and 1987 and a 502.46 point loss in 1997 ❑ Add to these the memory of back-to-back "massacres" in 1978 and 1979 and Friday the Thirteenth in 1989 and one can see why Halloween's month may be spooked in future years ❑ October is known as a "bear-killer," turning the tide in 8 major bear markets: 1946, 1957, 1960, 1962, 1966, 1974, 1987, and 1990 ❑ RECORD: S&P 27 up, 21 down since 1950 ❑ Big S&P percentage moves: 1987 off 21.8%, 1974 up 16.3% and 1982 up 11.0%.

OCTOBER DAILY POINT CHANGES DOW JONES INDUSTRIALS

Previous Month	1988	1989	1990	1991	1992	1993	1994	1995	1996	1997
Close	2112.91	2692.82	2452.48	3016.77	3271.66	3555.12	3843.19	4789.08	5882.17	7945.26
1	—	—	63.36	1.57	−17.29	25.99	—	—	22.73	70.24
2	—	20.90	−10.64	− 5.82	−53.76	—	—	−27.82	29.07	12.03
3	− 7.65	40.84	−15.84	−27.73	—	—	3.70	−11.56	− 1.12	11.05
4	− 3.20	16.53	27.47	−23.03	—	− 3.35	−45.76	− 9.03	60.01	—
5	4.45	2.47	− 6.19	—	−21.61	9.50	−13.79	22.04	—	—
6	1.24	11.96	—	—	− 0.81	11.73	−11.78	6.50	—	61.64
7	42.50	—	—	−19.01	−25.94	−15.36	21.87	—	−13.05	78.09
8	—	—	13.12	21.02	23.78	1.11	—	—	−13.04	− 83.25
9	—	5.89	−78.22	−17.44	−39.45	—	—	−42.99	−36.15	− 33.64
10	8.71	− 6.08	−37.62	30.19	—	—	23.89	− 5.42	− 8.95	− 16.21
11	− 2.49	− 11.97	−42.82	7.16	—	8.67	55.51	14.45	47.71	—
12	−30.23	− 13.52	32.92	—	37.83	− 0.28	− 1.68	29.63	—	—
13	7.12	−190.58	—	—	27.01	10.06	14.80	28.90	—	27.01
14	− 0.18	—	—	35.77	− 5.94	18.44	20.52	—	40.62	24.07
15	—	—	18.32	21.92	−20.80	8.10	—	—	− 5.22	− 38.31
16	—	88.12	−35.15	20.35	− 0.27	—	—	− 9.40	16.03	−119.10
17	7.29	− 18.65	6.68	− 8.72	—	—	13.46	11.56	38.39	− 91.85
18	19.38	4.92	64.85	24.15	—	12.58	− 6.39	−18.42	35.03	—
19	−22.58	39.55	68.07	—	14.04	− 6.99	18.50	24.93	—	—
20	43.92	5.94	—	—	− 2.43	9.78	−24.89	− 7.59	—	74.41
21	2.31	—	—	−16.77	1.08	− 8.94	−19.85	—	− 3.36	139.00
22	—	—	− 4.70	−20.58	13.78	13.14	—	—	−29.07	− 25.79
23	—	− 26.23	−22.03	1.12	6.76	—	—	−39.38	−25.34	−186.88
24	−13.16	− 3.69	10.15	−24.60	—	—	−36.00	28.18	−43.98	−132.36
25	3.02	− 5.94	−20.05	−11.40	—	24.31	− 4.71	−29.98	14.54	—
26	− 8.18	− 39.55	−48.02	—	36.47	− 1.12	− 2.36	−49.86	—	—
27	−24.35	− 17.01	—	—	− 8.38	− 7.83	26.92	37.93	—	−554.26
28	9.06	—	—	40.70	15.67	23.20	55.51	—	−34.29	337.17
29	—	—	− 5.94	16.32	− 5.13	− 7.27	—	—	34.29	8.35
30	—	6.76	17.82	9.84	−19.99	—	—	14.82	−13.79	−125.00
31	− 1.24	41.60	− 5.69	− 2.68	—	—	−22.54	− 1.09	36.15	61.13
Close	2148.65	2645.08	2442.33	3069.10	3226.28	3680.59	3908.12	4755.48	6029.38	7442.80
Change	35.74	− 47.74	−10.15	52.33	−45.38	125.47	64.93	−33.60	147.21	−502.46

SEPTEMBER/OCTOBER

MONDAY

 27

*The less a man knows about the past
and the present the more insecure must
be his judgment of the future.*
— Sigmund Freud

*Last 3 days in Sept. and first 5 in Oct. up 330.30 Dow points in 1997.
Should be bullish in 1999, prior to 2000 (page 88).*

TUESDAY

 28

*Marx's great achievement was to place the
system of capitalism on the defensive.*
— Charles A. Madison, 1977

WEDNESDAY

 29

*The word "crisis" in Chinese
is composed of two characters:
the first, the symbol of danger;
the second, opportunity.*
— Anonymous

THURSDAY

 30

*In the course of evolution and a higher
civilization we might be able to get
along comfortably without Congress,
but without Wall Street, never.*
— Henry Clews, 1900

FRIDAY

 1

*Let us have the courage to stop
borrowing to meet the continuing
deficits. Stop the deficits.*
— Franklin D. Roosevelt, 1932

SATURDAY

2

SUNDAY

3

A CORRECTION FOR ALL SEASONS

While there's a rally for every season (page 72), almost always there's a decline or correction, too. Fortunately, corrections tend to be smaller than rallies, and that's what gives the stock market its long-term upward bias. In each season the average bounce outdoes the average setback. On average the net gain between the rally and the correction is smallest in summer and fall.

The summer setback tends to be slightly outdone by the average correction in the fall. Tax selling and portfolio cleaning are the usual explanations—individuals sell to register a tax loss and institutions like to get rid of their losers before preparing year-end statements. The October jinx also plays a major part. Since 1964, there have been 11 fall declines of over 10%, and in seven of them (1966, 1974, 1978, 1979, 1987, 1990 and 1997) the worst damage was done in October, where so many bear markets end.

Most often, it has paid to buy after fourth quarter "waterfall declines" for a rally that may continue into January or even beyond.

SEASONAL CORRECTIONS IN DOW JONES INDUSTRIALS

	WINTER Nov/Dec High to 1 Q. Low	SPRING Feb/Mar High to 2 Q. Low	SUMMER May/Jun High to 3 Q. Low	FALL Aug/Sep High to 4 Q. Low
1964	— 0.15%	— 2.43%	— 0.97%	— 2.09%
1965	— 2.46	— 7.25	— 8.29	— 0.88
1966	— 6.00	—13.16	—17.70	—12.68
1967	— 4.20	— 3.91	— 5.50	— 9.92
1968	— 8.84	— 0.27	— 5.46	+ 0.43
1969	— 8.67	— 8.71	—17.23	— 8.10
1970	—13.79	—20.21	— 8.76	— 2.53
1971	— 1.36	— 4.77	—10.67	—13.35
1972	— 0.50	— 2.64	— 6.26	— 5.33
1973	—10.96	—12.80	—10.94	—17.30
1974	—15.27	—10.80	—29.79	—27.58
1975	— 6.33	— 5.55	— 9.93	— 6.66
1976	— 0.23	— 5.07	— 4.67	— 8.94
1977	— 8.51	— 7.16	—11.52	—10.20
1978	—12.27	— 4.04	— 7.01	—13.49
1979	— 2.51	— 5.76	— 3.74	—10.88
1980	—10.02	—16.01	— 1.72	— 6.78
1981	— 6.86	— 5.10	—18.58	—12.86
1982	—10.89	— 7.50	—10.62	— 3.34
1983	— 4.06	— 2.83	— 6.83	— 3.64
1984	—11.89	—10.46	— 8.43	— 6.17
1985	— 4.76	— 4.41	— 2.81	— 2.31
1986	— 3.27	— 4.73	— 7.27	— 7.58
1987	— 1.45	— 6.61	— 1.68	—36.13
1988	— 6.70	— 6.99	— 7.57	— 4.47
1989	— 1.74	— 2.35	— 3.12	— 6.64
1990	— 7.89	— 4.01	—17.32	—18.42
1991	— 6.33	— 3.63	— 4.52	— 6.26
1992	+ 0.11	— 3.31	— 5.42	— 7.62
1993	— 2.74	— 3.09	— 2.95	— 2.04
1994	— 4.42	— 9.61	— 4.41	— 7.06
1995	— 0.81	— 0.10	— 0.20	— 2.04
1996	— 3.52	— 4.62	— 7.47	+ 0.17
1997	— 1.80	— 9.79	— 2.23	—13.30
1998	— 6.98	— 0.43		
Totals	**—198.05%**	**—220.10%**	**—271.58%**	**—296.00%**
Average	**— 5.66%**	**— 6.29%**	**— 7.99%**	**— 8.71%**

OCTOBER

MONDAY
 4

No nation ought to be without debt.
A national debt is a national blessing.
— Thomas Paine, 1776

TUESDAY
 5

If I had my life to live over again, I
would elect to be a trader of goods
rather than a student of science. I
think barter is a noble thing.
— Albert Einstein, 1934

WEDNESDAY
  6

You must automate, emigrate,
or evaporate.
— James A. Baker, General Electric

THURSDAY
 7

If you don't know who you are, the stock
market is an expensive place to find out.
— George Goodman, 1959

FRIDAY
8

The worst trades are generally when
people freeze and start to pray and
hope rather than take some action.
— Robert Mnuchin, Goldman, Sachs

SATURDAY
9

SUNDAY
10

YEAR'S TOP INVESTMENT BOOKS

1. The Gorilla Game: Picking Winners In High Technology, Geoffrey A. Moore, Paul Johnson and Tom Kippola, HarperCollins, $26.00. Reveals the dynamics driving the market for high-tech stocks and outlines the forces that catapult a few select companies to "gorilla" status.

2. How To Retire Rich, James O'Shaughnessy, Broadway Books, $25.00. Identifies exactly which strategies have consistently beaten almost all active stock pickers over the past four decades—and are capable of transforming yearly $2,000 IRA contributions into more than $4 million over time.

3. The Death of Distance: How The Communications Revolution Will Change Our Lives, Frances Cairncross, Harvard Business School Press, $24.95. Geography, borders, time zones are all rapidly becoming irrelevant to the way we conduct our business and personal lives. This "death of distance"could be the single most important economic force shaping all of society over the next half century.

4. Every Investor's Guide To High-Tech Stocks And Mutual Funds, Michael Murphy, Broadway Books, $27.50. You don't have to be an engineer or research scientist to invest well in technology stocks. From software to communications to biotech, you are provided a clear, jargon-free analysis of the seven key technology industries, which could supercharge your portfolio's results.

5. Contrarian Investment Strategies: The Next Generation, David Dreman, Simon and Schuster, $25.00. How to outperform professional money managers and profit from Wall Street panics. Dreman offers investors four new proven contrarian strategies in addition to the low P/E method he pioneered in his earlier works.

6. Pit Bull: Lessons From Wall Street's Champion Trader, Martin Schwartz with Dave Morine and Paul Flint, Harper Business, $27.50. The true story of how Schwartz became the legendary "Pit Bull." Each chapter presents fascinating "lessons" Schwartz learned about the financial markets that will help you profit from his expertise.

7. Women Of The Street: Making It On Wall Street—The World's Toughest Business, Sue Herera, John Wiley & Sons, $16.95 (softcover). Interviews with fourteen of Wall Street's key professional women. The unfolding story of the ascension of women in one of the last bastions of male dominance—the Street.

8. Sector Funds For Trophy Returns: A Guide To Investing In Sector Mutual Funds, Marshall Schield, 21st Century Publishers, $24.95. How to harness the power potential of sector fund investing. Presents a workable concept for managing mutual fund investment funds with an investment strategy that can outperform 90% of all growth funds over time and with less risk.

9. Trading S&P Futures And Options: A Survival Manual And Study Guide, Humphrey E. D. Lloyd, Traders Press, $49.00 (softcover). An introduction to trading in the S&P 500 futures and index option markets, two markets which are very closely related. A good starting point for the neophyte

(continued on page 104)

OCTOBER

MONDAY
11

*A good trader has to have three things:
a chronic inability to accept things at
face value, to feel continuously
unsettled, and to have humility.*
— Michael Steinhardt

TUESDAY
12

*The pursuit of gain is the only way
in which people can serve the needs of
others whom they do not know.*
— Friedrich von Hayek, *Counterrevolution of Science*

WEDNESDAY
13

*Cheapening the cost of necessities and
conveniences of life is the most powerful
agent of civilization and progress.*
— Thomas Elliott Perkins, 1888

THURSDAY
14

*In the market, yesterday is a memory and
tomorrow is a vision. And looking back
is a lot easier than looking ahead.*
— Frankie Joe

FRIDAY
 ## 15

*The American system of ours gives
everyone of us a great opportunity if we
only seize it with both hands.*
— Al Capone, 1929

SATURDAY
16

SUNDAY
17

(continued from page 102)

investor in futures and options.

10. The Complete Book Of Business Plans, Joseph A. Covello and Brian J. Hazelgren, Sourcebooks, $19.95. Create a powerful, winning business plan based on the authors' more than two decades of combined experience writing business plans. Designed to assist anyone in preparing an effective business plan.

11. The Option Advisor Wealth Building: Techniques Using Equity & Index Options, Bernie Schaeffer, John Wiley & Sons, $59.95. This renowned options expert reveals the proven techniques for selecting the right stocks, assessing risk, managing your options portfolio and, most importantly, for reading market timing indicators.

12. So Far, So Good—The First 94 Years, An Autobiography, Roy R. Neuberger with Alfred and Roma Connable, John Wiley & Sons, $29.95. Share the secrets of the renowned life-long value investor who has made a profitable art of shorting the market. He founded the $34 billion money management firm of Neuberger & Berman in 1939 and in 1950 he began one of the first no-load mutual funds. A Wall Street legend.

13. The Millionaire Next Door, Thomas J. Stanley, Ph.D and William D. Danko, Ph.D, Longstreet Press, $22.00. Debunks many of the myths of how to become wealthy in America. Wealth is the result of hard work, diligent savings, and living below your means. Reveals the seven common denominators that define those who built their personal fortunes from scratch.

14. Hamilton's Blessing: The Extraordinary Life And Times Of Our National Debt, John Steele Gordon, Penguin Books, $11.95 (softcover). Chronicles our national debt and how it helped launch America's economy. In 1916, the richest man in the country, John D. Rockefeller, could have paid off the national debt by himself. In 1997, Bill Gates and Warren Buffet together could not pay two months interest on it—about $50 billion—without going broke.

15. How I Found Freedom In An Unfree World: A Handbook For Personal Liberty, Harry Browne, LiamWorks, $24.95. Originally published in 1973, this timeless manifesto for personal liberty has helped thousands of readers break free from the constrictions imposed by traditional thought.

Broadway Books
1540 Broadway
New York NY 10036

HarperCollins
10 East 53rd Street
New York NY 10022

Harvard Business School Press
60 Harvard Way
Boston MA 02163

LiamWorks
P O Box 2165
1219 Central Avenue
Great Falls MT 59403

Longstreet Press
2140 Newmarket Parkway
Suite 122
Marietta GA 30067

Penguin Books
375 Hudson Street
New York, NY 10014

Simon and Schuster
Rockefeller Center
1230 Avenue of the Americas
New York NY 10020

Sourcebooks
P O Box 372
Naperville IL 60566

Traders Press
P.O. Box 6206
Greenville SC 29606

21st Century Publishers
1320 Curt Gowdy Drive
Cheyenne WY 82009

John Wiley & Sons
605 Third Avenue
New York NY 10158

OCTOBER

MONDAY
18

*If you don't profit from your investment
mistakes, someone else will.*
— Yale Hirsch

TUESDAY
19

*Major bottoms are usually made when
analysts cut their earnings estimates
and companies report earnings
which are below expectations.*
— Edward Babbitt, Jr., Avatar Associates

WEDNESDAY
20

*The worst bankrupt in the world is the person
who has lost his enthusiasm.*
—H.W. Arnold

THURSDAY
21

*Italians come to ruin most generally in three ways:
women, gambling and farming.
My family chose the slowest one.*
— Pope John XXIII, 1961

FRIDAY
22

*It's no coincidence that three of the top
five stock option traders in a recent
trading contest were all ex-Marines.*
—Robert Prechter, Jr., *Elliott Wave Theorist*

SATURDAY
23

SUNDAY
24

Two days pre-Thanksgiving, one day more
A rally we can all be thankful for

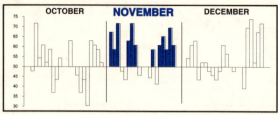

NOVEMBER ALMANAC

NOVEMBER						
S	M	T	W	T	F	S
				1	2	3	4	5	6
7	8	9	10	11	12	13
14	15	16	17	18	19	20
21	22	23	24	25	26	27
28	29	30				

DECEMBER						
S	M	T	W	T	F	S
					1	2	3	4
5	6	7	8	9	10	11
12	13	14	15	16	17	18
19	20	21	22	23	24	25
26	27	28	29	30	31	

See Market Probability Chart on page 125.

❑ Third best percentage gainer in 48 years based on S&P, up an average 1.6% per year ❑ Up 31 times, down 17 ❑ Hefty losses in 1987, 1991, and 1994 but big Dow gains in 1995, 1996 and 1997 ❑ Day before and day after Thanksgiving combined 21 years without a loss until 1987 (page 114) ❑ Anticipators pushed up preceding Tuesday 7 years in a row until 1990 ❑ November, December, and January comprise Best 3 Months of the Year ❑ November begins the Best 6 Months of the Year (page 54).

NOVEMBER DAILY POINT CHANGES DOW JONES INDUSTRIALS

Previous Month Close	1988	1989	1990	1991	1992	1993	1994	1995	1996	1997
	2148.65	2645.08	2442.33	3069.10	3226.28	3680.59	3908.12	4755.48	6029.38	7442.80
1	2.31	0.82	12.62	− 12.75	—	12.02	−44.75	11.20	− 7.45	—
2	5.87	−14.34	35.89	—	35.93	5.03	−26.24	41.91	—	—
3	13.51	− 2.05	—	—	− 9.73	−35.77	8.75	16.98	—	231.59
4	−24.54	—	—	− 10.73	−29.44	−36.89	−38.36	—	19.75	14.74
5	—	—	11.39	− 14.31	20.80	18.45	—	—	39.50	3.44
6	—	−47.34	−17.08	7.15	− 3.78	—	—	−11.56	96.53	− 9.33
7	−21.16	14.96	−44.31	15.65	—	−	1.35	−16.98	28.33	−101.92
8	2.85	26.23	2.97	− 8.49	—	4.47	21.87	55.64	13.78	—
9	− 9.25	−19.67	44.80	—	0.81	− 7.83	1.01	11.56	—	—
10	− 3.55	21.92	—	—	−15.40	23.48	− 9.76	6.14	—	− 28.73
11	−47.66	—	—	− 3.36	14.86	− 1.12	−20.52	—	35.78	6.14
12	—	—	51.74	11.85	− 0.54	22.08	—	—	10.44	−157.41
13	—	0.82	− 4.95	11.19	− 6.76	—	—	2.53	8.20	86.44
14	− 1.95	−16.18	24.25	− 1.79	—	—	28.26	− 1.09	38.76	84.72
15	12.09	22.33	−14.60	−120.31	—	− 6.99	− 3.37	50.94	35.03	—
16	−38.59	3.08	5.20	—	−27.29	33.25	18.84	46.61	—	—
17	13.87	17.00	—	—	−12.42	− 6.42	−17.15	20.59	—	125.74
18	9.96	—	—	29.52	14.05	−19.01	−12.79	—	− 1.12	− 47.40
19	—	—	15.10	− 41.15	2.16	8.67	—	—	50.69	73.92
20	—	−20.62	−35.15	− 1.56	17.83	—	—	− 6.86	32.42	101.87
21	3.56	7.25	9.16	2.68	—	—	−45.75	40.46	−11.55	54.46
22	11.73	17.49	H	− 29.96	—	−23.76	−91.52	18.06	53.29	—
23	14.58	H	−12.13	—	− 4.32	3.92	− 3.36	H	—	—
24	H	18.77	—	− 0.67	25.66	13.41	H	7.23*	—	−113.15
25	−17.60	—	—	14.08	17.56	H	33.64	—	76.03	41.03
26	—	—	5.94	H	H	− 3.63	—	—	−19.38	− 14.17
27	—	19.42	10.64	− 16.10	15.94	—	—	22.04	−29.07	H
28	6.76	7.04	− 8.66	H	—	—	31.29	7.22	H	28.35*
29	20.09	−13.23	−16.34	− 5.36	—	− 6.15	− 1.01	27.46	22.36*	—
30	12.98	17.49	40.84	—	22.96	6.15	0.68	−31.07	—	—
Close	2114.51	2706.27	2559.65	2894.68	3305.16	3683.95	3739.23	5074.49	6521.70	7823.13
Change	−34.14	61.19	117.32	−174.42	78.88	3.36	−168.89	319.01	492.32	380.33

*Shortened trading day.

OCTOBER

MONDAY
25

*In nature there are no rewards or
punishments; there are consequences.*
— Horace Annesley Vachell, *The Force of Clay*

TUESDAY
 # 26

*A loss never bothers me after I take it.
I forget it overnight. But being wrong—
not taking the loss— that is what does
damage to the pocketbook and to the soul.*
— Jesse Livermore

WEDNESDAY
 # 27

*The facts are unimportant! It's what they
are perceived to be that determines the
course of events.*
— R. Earl Hadady

*Next seven trading days should be bullish in 1999 unless Millennium fever
has caused spectacular Dow rise.*

THURSDAY
 # 28

*The commodity futures game is a
money game— not a game involving
the supply-demand of the actual
commodity as commonly depicted.*
— R. Earl Hadady

FRIDAY
 # 29

*Regulatory agencies within five
years become controlled by industries they
were set up to regulate.*
— Gabriel Kolko

SATURDAY
30

Halloween

SUNDAY
31

PERFECT MARKET TIMERS $1,000 TO $85,937
PERFECT SECTOR SELECTORS $1,000 TO $4,357,000,000

According to Charles D. Ellis in *Winning the Loser's Game* (McGraw-Hill, $24.95):

"A delightful comparative analysis of two kinds of investment perfection for the period 1940-73 gives a sense of the seductive potential of market timing. The first record was the result of perfect market timing with 100 percent in equities in all rising markets and 100 percent in cash in all falling markets."

"With 22 transactions (11 buys and 11 sells) in 34 years, using the Dow Jones Industrial Average as a proxy for equities, $1,000 was expanded into $85,937.

"During the same 34-year period, with the hypothetical portfolio always 100 percent invested and always invested in the one best industry group, the same $1,000 (with 28 buys and 28 sells) exploded into $4,357,000,000!"

Sam Stovall, in the introduction to his book. *Standard & Poor's Guide To Sector Investing* (McGraw-Hill, but no longer in print) cites another study performed by CDA/Weisenberger, an investment research firm out of Rockville, Maryland. They compared the performances of three investment strategies—market timing, sector investing, and "buy and hold" over a 10-year period.

"Each investment technique started with $1,000. At the end of the 10-year period, the buy-and-hold investor walked away with a little more than $6,000, while the market timer netted almost $15,000. Yet the sector selector amassed nearly $63,000!"

Thomas J. Dorsey, another sector enthusiast, in his book, *Point & Figure Charting: The Essential Application for Forecasting and Tracking Market Prices* (John Wiley, $55.00), also notes that most stocks are more influenced by market and industry group trends than fundamental developments at the company.

Dorsey places a lot of emphasis on sector analysis—how strong is each industry group, and which ones are attracting new money? A sector is rated by keeping track of the charts of all stocks in the group, at **www.dorseywright.com**.

See all the companies in each industry arranged across a bell curve to easily identify those that are overbought or oversold. Dorsey's Breakout Report separates breakouts (to the upside or downside) by sector. This way when a large number of stocks start to break out in one sector, this obvious signal will jump out at you.

There's a lot of information available online, and more sites are being developed all the time. **www.marketguide.com** updates a series of industry groups every day, giving the one-day and five-day price change for each and ranking them. A table also shows fundamental data for each group, including average P/E, yield, price to book, one-year earnings growth and more.

Bring up an extensive list of the stocks in each industry, with basic fundamental information. Marketguide also lists the hottest industry groups, as well as the hottest stocks—and the coolest (meaning down in price). A must for wired investors to check out. Much of it is free; there's a charge for certain extra information.

If you're still dependent on the print world, there's plenty of data to work with. *Investor's Business Daily* keeps track of 197 industry groups showing how they ranked on performance in the last week, previous week, last month, and the year so far. There's still more, including a rundown of the groups with the most stocks making new highs. The paper keeps track of how a number of indexes are doing. Some are general or specialized market averages. Others are specific, such as the medical/healthcare, consumer, insurance, bank and high-tech indexes.

NOVEMBER

MONDAY

Charts not only tell what was, they tell what is; and a trend from was to is (projected linearly into the will be) contains better percentages than clumsy guessing.
— R.A. Levy

Election Day

TUESDAY

If a battered stock refuses to sink any lower no matter how many negative articles appear in the papers, that stock is worth a close look.
— James L. Fraser, *Contrary Investor*

WEDNESDAY

I know but one sure tip from a broker…your margin call.
— Jesse Livermore

THURSDAY

The business world worships mediocrity. Officially we revere free enterprise, initiative, and individuality. Unofficially, we fear it.
— George Lois, *Art of Advertising*, 1977

FRIDAY

When a falling stock becomes a screaming buy because it cannot conceivably drop further, try to buy it 30 percent lower.
— Al Rizzo, 1986

SATURDAY

6

SUNDAY

7

"JANUARY EFFECT" FAVORS SMALL STOCKS

My research on the January Effect since 1953 using the S&P Low-Priced stock index as a proxy for small stocks vs. the blue-chip S&P 500 is shown in the table.

Simply stated, the January Effect is the tendency for small stocks to outperform large stocks in January. Hundreds have studied this effect. Two professors, Robert A. Haugen and Josef Lakonichok, analyzed all the research and wrote *The Incredible January Effect* (Irwin Professional Publishing).

JANUARY % CHANGES
(Based on Monthly Averages)

	Daily S&P 500 Index	Weekly Low–Priced Index	Difference
1953	0.5%	4.6%	4.1%
1954	2.5	7.6	5.1
1955	1.8	7.8	6.0
1956	−2.7	0.9	3.6
1957	−2.2	4.0	6.2
1958	2.0	8.7	6.7
1959	4.0	6.9	2.9
1960	−1.7	3.1	4.8
1961	5.1	10.0	4.9
1962	−3.7	2.2	5.9
1963	3.9	4.8	0.9
1964	3.1	5.7	2.6
1965	2.6	6.1	3.5
1966	1.7	3.2	1.5
1967	3.8	7.1	3.3
1968	−0.3	15.1	15.4
1969	−4.2	−4.7	−0.5
1970	−8.7	3.7	12.4
1971	3.3	14.4	11.1
1972	4.2	13.1	8.9
1973	0.8	−3.6	−4.4
1974	1.4	14.7	13.3
1975	8.2	28.5	20.3
1976	9.2	16.8	7.6
1977	−0.9	6.3	7.2
1978	−3.8	−1.4	2.4
1979	3.7	11.9	8.2
1980	3.5	7.3	3.8
1981	−0.4	2.9	3.3
1982	−5.3	−0.3	5.0
1983	3.5	6.1	2.6
1984	1.2	4.7	3.5
1985	4.3	9.0	4.7
1986	0.4	1.9	1.5
1987	6.4	8.4	2.0
1988	4.0	7.1	3.1
1989	3.2	7.4	4.2
1990	−2.5	−3.8	−1.3
1991	4.2*	21.0*	16.8
1992	−2.0	14.3	16.3
1993	0.7	8.5	7.8
1994	3.2	3.8	0.6
1995	2.4	6.3	3.9
1996	3.3	2.2	−1.1
1997	6.1	2.8	−3.3
1998	1.0	−4.7	−5.7
46 year Average	**1.5%**	**6.6%**	**5.1%**

*Month–end prices now available

Some of their conclusions:

• Average returns to the stocks of small companies in January are typically larger than those of the biggest companies.

• In January buying the Value Line index futures contract while selling the S&P 500 contract is a profitable hedge strategy.

• Low-grade bonds beat higher-grade bonds and non-dividend paying stocks outperform the dividend payers in January.

• The January Effect has been in operation since the introduction of the income tax and it's even more prevalent in foreign countries.

Low-priced stocks had double-digit gains and a better "batting average" than the S&P 500 in 1961, 1968, 1971, 1972, 1974, 1975, 1976, 1979, 1991 and 1992. These were Januarys following bear markets or when the stock market was clobbered late in the year.

Though the low-priced stock index outperformed the S&P 500 in 40 out of the past 46 Januarys by 5.1 percentage points on average, note that the margin between the two has been smaller in recent years until 1991 and 1992.

January losses for low-priced stocks resulted in 1969, 1973, 1978, 1982, and 1990 when bear markets began or were in progress, at least for the smaller capitalization issues.

Surprisingly quick military victories in Kuwait in mid-January 1991 and a one-point discount rate reduction prior to January 1992 led to the best two consecutive January Effects since 1975 and 1976.

The January Effect has now failed to materialize three years in a row as blue chips continued to leave small stocks in the dust.

Can this be the end of the January Effect? Or, has the greatest bull market ever just put the January Effect on hold temporarily? We'll just have to wait and see!

NOVEMBER

Loscalzo Assoc. I 11/19/99

MONDAY
8

A great pleasure in life is doing what most people say you cannot do.
—Walter Bagehot

TUESDAY
9

The "whole" or "cash-value" life policy is certainly in its time one of the most cleverly designed financial products (from the insurance industry's viewpoint) of all time.
— Chris Welles

WEDNESDAY
10

Wall Street's graveyards are filled with men who were right too soon.
— William Hamilton

Veteran's Day

THURSDAY
11

Murphy & Murphy   2 HRS

Review and Correct
September & October Activity

Look for an impending crash in the economy when the best seller lists are filled with books on business strategies and quick-fix management ideas.
— Peter Drucker

FRIDAY
12

The stock market is that creation of man which humbles him the most.
— Anonymous

SATURDAY
13

SUNDAY
14

REVELATIONS FROM NEW INVESTMENT RESEARCH

1. Stocks decline prior to negative earnings surprises
And stay flat prior to positive earnings surprises
The most revealing study of the year appeared in the *Wall Street Journal* on April 24, 1998 (by Robert Butman, president of TQA Investors LLC, a New York hedge fund). The research showed stocks with negative earnings surprises in the last four years dropping an average 8% within two days of the report. During the 1980s, it took three to four weeks for that response. Similarly, positive surprises saw 8% gains on average very quickly compared to the past. What's most amazing though is that negative surprises were preceded by a 4% decline over a three-week period relative to the S&P. In contrast, stocks were relatively flat prior to positive surprises. Somehow, bad news leaks out faster than good news.

2. Friday market action often a tip-off
There are tens or maybe hundreds of thousands of day traders boldly moving billions of dollars into and out of the market, often changing course on a dime. When they're nervous, they won't keep long positions over the weekend and may even go short. Look at 1997's *Daily Dow Point Changes* on page 58 (or on our website) and you'll see eight down Fridays in a row starting in mid-July as the Southeast Asian crisis began to unfold. The market held its ground for three months but during three weeks in October 1000 Dow points were peeled off. Another Friday phenomenon can be seen in 1998's point changes which are updated every day on our website *www.hirschorganization.com.* You rarely see a cluster of down-Fridays followed by down-Mondays (or Tuesdays if Monday is a holiday) in a bull market. But this negative pattern occurred in April/May 1998 as worries about Southeast Asian fallout and Russian Ruble weakness affected the market.

3. Unpopular funds trounce popular funds in following 1, 2 and 3 years
Morningstar examined the cash flows of mutual funds since 1987 and discovered that unpopular funds suffering redemptions outperformed the average fund during the next one-, two-, and three-year periods 78% of the time. Popular funds with swelling coffers were beaten 89% of the time.

4. Triple-witching weeks tend to be up, weeks after tend to be down
Dow points were gained in 16 of the past 18 triple-witching expiration weeks (March, June, September and December). Following weeks were only up 7 out of 18 times. If you go back to September 1990, You'll find that only 8 expiration weeks out of 31 were down, while 22 of 31 following weeks were down. For what it's worth every down triple-witching week lost further ground in the following week except June 1998.

5. Best time to buy high-tech stocks is late October
Michael Murphy reveals this unique seasonal phenomenon in his new book, *Every Investor's Guide to High-Tech Stocks And Mutual Funds* (Broadway Books, $27.50). This is corroborated by a Ned Davis 1979–1997 study showing December through February being the best three-month period for technology stocks with an average 9.6% gain. November through January and January through March were tied for second place with average 7.3% gains.

6. Sectors that do well in January outperform others in the rest of the year
I read about this seasonal pattern in *Investors Intelligence* some time ago and was intrigued. This will be a project for the 2000 edition of the *Stock Trader's Almanac.*

NOVEMBER

MONDAY
15

*We pay the debts of the last generation
by issuing bonds payable by
the next generation.*
— Lawrence J. Peter

TUESDAY
16

*Fortune 500 companies have shrunk by
over one million workers while non-
manufacturing sectors dominated by small
entrepreneurial companies have added
more than 9 million workers in the 1980s.*
— John Rutledge

WEDNESDAY
17

*Small business has been the first rung
on the ladder upward for every minority
group in the nation's history.*
— S. I. Hayakawa, 1947

THURSDAY
18

*The inherent vice of capitalism is the
unequal sharing of blessings;
the inherent virtue of socialism
is the equal sharing of miseries.*
— Winston Churchill

Lose 3/20 Assoc. Seminar

 ## FRIDAY
19

*It's not what you say.
It's what they hear.*
— A sign in an advertising office.

SATURDAY
20

SUNDAY
21

THANKSGIVING MARKET—NO TURKEY!
SURE WAY TO WIN THE TURKEY SHOOT

Easy! Be invested on the day before and after Thanksgiving. These two days combined gained about nine Dow points on average for 21 straight years without a loss until 1987's crash. In 46 years there were only seven losses. Thanksgiving strength may be attributed to the "holiday spirit," but November has been a top performer since 1950. Notice in recent years Tuesdays were up thanks to anticipators and seven of the last thirteen Fridays were down because of too many "game" players. I would go long prior to the Tuesday before Thanksgiving and exit sometime the following Monday.

WHAT DOW JONES INDUSTRIALS DID ON
THE DAY BEFORE AND AFTER THANKSGIVING

	2 Days Before	Day Before	Day After	Total Gain Dow Points	Dow Close	Next Monday
1952	— 0.18	1.54	1.22	2.76	283.66	0.04
1953	1.71	0.65	2.45	3.10	280.23	1.14
1954	3.27	1.89	3.16	5.05	387.79	0.72
1955	4.61	0.71	0.26	0.97	482.88	— 1.92
1956	— 4.49	— 2.16	4.65	2.49	472.56	— 2.27
1957	— 9.04	10.69	3.84	14.53	449.87	— 2.96
1958	— 4.37	8.63	8.31	16.94	557.46	2.61
1959	2.94	1.41	1.42	2.83	652.52	6.66
1960	— 3.44	1.37	4.00	5.37	606.47	— 1.04
1961	— 0.77	1.10	2.18	3.28	732.60	— 0.61
1962	6.73	4.31	7.62	11.93	644.87	— 2.81
1963	32.03	— 2.52	9.52	7.00	750.52	1.39
1964	— 1.68	— 5.21	— 0.28	— 5.49	882.12	— 6.69
1965	2.56	N/C	— 0.78	— 0.78	948.16	— 1.23
1966	— 3.18	1.84	6.52	8.36	803.34	— 2.18
1967	13.17	3.07	3.58	6.65	877.60	4.51
1968	8.14	— 3.17	8.76	5.59	985.08	— 1.74
1969	— 5.61	3.23	1.78	5.01	812.30	— 7.26
1970	5.21	1.98	6.64	8.62	781.35	12.74
1971	— 5.18	0.66	17.96	18.62	816.59	13.14
1972	8.21	7.29	4.67	11.96	1025.21	— 7.45
1973	—17.76	10.08	— 0.98	9.10	854.00	—29.05
1974	5.32	2.03	— 0.63	1.40	618.66	—15.64
1975	9.76	3.15	2.12	5.27	860.67	— 4.33
1976	— 6.57	1.66	5.66	7.32	956.62	— 6.57
1977	6.41	0.78	1.12	1.90	844.42	— 4.85
1978	— 1.56	2.95	3.12	6.07	810.12	3.72
1979	— 6.05	— 1.80	4.35	2.55	811.77	16.98
1980	3.93	7.00	3.66	10.66	993.34	—23.89
1981	18.45	7.90	7.80	15.70	885.94	3.04
1982	— 9.01	9.01	7.36	16.37	1007.36	— 4.51
1983	7.01	— 0.20	1.83	1.63	1277.44	— 7.62
1984	9.83	6.40	18.78	25.18	1220.30	— 7.95
1985	0.12	18.92	— 3.56	15.36	1472.13	—14.22
1986	6.05	4.64	— 2.53	2.11	1914.23	— 1.55
1987	40.45	—16.58	—36.47	—53.05	1910.48	—76.93
1988	11.73	14.58	—17.60	— 3.02	2074.68	6.76
1989	7.25	17.49	18.77	36.26	2675.55	19.42
1990	—35.15	9.16	—12.13	— 2.97	2527.23	5.94
1991	14.08	—16.10	— 5.36	—21.46	2894.68	40.70
1992	25.66	17.56	15.94	33.50	3282.20	22.96
1993	3.92	13.41	— 3.63	9.78	3683.95	— 6.15
1994	—91.52	— 3.36	33.64	30.28	3708.27	31.29
1995	40.46	18.06	7.23*	25.29	5048.84	22.04
1996	—19.38	—29.07	22.36*	— 6.71	6521.70	N/C
1997	41.03	—14.17	28.35*	14.18	7823.13	189.98

* Shortened trading day

NOVEMBER

MONDAY
22

I believe in the exceptional man— the entrepreneur who is always out of money, not the bureaucrat who generates cash flow and pays dividends.
— Armand Erpf

TUESDAY
 ## 23

History is a collection of agreed upon lies.
— Voltaire

WEDNESDAY
 ## 24

When I have to depend upon hope in a trade, I get out of it.
— Jesse Livermore

Thanksgiving (Market Closed) THURSDAY
25

Statements by high officials are practically always misleading when they are designed to bolster a falling market.
— Gerald M. Loeb

FRIDAY
  ## 26

Companies which do well generally tend to report (their quarterly earnings) earlier than those which do poorly.
— Alan Abelson, *Barron's*

SATURDAY
27

SUNDAY
28

If Santa Claus should fail to call
Bears may come to Broad and Wall

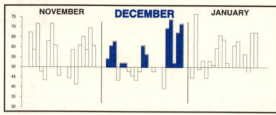

DECEMBER ALMANAC

See Market Probability Chart on page 125.

❑ Inferior Decembers often precede bear market years or are hit by tax loss selling after bear markets have ended ❑ "Free lunch" served on Wall Street at mid-month (page 118) ❑ RECORD: S&P up 36, down 12 times ❑ December is best month, with average 1.7% S&P gain but ranks sixth in Dow with total gain of 1140.19 points since 1950 ❑ SEC changing from 5-day to 3-day settlement date after trades may be affecting month-end seasonality.

DECEMBER DAILY POINT CHANGES DOW JONES INDUSTRIALS

Previous Month Close	1988 2114.51	1989 2706.27	1990 2559.65	1991 2894.68	1992 3305.16	1993 3683.95	1994 3739.23	1995 5074.49	1996 6521.70	1997 7823.13
1	−12.63	41.38	—	—	−10.80	13.13	−38.36	12.64	—	189.98
2	− 9.60	—	—	40.7	− 8.11	5.03	44.75	—	N/C	5.72
3	—	—	5.94	− 5.82	− 9.72	1.96	—	—	− 79.01	13.18
4	—	5.98	14.11	−17.89	12.15	—	—	52.39	− 19.75	18.15
5	31.48	−11.95	30.7	−22.58	—	—	− 3.70	37.93	14.16	98.97
6	25.6	− 4.91	− 7.92	− 2.69	—	6.14	4.03	21.68	− 55.16	—
7	4.27	−15.99	−12.38	—	18.65	8.67	−10.43	− 39.74	—	—
8	−11.92	10.66	—	—	14.85	15.65	−49.79	− 2.53	—	− 38.29
9	1.78	—	—	−14.75	1.63	− 4.75	5.38	—	82	− 61.18
10	—	—	6.68	− 7.83	−11.62	10.89	—	—	9.31	− 70.87
11	—	− 3.20	−10.64	1.56	− 8.11	—	—	27.46	− 70.73	− 129.8
12	− 3.91	23.89	36.14	29.75	—	—	27.26	− 9.4	− 98.81	− 10.69
13	3.91	8.96	− 7.92	19.23	—	23.76	− 3.03	41.55	1.16	—
14	− 9.24	− 7.46	−20.55	—	−11.88	− 21.8	30.95	− 34.32	—	—
15	− 1.25	−14.08	—	—	− 7.84	−25.71	19.18	− 5.42	—	84.29
16	17.71	—	—	4.69	−29.18	9.22	41.72	—	− 36.52	53.72
17	—	—	− 0.49	−16.77	14.05	25.43	—	—	39.98	− 18.90
18	—	−42.02	33.41	5.81	44.04	—	—	−101.52	38.44	−110.91
19	21.97	− 1.92	N/C	6.27	—	—	−16.49	34.68	126.87	− 90.21
20	− 6.61	− 7.68	2.73	20.12	—	3.64	−23.55	− 50.57	10.76	—
21	− 1.43	3.20	4.2	—	− 0.81	−10.06	34.65	37.21	—	—
22	− 4.28	20.26	—	—	8.64	17.04	13.12	1.44	—	63.02
23	8.57	—	—	88.1	− 7.56	− 4.47	18.51	—	4.62	−127.54
24	—	—	−12.37	28.4	12.7	—	—	—	33.83*	− 31.64*
25	H	H	H	H	H	H	H	H	H	H
26	—	− 2.13	15.84	31.98	—	—	—	12.29	23.83	19.18*
27	− 6.25	15.14	−11.63	18.56	—	35.21	28.26	− 4.34	14.23	—
28	3.75	7.9	3.71	—	7.02	0.84	− 22.2	− 10.12	—	—
29	16.25	20.9	—	—	10.26	0.56	− 6.06	21.32	—	113.1
30	−14.11	—	—	62.39	10.26	−18.45	1.01	—	− 11.54	123.56
31	—	—	4.45	4.92	−19.99	−21.79	—	—	−101.10	− 7.72
Close	2168.57	2753.20	2633.66	3168.83	3301.11	3754.09	3834.44	5117.12	6448.27	7908.25
Change	54.06	46.93	74.01	274.15	−4.05	70.14	95.21	42.63	−73.43	85.12

* Shortened trading day

MONDAY

 29

No profession requires more hard work, intelligence, patience, and mental discipline than successful speculation.
— Robert Rhea

TUESDAY

 30

Live beyond your means; then you're forced to work hard, you have to succeed.
— Edward G. Robinson

WEDNESDAY

 1

I have a simple philosophy. Fill what's empty. Empty what's full. And scratch where it itches.
— Alice Roosevelt Longworth

THURSDAY

 2

Lack of money is the root of all evil.
— George Bernard Shaw

FRIDAY

3

A statistician is someone who can draw a straight line from an unwarranted assumption to a foregone conclusion.
— Anonymous

Chanukah   **SATURDAY**

4

SUNDAY

5

MID-DECEMBER NEW LOWS
THE ONLY FREE LUNCH ON WALL STREET

Several shrewd observers note that many depressed issues sell at "bargain" levels near the close of each year as investors rid their portfolios of these "losers" for tax purposes. Stocks hitting new lows for the year around December 15 tend to out-perform the market handsomely by February 15 in the following year.

BARGAIN STOCKS VS. THE MARKET

60-Day Period Dec 15 - Feb 15	New Lows Around Dec 15	% Change Around Feb 15	% Change NYSE Composite	Bargain Stocks Advantage
1966-67	45	18.0%	8.9%	9.1%
1967-68	45	7.4	— 4.7	12.1
1968-69	24	5.0	— 3.4	8.4
1974-75	112	48.9	22.1	26.8
1975-76	21	34.9	14.9	20.0
1976-77	2	1.3	— 3.3	4.6
1977-78	15	2.8	— 4.5	7.3
1978-79	43	11.8	3.9	7.9
1979-80	5	9.3	6.1	3.2
1980-81	14	7.1	— 2.0	9.1
1981-82	21	— 2.6	— 7.4	4.8
1982-83	4	33.0	9.7	23.3
1983-84	13	— 3.2	— 3.8	0.6
1984-85	32	19.0	12.1	6.9
1985-86	4	— 22.5	3.9	— 26.4
1986-87	22	9.3	12.5	— 3.2
1987-88	23	13.2	6.8	6.4
1988-89	14	30.0	6.4	23.6
1989-90	25	— 3.1	— 4.8	1.7
1990-91	18	18.8	12.6	6.2
1991-92	23	51.1	7.7	43.4
1992-93	9	8.7	0.6	8.1
1993-94	10	— 1.4	2.0	— 3.4
1994-95	25	14.6	5.7	8.9
1995-96	5	— 11.3	5.5	— 16.8
1996-97	16	13.9	11.2	2.7
1997-98	29	9.9	5.7	4.2
27-Year Totals		323.9%	124.4%	199.5%
Average		12.0%	4.6%	7.4%

Remember this is a trading—not an investing—strategy. Select stocks that are making mid-December new lows by first eliminating preferred stocks, closed-end funds, splits, new issues, etc. Then buy stocks that are down the most. There is some risk as these companies are down for a reason. They do tend to bounce back after tax-selling season is over.

Understandably, lower quality stocks tend to bounce back even higher than their blue-chip brethren. Santa Claus seems to reward pre-Christmas "scavengers" on Wall Street. The biggest bull market of all time has favored the big blue chip Dow type stocks, leaving smaller, depressed issues behind.

Examination of December trades by NYSE members through the years shows they tend to buy on balance during this month contrary to other months.

DECEMBER

BUY VERTEX

MONDAY
6

*In investing, the return you want
should depend on whether you
want to eat well or sleep well.*
— J. Kenfield Morley

TUESDAY
7

*Those who are of the opinion that money
will do everything may very well be
suspected to do everything for money.*
— Sir George Savile

WEDNESDAY
8

*All you need is to look over the earnings
forecasts publicly made a year ago to
see how much care you need to give
those being made now for next year.*
— Gerald M. Loeb

THURSDAY
9

*The miracle, or the power, that elevates the few is
to be found in their perseverance under the
promptings of a brave, determined spirit.*
—Mark Twain

FRIDAY
10

*When a company reports higher earnings
for its first quarter (over its previous
year's first quarter), chances are almost
five to one it will also have increased
earnings in its second quarter.*
— Niederhoffer, Cross & Zeckhauser

SATURDAY
11

SUNDAY
12

THE SANTA CLAUS RALLY

Santa Claus used to come to Wall Street nearly every year, bringing a short, sweet, respectable rally within the last five days of the year (four prior to 1969) and the first two in January. This was good for an average 1.6% gain. In the 38 years prior to 1990, the market was down just seven times and eked out subpar gains (0.8% or less) six times. But in the last eight years of a giant bull market, only thrice did Santa bring juicy rallies. Scrooge came in his place on the other five occasions.

DAILY % CHANGE IN S&P COMPOSITE INDEX AT YEAR END

	Trading Days Before Year-End						First Days in Jan			Rally % Change
	6	5	4	3	2	1	1	2	3	
1952	—0.4	0.1	0.2	0.6	0.7	—0.1	—0.1	0.5	—0.7	1.7
1953	—0.3	0.4	—0.4	—0.6	0.9	0.2	0.6	0.6	0.2	1.2
1954	0.1	—0.8	1.0	0.9	0.0	0.7	2.1	—0.9	—2.5	3.8
1955	0.2	0.2	—0.6	—0.4	0.2	0.7	—0.7	—0.4	—0.1	—1.1
1956	—0.8	0.7	0.0	—0.1	0.5	0.2	—1.0	0.9	0.1	0.5
1957	0.0	0.1	1.0	—0.4	—0.5	1.0	0.9	1.3	—0.5	3.4
1958	—0.7	—0.5	1.3	1.2	0.3	0.5	0.4	0.4	—0.1	4.2
1959	—0.3	0.1	0.0	0.5	0.8	0.2	0.0	0.8	—0.4	2.4
1960	—0.3	0.1	0.1	0.5	0.5	0.1	—0.9	1.4	0.4	1.6
1961	—0.4	0.1	0.2	0.9	0.1	—0.2	—0.8	0.2	—0.7	0.3
1962	—0.3	0.0	0.6	—0.1	0.05	0.2	—0.6	1.6	0.6	1.7
1963	—0.6	0.2	0.5	0.2	0.2	0.6	0.5	0.1	0.2	2.1
1964	—0.2	0.0	—0.1	—0.3	0.6	0.5	—0.6	0.5	0.3	0.6
1965	—0.1	—0.7	0.0	0.3	0.4	0.2	—0.3	0.1	0.6	0.8
1966	0.4	—0.3	—0.6	—0.5	—0.3	0.0	0.1	0.2	1.3	—1.1
1967	0.2	—0.2	0.1	0.7	0.0	0.6	—0.4	—0.5	—0.3	0.5
1968	—1.1	—0.2	0.1	—0.4	—0.9	0.1	0.1	0.1	—1.5	—1.0
1969	—0.4	1.1	0.8	—0.7	0.4	0.5	1.0	0.5	—0.7	3.6**
1970	0.1	0.6	0.5	1.1	0.2	—0.1	—1.1	0.7	0.6	1.9
1971	—0.4	0.2	1.0	0.3	—0.4	0.3	—0.4	0.4	1.0	1.3
1972	—0.3	—0.7	0.6	0.4	0.5	1.0	0.9	0.4	—0.1	3.1
1973	—1.1	—0.7	3.1	2.1	—0.2	0.0	0.1	2.2	—0.9	6.7
1974	—1.4	1.4	0.8	—0.4	0.03	2.1	2.4	0.7	0.5	7.2
1975	0.7	0.8	0.9	—0.1	—0.4	0.5	0.8	1.8	1.0	4.3
1976	0.1	1.2	0.7	—0.4	0.5	0.5	—0.4	—1.2	—0.9	0.8
1977	0.8	0.9	0.0	0.1	0.2	0.2	—1.3	—0.3	—0.8	—0.3
1978	0.0	1.7	1.3	—0.9	—0.4	—0.2	0.6	1.1	0.8	3.3
1979	—0.6	0.1	0.1	0.2	—0.1	0.1	—2.0	—0.5	1.2	—2.2
1980	—0.4	0.4	0.5	—1.1	0.2	0.3	0.4	1.2	0.1	2.0
1981	—0.5	0.2	—0.2	—0.5	0.5	0.2	0.2	—2.2	—0.7	—1.8
1982	0.6	1.8	—1.0	0.3	—0.7	0.2	—1.6	2.2	0.4	1.2
1983	—0.2	0.0	0.9	0.3	—0.2	0.0	—0.5	1.7	1.2	2.1
1984	—0.5	0.8	—0.2	—0.4	0.3	0.6	—1.1	—0.5	—0.5	—0.6
1985	—1.1	—0.7	0.2	0.9	0.5	0.3	—0.8	0.6	—0.1	1.1
1986	—1.0	0.2	0.1	—0.9	—0.5	—0.5	1.8	2.3	0.2	2.4
1987	1.3	—0.5	—2.6	—0.4	1.3	—0.3	3.6	1.1	0.1	2.2
1988	—0.2	0.3	—0.4	0.1	0.8	—0.6	—0.9	1.5	0.2	0.9
1989	0.6	0.8	—0.2	0.6	0.5	0.8	1.8	—0.3	—0.9	4.1
1990	0.5	—0.6	0.3	—0.8	0.1	0.5	—1.1	—1.4	—0.3	—3.0
1991	2.5	0.6	1.4	0.4	2.1	0.5	0.04	0.5	—0.3	5.7
1992	—0.3	0.2	—0.1	—0.3	0.2	—0.7	—0.1	—0.2	0.0	—1.1
1993	0.0	0.7	0.1	—0.1	—0.4	—0.5	—0.2	0.3	0.1	—0.1
1994	0.0	0.2	0.4	—0.3	0.1	—0.4	0.0	0.3	—0.1	0.2
1995	0.8	0.2	0.4	0.04	—0.1	0.3	0.8	0.1	—0.6	1.8
1996	—0.3	0.5	0.6	0.1	—0.4	—1.7	—0.5	1.5	—0.1	0.1
1997	—1.5	—0.7	0.4	1.8	1.8	0.0	0.5	0.2	—1.1	4.0
Avg	—0.15	0.36*	0.30	0.09	0.22	0.20	0.04	0.47	—0.08	1.6%

*From 1968 to date; **Seven days   **Average 7-Day Gain 1.6%**

Santa's failure to show usually preceded bear markets or times stocks could be purchased at much lower prices later in the new year. Only 1966, 1984, 1992, and 1994 were in error, and 1990 has to be excluded as Saddam Hussein cancelled Christmas by invading Kuwait in August.

I think it's still a dandy couplet: **If Santa Claus should fail to call**
Bears may come to Broad & Wall

DECEMBER

MONDAY
13

*I'm a great believer in luck, and I find the
harder I work the more I have of it.*
— Thomas Jefferson

TUESDAY
14

*The price of a stock varies inversely with
the thickness of its research file.*
— Martin Sosnoff

WEDNESDAY
15

*Money makes money. And the money that
money makes makes more money.*
— Benjamin Franklin

THURSDAY
16

*The fewer analysts who follow a situation,
the more pregnant its possibilities…if
Wall Street hates a stock, buy it.*
— Martin T. Sosnoff

FRIDAY
 # 17

*A bank is a place where they lend you an
umbrella in fair weather and ask for it
back again when it begins to rain.*
— Robert Frost

SATURDAY
18

SUNDAY
19

DECEMBER

MONDAY
20

If you destroy a free market you create a black market. If you have ten thousand regulations you destroy all respect for the law.
— Winston Churchill

TUESDAY
21

A gold mine is a hole in the ground with a liar on top.
— Mark Twain

WEDNESDAY
22

Market should do well rest of 1999 unless year 2000 has already been discounted.

If buying equities seem the most hazardous and foolish thing you could possibly do, then you are near the bottom that will end the bear market.
— Joseph E. Granville

THURSDAY
23

If a man can see both sides of a problem, you know that none of his money is tied up in it.
— Verda Ross

FRIDAY
24

(Market Closed)

Knowledge born from actual experience is the answer to why one profits; lack of it is the reason one loses.
— Gerald M. Loeb

SATURDAY
25

Christmas Day

SUNDAY
26

Buy Sterling Software
this week
or on Jan. 3

MONDAY

27

TUESDAY

28

WEDNESDAY

29

THURSDAY

30

FRIDAY
31

A Happy and Prosperous New Century—Y.H.

New Year's Day

SATURDAY
1

SUNDAY
2

MARKET PROBABILITY CALENDAR 1999

The chance of the market rising on any trading day of the year*

(Based on the number of times the S&P 500 rose on a particular trading day during January 1953–December 1997)

Date	Jan	Feb	Mar	Apr	May	Jun	Jul	Aug	Sep	Oct	Nov	Dec
1	H	54.3	62.2	60.0	S	55.3	67.4	S	63.0	48.9	66.7	48.9
2	S	62.2	67.4	H	S	58.7	65.2	48.9	60.0	S	54.2	53.3
3	S	48.9	58.7	S	51.1	55.6	S	42.2	63.0	S	71.1	62.2
4	46.7	51.1	46.7	S	73.9	55.6	S	48.9	S	71.1	45.7	S
5	75.6	52.2	45.7	55.6	64.4	S	H	52.2	S	54.3	44.4	S
6	48.9	S	S	56.5	44.4	S	53.3	57.8	H	62.2	S	63.0
7	51.1	S	S	54.3	42.2	48.9	60.0	S	44.4	53.3	S	42.2
8	44.4	39.1	57.8	57.8	S	40.0	66.0	S	48.9	55.3	64.4	51.1
9	S	40.0	62.2	64.4	S	40.0	55.6	42.2	51.1	S	71.1	51.1
10	S	62.2	50.0	S	51.1	62.2	S	57.8	55.6	S	60.0	46.7
11	50.0	48.9	62.2	S	53.3	66.7	S	44.4	S	37.8	44.4	S
12	48.9	44.4	50.0	64.4	51.1	S	52.2	47.8	S	44.4	47.8	S
13	57.8	S	S	53.3	45.7	S	40.0	66.7	62.2	55.6	S	46.7
14	63.0	S	S	54.3	55.6	53.3	71.1	S	48.9	51.1	S	42.2
15	64.4	H	60.9	65.2	S	51.1	58.7	S	55.6	51.1	48.9	45.7
16	S	43.5	64.4	62.2	S	44.4	42.2	60.0	51.1	S	55.6	51.1
17	S	37.8	47.8	S	53.3	53.3	S	51.1	50.0	S	56.5	47.8
18	H	51.1	51.1	S	46.7	40.0	S	48.9	S	64.4	40.0	S
19	51.1	50.0	46.7	55.6	46.7	S	28.9	46.7	S	50.0	60.0	S
20	47.8	S	S	40.0	56.5	S	45.7	58.7	40.0	46.7	S	47.8
21	62.2	S	S	48.9	42.2	52.2	42.2	S	53.3	34.8	S	48.9
22	64.4	40.4	42.2	48.9	S	56.5	48.9	S	54.3	41.3	66.7	39.1
23	S	41.3	44.4	45.7	S	46.7	46.8	46.7	41.3	S	60.0	67.4
24	S	60.9	48.9	S	53.3	35.6	S	46.7	51.1	S	68.9	H
25	51.1	48.9	39.1	S	46.7	45.7	S	44.4	S	28.9	H	S
26	55.6	62.2	54.3	51.1	43.5	S	56.5	44.4	S	60.9	62.2	S
27	45.7	S	S	57.8	53.3	S	56.5	56.5	51.1	60.0	S	71.7
28	66.7	S	S	53.2	62.2	48.9	52.2	S	60.0	57.8	S	51.1
29	66.7		57.8	43.5	S	59.6	67.4	S	45.7	51.1	53.3	65.2
30	S		35.6	62.2	S	52.2	68.9	52.2	48.9	S	57.8	73.3
31	S		39.1		H		S	66.7		S		71.7

* See new trends developing on pages 56, 64, 66, and 134.

MARKET PROBABILITY CHART*

The chances of the market rising on any trading day of the year

(Based on the number of times the S&P 500 rose on a particular trading day during January 1953–December 1997)

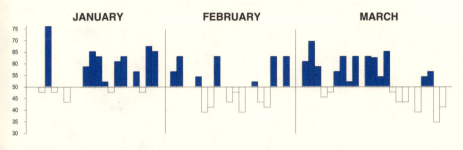

JANUARY FEBRUARY MARCH

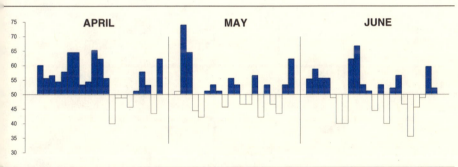

APRIL MAY JUNE

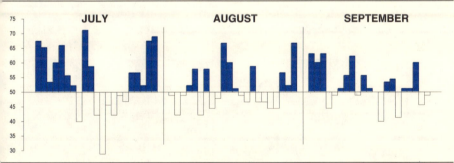

JULY AUGUST SEPTEMBER

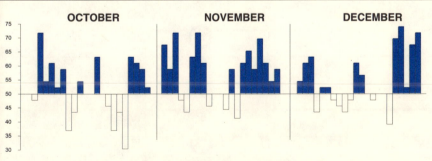

OCTOBER NOVEMBER DECEMBER

Shows the number of trading days in each month (Saturdays, Sundays, and holidays excluded) for 1998
Graphic representation of page 124
* See new trends developing on pages 56, 64, 66, and 134.

2000 STRATEGY CALENDAR
(Option expiration dates encircled)

	MONDAY	TUESDAY	WEDNESDAY	THURSDAY	FRIDAY	SATURDAY	SUNDAY
	27	28	29	30	31	1 JANUARY New Year's Day	2
JANUARY	3	4	5	6	7	8	9
	10	11	12	13	14	15	16
	17 Martin Luther King Day	18	19	20	(21)	22	23
	24	25	26	27	28	29	30
FEBRUARY	31	1 FEBRUARY	2	3	4	5	6
	7	8	9	10	11	12	13
	14 ♥	15	16	17	(18)	19	20
	21 Presidents' Day	22	23	24	25	26	27
MARCH	28	29	1 MARCH	2	3	4	5
	6	7	8 Ash Wednesday	9	10	11	12
	13	14	15	16	(17) ♣	18	19
	20	21	22	23	24	25	26
APRIL	27	28	29	30	31	1 APRIL	2
	3	4	5	6	7	8	9
	10	11	12	13	14	15	16
	17	18	19	(20) Passover	21 Good Friday	22	23 Easter
	24	25	26	27	28	29	30
MAY	1 MAY	2	3	4	5	6	7
	8	9	10	11	12	13	14 Mother's Day
	15	16	17	18	(19)	20	21
	22	23	24	25	26	27	28
JUNE	29 Memorial Day	30	31	1 JUNE	2	3	4
	5	6	7	8	9	10	11
	12	13	14	15	(16)	17	18 Father's Day
	19	20	21	22	23	24	25

Market closed on shaded weekdays; closes early when half-shaded.

2000 STRATEGY CALENDAR
(Option expiration dates encircled)

MONDAY	TUESDAY	WEDNESDAY	THURSDAY	FRIDAY	SATURDAY	SUNDAY	
26	27	28	29	30	1 JULY	2	
3	4 Independence Day	5	6	7	8	9	JULY
10	11	12	13	14	15	16	
17	18	19	20	⃝21	22	23	
24	25	26	27	28	29	30	
31	1 AUGUST	2	3	4	5	6	
7	8	9	10	11	12	13	AUGUST
14	15	16	17	⃝18	19	20	
21	22	23	24	25	26	27	
28	29	30	31	1 SEPTEMBER	2	3	SEPTEMBER
4 Labor Day	5	6	7	8	9	10	
11	12	13	14	⃝15	16	17	
18	19	20	21	22	23	24	
25	26	27	28	29	30 Rosh Hashanah	1 OCTOBER	
2	3	4	5	6	7	8	OCTOBER
9 Columbus Day	10 Yom Kippur	11	12	13	14	15	
16	17	18	19	⃝20	21	22	
23	24	25	26	27	28	29	
30	31 Boo!	1 NOVEMBER	2	3	4	5	NOVEMBER
6	7 Election Day	8	9	10	11 Veteran's Day	12	
13	14	15	16	⃝17	18	19	
20	21	22	23 Thanksgiving	24	25	26	
27	28	29	30	1 DECEMBER	2	3	DECEMBER
4	5	6	7	8	9	10	
11	12	13	14	⃝15	16	17	
18	19	20	21	22 Chanukah	23	24	
25 Christmas	26	27	28	29	30	31	

WINTER PORTFOLIO REVIEW

NO. OF SHARES	SECURITY	A ORIGINAL COST	B CURRENT VALUE	C GAIN (B – A) OR LOSS (A – B)	D % CHANGE (C ÷ A)	E MONTHS HELD	F CHANGE PER MO. (D ÷ E)	G ANNUAL RETURN (F × 12)
200	Sample Corp.	$10,000	$10,400	$400	4.0%	8	0.5%	6.0%
TOTALS								

Stocks which have achieved their potential
1
2
3

Candidates for addition to portfolio
1
2
3

Stocks which have been disappointments
1
2
3

Investment decisions
1
2
3

DIRECTORY OF SEASONAL AND TRADING PATTERNS

CONTENTS

A TYPICAL DAY IN THE MARKET

Half hourly reporting began January 1987. The NYSE switched from 10:00 AM openings to 9:30 AM in October 1985. Compared to the typical day during 1963 to 1985, prior to half-hourly reporting, the major difference now is stronger openings and closings in a more bullish market dominated by professionals. Morning and afternoon weakness appears one hour earlier.

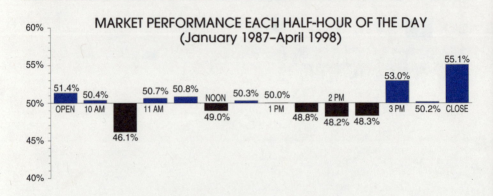

MARKET PERFORMANCE EACH HALF-HOUR OF THE DAY (January 1987–April 1998)

Based on the number of times the Dow Jones industrial average increased over previous half-hour.

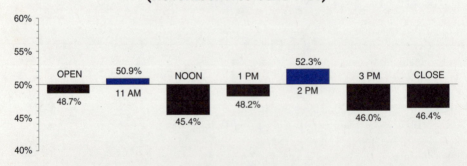

MARKET PERFORMANCE EACH HOUR OF THE DAY (November 1963–June 1985)

Based on the number of times the Dow Jones industrial average increased over previous hour.

On the opposite page, half-hourly movements since January 1987 have been separated by day of the week. Visible proof of my discovery that Monday is the strongest comeback day of the week is evident. This is not surprising in as much as Monday used to be the most massacred trading day. Since 1990 Monday has been the strongest day of the week. (See page 56.) Other days tended to rise most often at the open. Tuesdays and Fridays after lunch were two of the weakest hours of the week. Stocks tend to firm at the close more often than weaken.

THROUGH THE WEEK ON A HALF-HOURLY BASIS

From the chart showing the percentage of times the Dow Jones industrial average rose over the preceding half-hour (January 1987–April 1998*) the typical week unfolds.

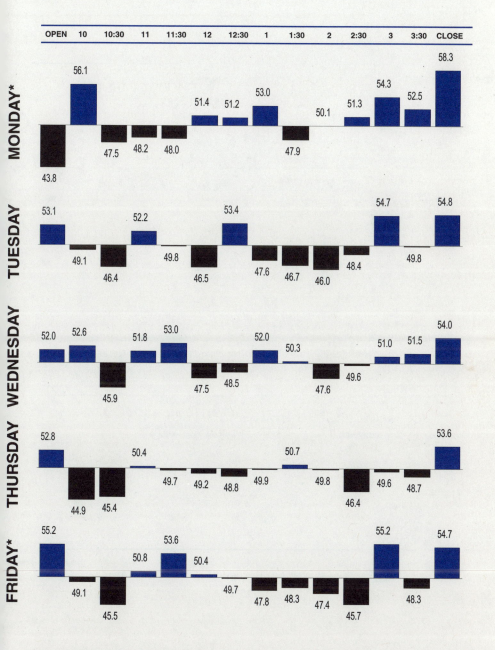

*Research indicates that where Tuesday is the first trading day of the week, it follows the Monday pattern. Therefore, all such Tuesdays were combined with the Mondays here. Thursdays that are the final trading day of a given week behave like Fridays, and were similarly grouped with the Fridays.

MONDAY IS NOW WINNINGEST DAY OF WEEK

Between 1952 and 1989 Monday was the worst trading day of the week. The first trading day of the week (including Tuesday, when Monday is a holiday) rose only 44.5% of the time, while the other trading days of the week closed higher 54.7% of the time.

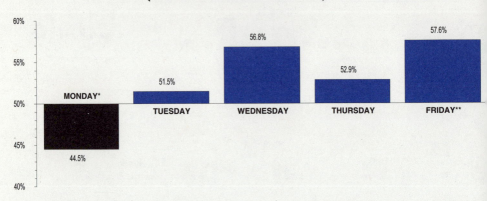

MARKET PERFORMANCE EACH DAY OF THE WEEK
(June 1952–December 1989)

A dramatic reversal occurred starting in 1990. Since then Monday became the most powerful day of the week. Friday slipped to second place and Wednesday dropped to third place.

To see how the Dow Jones industrial average performed on different days of the week each year in points gained or lost, see page 56.

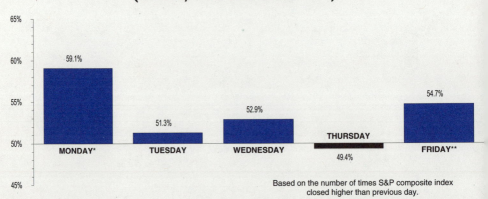

MARKET PERFORMANCE EACH DAY OF THE WEEK
(January 1990–December 1997)

Based on the number of times S&P composite index closed higher than previous day.

*On Monday holidays, the following Tuesday is included in the Monday figure.
**On Friday holidays, the preceding Thursday is included in the Friday figure.

DAILY PERFORMANCE EACH YEAR SINCE 1952

To determine if market trend alters performance of different days of the week, I separated the fourteen bear years of 1953, '57, '60, '62, '66, '69, '70, '73, '74, '77, '81, '84, '90 and '94 from the 32 bull market years. While middle days— Tuesday, Wednesday and Thursday—did not vary much on average between bull and bear years, Mondays and Fridays were sharply affected. There was a swing of 11.7 percentage points in Monday's performance and 10.3 percentage points in Friday's. Mondays have been stronger in recent years.

PERCENTAGE OF TIMES MARKET
CLOSED HIGHER THAN PREVIOUS DAY

	Monday	Tuesday	Wednesday	Thursday	Friday
1952	48.4%	55.6%	58.1%	51.9%	66.7%
1953	34.6	52.1	54.9	59.6	54.7
1954	50.0	57.4	63.5	59.2	73.1
1955	50.0	45.7	63.5	60.0	78.8
1956	37.7	39.6	45.8	50.0	59.6
1957	26.9	54.0	66.7	48.9	44.2
1958	59.6	52.0	58.8	68.1	73.1
1959	40.4	53.1	55.8	48.9	69.8
1960	34.6	50.0	44.2	54.0	59.6
1961	53.8	52.2	64.0	56.0	63.5
1962	28.3	52.1	54.0	53.1	48.1
1963	46.2	63.3	51.0	57.4	69.2
1964	40.4	48.0	61.5	58.7	77.4
1965	46.2	57.4	55.8	51.0	71.2
1966	36.5	47.8	53.8	42.0	57.7
1967	38.5	50.0	60.8	64.0	69.2
1968*	49.1	55.3	63.0	40.4	55.8
1969	32.7	45.8	50.0	67.4	50.0
1970	40.4	44.0	65.4	46.8	52.8
1971	44.2	62.5	55.8	57.1	50.0
1972	38.5	60.9	57.7	51.0	67.3
1973	32.1	51.1	52.9	44.9	44.2
1974	32.7	57.1	51.0	36.7	30.8
1975	53.8	38.8	61.5	56.3	55.8
1976	55.8	55.3	55.8	40.8	58.5
1977	40.4	40.4	46.2	53.1	53.8
1978	51.9	43.5	59.6	54.0	48.1
1979	54.7	53.2	58.8	66.0	44.2
1980	55.8	56.3	69.8	35.4	55.8
1981	44.2	38.8	55.8	53.2	47.2
1982	46.2	39.6	44.2	44.9	50.0
1983	55.8	46.8	61.5	50.0	55.8
1984	39.6	63.8	31.4	46.0	44.2
1985	44.2	61.2	54.9	56.3	53.8
1986	51.9	44.9	67.3	58.3	55.8
1987	51.9	57.1	63.5	61.7	49.1
1988	51.9	61.7	51.9	48.0	59.6
1989	51.9	47.8	69.2	58.0	69.2
1990	67.9	53.2	52.9	40.0	51.9
1991	44.2	46.9	52.9	49.0	51.9
1992	51.9	49.0	53.8	56.3	45.3
1993	65.4	41.7	55.8	44.9	48.1
1994	55.8	46.8	52.9	48.0	59.6
1995	63.5	56.5	63.5	62.0	63.5
1996	54.7	44.9	51.0	57.1	63.5
1997	69.2	71.4	40.4	37.5	53.8
1998**	58.8	73.3	58.8	37.5	58.8
Average	47.3%	51.9%	56.2%	51.9%	57.1%
32 Bull Years	50.8%	52.8%	57.9%	53.0%	60.2%
14 Bear Years	39.1%	49.8%	52.3%	49.6%	49.9%

*Excludes last six months of four-day market weeks.

**Four months only. Not included in averages.

Based on S&P composite index.

133

END-OF-MONTH CASH INFLOWS INTO STOCKS

For many years, the best market days of the month were the last day of the month plus the first four trading days of the following month. This pattern is quite clear in the first chart showing these five consecutive trading days towering above the other 16 trading days of the average month in the 1953-1981 period.

The rationale was that individuals and institutions tended to operate similarly, causing a massive flow of cash out of banks, mutual funds and insurance companies into stocks near beginnings of months.

MARKET PERFORMANCE EACH DAY OF THE MONTH
(January 1953–December 1981)
Based on the number of times the S&P composite closed higher than previous day

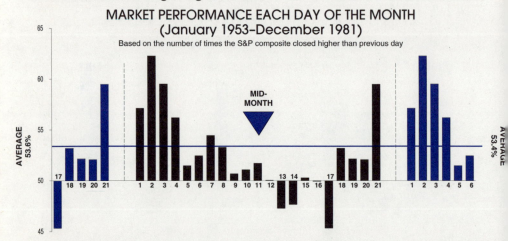

It is quite clear that "front-running" traders and money managers have been taking advantage of this bullish phenomenon in recent years, drastically altering the previous pattern. The second chart from 1982 shows the trading shift caused by these "anticipators" to the last four trading days of the month plus the first two. Another astonishing development shows the ninth and tenth trading days rising more often than any other consecutive two. Perhaps the enormous growth of 401k retirement plans is responsible for this new mid-month bulge. As most participants' salaries are usually paid twice monthly, it follows contributions need to be invested twice monthly.

(January 1982–December 1997)

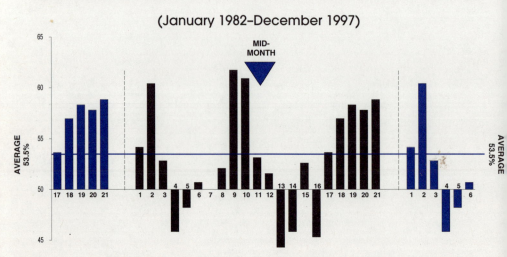

TRADING DAYS (excluding Saturdays, Sundays, and holidays)

NOVEMBER, DECEMBER, AND JANUARY
YEAR'S BEST THREE-MONTH SPAN

The most important observation to be made from a chart showing the average monthly percent change in market prices since 1950 is that institutions (mutual funds, pension funds, banks, etc.) determine the trading patterns in today's market.

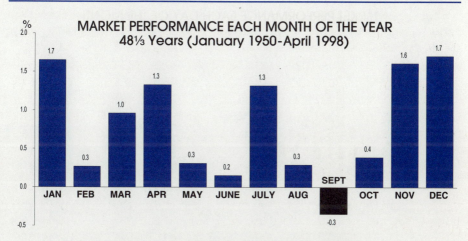

MARKET PERFORMANCE EACH MONTH OF THE YEAR
48⅓ Years (January 1950-April 1998)

Average month-to-month % change in Standard & Poor's composite index
(Based on monthly closing prices)

The "investment calendar" reflects the annual, semi-annual and quarterly operations of institutions during January, April and July. October, besides being a "tight money" month, and the last campaign month before elections, is also the time when most bear markets seem to end, as in 1946, 1957, 1960, 1966, 1974, 1987, and 1990. (August was most favored in 1982 and 1984.)

Unusual year-end strength comes from corporate and private pension funds producing a 5.0% gain on average between November 1 and January 31.

September's dismal performance makes it the worst month of the year and the only month with a loss. In the last thirteen years it has only been up five times. In midterm election years, Septembers have been down nine times in a row.

In the last ten years (see page 140) May was the best month while November was third from the bottom.

See page 50 for monthly performance tables for the S&P 500 and the Dow Jones industrials. See page 54 for unique six-month switching strategy.

On page 74 you can see how the first month of the first three quarters far outperforms the second and the third months since 1950. Individual monthly performance is also shown for each year starting with 1991.

20TH CENTURY BULL AND BEAR MARKETS

— Beginning —		— Ending —		Bull		Bear	
Date	DJIA	Date	DJIA	% Gain	Days	% Change	Days
09/24/00	52.96	06/17/01	78.26	47.8	266	— 46.1	875
11/09/03	42.15	01/19/06	103.00	144.4	802	— 48.5	665
11/15/07	53.00	11/19/09	100.53	89.7	735	— 27.4	675
09/25/11	72.94	09/30/12	94.15	29.1	371	— 43.5	668
12/24/14	53.17	11/21/16	110.15	107.2	698	— 40.1	393
12/19/17	65.95	11/03/19	119.62	81.4	684	— 46.6	660
08/24/21	63.90	03/20/23	105.38	64.9	573	— 18.6	221
10/27/23	85.76	09/03/29	381.17	344.5	2138	— 47.9	71
11/13/29	198.69	04/17/30	294.07	48.0	155	— 86.0	813
07/08/32	41.22	09/07/32	79.93	93.9	61	— 37.2	173
02/27/33	50.16	02/05/34	110.74	120.8	343	— 22.8	171
07/26/34	85.51	03/10/37	194.40	127.3	958	— 49.1	386
03/31/38	98.95	11/12/38	158.41	60.1	226	— 23.3	147
04/08/39	121.44	09/12/39	155.92	28.4	157	— 40.4	959
04/28/42	92.92	05/29/46	212.50	128.7	1492	— 23.2	353
05/17/47	163.21	06/15/48	193.16	18.4	395	— 16.3	363
06/13/49	161.60	01/05/53	293.79	81.8	1302	— 13.0	252
09/14/53	255.49	04/06/56	521.05	103.9	935	— 19.4	564
10/22/57	419.79	01/05/60	685.47	63.3	805	— 17.4	294
10/25/60	566.05	12/31/61	734.91	29.8	414	— 27.1	195
06/26/62	535.76	02/09/66	995.15	85.7	1324	— 25.2	240
10/07/66	744.32	12/03/68	985.21	32.4	788	— 35.9	539
05/26/70	631.16	04/28/71	950.82	50.6	337	— 16.1	209
11/23/71	797.97	01/11/73	1051.70	31.8	415	— 45.1	694
12/06/74	577.60	09/21/76	1014.79	75.7	655	— 26.9	525
02/28/78	742.12	09/08/78	907.74	22.3	192	— 16.4	591
04/21/80	759.13	04/27/81	1024.05	34.9	371	— 24.1	472
08/12/82	776.92	11/29/83	1287.20	65.7	474	— 15.6	238
07/24/84	1086.57	08/25/87	2722.42	150.6	1127	— 36.1	55
10/19/87	1738.74	07/17/90	2999.75	72.5	1002	— 21.2	86
10/11/90	2365.10						

Data: Ned Davis Research
Based on Dow Jones industrial average

Bear markets begin at the end of one bull market and end at the start of the next bull market (7/17/90 to 10/11/90 as an example). The high at Dow 3978.36 on January 31, 1994 was followed by a 9.7 percent correction. A 10.3 percent correction occurred between the May 22, 1996 closing high of 5778 and the intraday low on July 16, 1996. We are now in the eighth year of the longest bull market on record.

STOCK FRACTIONS IN DECIMALS AND CENTS

The table below is for investors who want to quickly convert stock price quotations into dollars and cents equivalents. One simple method to find an approximate price is to multiply the numerator by 3¢ for 32nds ($^{11}/_{32}$: 11 x 3¢ = 33¢). For 16ths, multiply the numerator by 6¢.

FRACTIONS	DECIMALS	CENTS	FRACTIONS	DECIMALS	CENTS
$^{1}/_{32}$	.03125	3⅛¢	$^{17}/_{32}$	.53125	53⅛¢
$^{1}/_{16}$	.0625	6¼¢	$^{9}/_{16}$	.5625	56¼¢
$^{3}/_{32}$	.09375	9⅜¢	$^{19}/_{32}$	.59375	59⅜¢
⅛	.125	12½¢	⅝	.625	62½¢
$^{5}/_{32}$	.15625	15⅝¢	$^{21}/_{32}$	.65625	65⅝¢
$^{3}/_{16}$	.1875	18¾¢	$^{11}/_{16}$	.6875	68¾¢
$^{7}/_{32}$	.21875	21⅞¢	$^{23}/_{32}$	.71875	71⅞¢
¼	.25	25¢	¾	.75	75¢
$^{9}/_{32}$	.28125	28⅛¢	$^{25}/_{32}$	.78125	78⅛¢
$^{5}/_{16}$	.3125	31¼¢	$^{13}/_{16}$	.8125	81¼¢
$^{11}/_{32}$	.34375	34⅜¢	$^{27}/_{32}$	.84375	84⅜¢
⅜	.375	37½¢	⅞	.875	87½¢
$^{13}/_{32}$	.40625	40⅝¢	$^{29}/_{32}$	.90625	90⅝¢
$^{7}/_{16}$	.4375	43¾¢	$^{15}/_{16}$	.9375	93¾¢
$^{15}/_{32}$	.46875	46⅞¢	$^{31}/_{32}$	.96875	96⅞¢
½	.50	50¢	1	1.0	100¢

DECENNIAL CYCLE: A MARKET PHENOMENON

By arranging each year's market gain or loss so the first years of a decade fall into the same column, certain interesting patterns emerge—strong fifth and eighth years, negative seventh and zero years.

This fascinating phenomenon was first presented by Edgar Lawrence Smith in *Common Stocks and Business Cycles* (William-Frederick Press, 1959). Anthony Gaubis co-pioneered the decennial pattern with Smith.

When Smith first cut graphs of market prices into ten-year segments and placed them above one another, he observed that each decade tended to have three bull market cycles and that the longest and strongest bull markets seem to favor the middle years of a decade.

It's difficult to place too much emphasis on the decennial cycle nowadays, other than the extraordinary fifth and zero years, as the stock market is more influenced by the quadrennnial presidential election cycle, shown on page 139.

The greatest bull market streak in history rolls on. Since the 1982 major bottom, we've experienced just two mini bear interruptions in the Dow in 1984 and 1990. The year before the Milennium augurs well for 1999. The question remains, will 2000 escape the zero jinx as its century predecessor, 1900, did? Or, will its arrival be anti-climactic?

THE TEN-YEAR STOCK MARKET CYCLE

Annual % change in Dow Jones industrial average

DECADES	Year of Decade									
	1st	2nd	3rd	4th	5th	6th	7th	8th	9th	10th
1881-1890	3.0	− 2.9	− 8.5	−18.8	20.1	12.4	− 8.4	4.8	5.5	−14.1
1891-1900	17.6	− 6.6	−24.6	− 0.6	2.3	− 1.7	21.3	22.5	9.2	7.0
1901-1910	− 8.7	− 0.4	−23.6	41.7	38.2	− 1.9	−37.7	46.6	15.0	−18.0
1911-1920	0.5	7.6	−10.3	− 5.1	81.7	− 4.2	−21.7	10.5	30.5	−32.9
1921-1930	12.7	21.7	− 3.3	26.2	30.0	0.3	28.8	48.2	−17.2	−33.8
1931-1940	−52.7	−23.1	66.7	4.1	38.5	24.8	−32.8	28.1	− 2.9	−12.7
1941-1950	−15.4	7.6	13.8	12.1	26.6	− 8.1	2.2	− 2.1	12.9	17.6
1951-1960	14.4	8.4	− 3.8	44.0	20.8	2.3	−12.8	34.0	16.4	− 9.3
1961-1970	18.7	−10.8	17.0	14.6	10.9	−18.9	15.2	4.3	−15.2	4.8
1971-1980	6.1	14.6	−16.6	−27.6	38.3	17.9	−17.3	− 3.1	4.2	14.9
1981-1990	− 9.2	19.6	20.3	− 3.7	27.7	22.6	2.3	11.8	27.0	− 4.3
1991-2000	20.3	4.2	13.7	2.1	33.5	26.0	22.6			
Total % Change	7%	40%	41%	89%	369%	72%	−38%	206%	85%	−81%
Up Years	8	7	5	7	12	7	6	9	8	4
Down Years	4	5	7	5	0	5	6	2	3	7

Based on annual close.
Cowles indices 1881–1885.

PRESIDENTIAL ELECTION/STOCK MARKET CYCLE THE 166-YEAR SAGA CONTINUES

It is no mere coincidence that the last two years (pre-election year and election year) of the 42 administrations since 1832 produced a total net market gain of 703.2%, dwarfing the 235.7% gain of the first two years of these administrations.

The presidential election every four years has a profound impact on the economy and the stock market. Wars, recessions and bear markets tend to start or occur in the first half of the term; prosperous times and bull markets, in the latter half.

We are witnessing the greatest bull market ever, which is temporarily putting the presidential election/stock market cycle on hold.

STOCK MARKET ACTION SINCE 1832
Annual % change in Dow Jones industrial average

4-Year Cycle Beginning	Election Year	President Elected	Post-Election Year	Midterm Year	Pre-Election Year
1832	4.8%	Jackson (D)	— 0.9%	13.0%	3.1%
1836	—11.7	Van Buren (D)	—11.5	1.6	—12.3
1840*	5.5	W.H. Harrison (W)**	—13.3	—18.1	45.0
1844*	15.5	Polk (D)	8.1	—14.5	1.2
1848*	— 3.6	Taylor (W)**	0.0	18.7	— 3.2
1852*	19.6	Pierce (D)	—12.7	—30.2	1.5
1856	4.4	Buchanan (D)	—31.0	14.3	—10.7
1860*	14.0	Lincoln (R)	— 1.8	55.4	38.0
1864	6.4	Lincoln (R)**	— 8.5	3.6	1.6
1868	10.8	Grant (R)	1.7	5.6	7.3
1872	6.8	Grant (R)	—12.7	2.8	— 4.1
1876	—17.9	Hayes (R)	— 9.4	6.1	43.0
1880	18.7	Garfield (R)**	3.0	— 2.9	— 8.5
1884*	—18.8	Cleveland (D)	20.1	12.4	— 8.4
1888*	4.8	B. Harrison (R)	5.5	—14.1	17.6
1892*	— 6.6	Cleveland (D)	—24.6	— 0.6	2.3
1896*	— 1.7	McKinley (R)	21.3	22.5	9.2
1900	7.0	McKinley (R)**	— 8.7	— 0.4	—23.6
1904	41.7	T. Roosevelt (R)	38.2	— 1.9	—37.7
1908	46.6	Taft (R)	15.0	—18.0	0.5
1912*	7.6	Wilson (D)	—10.3	— 5.1	81.7
1916	— 4.2	Wilson (D)	—21.7	10.5	30.5
1920*	—32.9	Harding (R)**	12.7	21.7	— 3.3
1924	26.2	Coolidge (R)	30.0	0.3	28.8
1928	48.2	Hoover (R)	—17.2	—33.8	—52.7
1932*	—23.1	F. Roosevelt (D)	66.7	4.1	38.5
1936	24.8	F. Roosevelt (D)	—32.8	28.1	— 2.9
1940	—12.7	F. Roosevelt (D)	—15.4	7.6	13.8
1944	12.1	F. Roosevelt (D)**	26.6	— 8.1	2.2
1948	— 2.1	Truman (D)	12.9	17.6	14.4
1952*	8.4	Eisenhower (R)	— 3.8	44.0	20.8
1956	2.3	Eisenhower (R)	—12.8	34.0	16.4
1960*	— 9.3	Kennedy (D)**	18.7	—10.8	17.0
1964	14.6	Johnson (D)	10.9	—18.9	15.2
1968*	4.3	Nixon (R)	—15.2	4.8	6.1
1972	14.6	Nixon (R)***	—16.6	—27.6	38.3
1976*	17.9	Carter (D)	—17.3	— 3.1	4.2
1980*	14.9	Reagan (R)	— 9.2	19.6	20.3
1984	— 3.7	Reagan (R)	27.7	22.6	2.3
1988	11.8	Bush (R)	27.0	— 4.3	20.3
1992*	4.2	Clinton (D)	13.7	2.1	33.5
1996	26.0	Clinton (D)	22.6		
% Gain	**296.2%**		**75.1%**	**160.6%**	**407.0%**
# Up	29		19	24	30
# Down	13		22	17	11

*Party in power ousted   **Death in office   ***Resigned   D—Democrat, W—Whig, R—Republican

Based on annual close. Prior to 1886 based on Cowles and other indices.

MONTHLY PERCENT CHANGES IN STANDARD & POOR'S 500

	JAN	FEB	MAR	APR	MAY	JUN
1950	1.7%	1.0%	0.4%	4.5%	3.9%	— 5.8%
1951	6.1	0.6	— 1.8	4.8	— 4.1	— 2.6
1952	1.6	— 3.6	4.8	— 4.3	2.3	4.6
1953	— 0.7	— 1.8	— 2.4	— 2.6	— 0.3	— 1.6
1954	5.1	0.3	3.0	4.9	3.3	0.1
1955	1.8	0.4	— 0.5	3.8	— 0.1	8.2
1956	— 3.6	3.5	6.9	— 0.2	— 6.6	3.9
1957	— 4.2	— 3.3	2.0	3.7	3.7	— 0.1
1958	4.3	— 2.1	3.1	3.2	1.5	2.6
1959	0.4	0.0	0.1	3.9	1.9	— 0.4
1960	— 7.1	0.9	— 1.4	— 1.8	2.7	2.0
1961	6.3	2.7	2.6	0.4	1.9	— 2.9
1962	— 3.8	1.6	— 0.6	— 6.2	— 8.6	— 8.2
1963	4.9	— 2.9	3.5	4.9	1.4	— 2.0
1964	2.7	1.0	1.5	0.6	1.1	1.6
1965	3.3	— 0.1	— 1.5	3.4	— 0.8	— 4.9
1966	0.5	— 1.8	— 2.2	2.1	— 5.4	— 1.6
1967	7.8	0.2	3.9	4.2	— 5.2	1.8
1968	— 4.4	— 3.1	0.9	8.2	1.1	0.9
1969	— 0.8	— 4.7	3.4	2.1	— 0.2	— 5.6
1970	— 7.6	5.3	0.1	— 9.0	— 6.1	— 5.0
1971	4.0	0.9	3.7	3.6	— 4.2	0.1
1972	1.8	2.5	0.6	0.4	1.7	— 2.2
1973	— 1.7	— 3.7	— 0.1	— 4.1	— 1.9	— 0.7
1974	— 1.0	— 0.4	— 2.3	— 3.9	— 3.4	— 1.5
1975	12.3	6.0	2.2	4.7	4.4	4.4
1976	11.8	— 1.1	3.1	— 1.1	— 1.4	4.1
1977	— 5.1	— 2.2	— 1.4	0.02	— 2.4	4.5
1978	— 6.2	— 2.5	2.5	8.5	0.5	— 1.8
1979	4.0	— 3.7	5.5	0.2	— 2.6	3.9
1980	5.8	— 0.4	—10.2	4.1	4.7	2.7
1981	— 4.6	1.3	3.6	— 2.3	— 0.2	— 1.0
1982	— 1.8	— 6.1	— 1.0	4.0	— 3.9	— 2.0
1983	3.3	1.9	3.3	7.5	— 1.2	3.5
1984	— 0.9	— 3.9	1.3	0.5	— 5.9	1.7
1985	7.4	0.9	— 0.3	— 0.5	5.4	1.2
1986	0.2	7.1	5.3	— 1.4	5.0	1.4
1987	13.2	3.7	2.6	— 1.1	0.6	4.8
1988	4.0	4.2	— 3.3	0.9	0.3	4.3
1989	7.1	— 2.9	2.1	5.0	3.5	— 0.8
1990	— 6.9	0.9	2.4	— 2.7	9.2	— 0.9
1991	4.2	6.7	2.2	0.03	3.9	— 4.8
1992	— 2.0	1.0	— 2.2	2.8	0.1	— 1.7
1993	0.7	1.0	1.9	— 2.5	2.3	0.1
1994	3.3	— 3.0	— 4.6	1.2	1.2	— 2.7
1995	2.4	3.6	2.7	2.8	3.6	2.1
1996	3.3	0.7	0.8	1.3	2.3	0.2
1997	6.1	0.6	— 4.3	5.8	5.9	4.3
1998	1.0	7.0	5.0	0.9	— 1.9	3.9

MONTHLY PERCENT CHANGES IN STANDARD & POOR'S 500

JUL	AUG	SEP	OCT	NOV	DEC		Year's Change
0.8%	3.3%	5.6%	0.4%	— 0.1%	4.6%	1950	21.8%
6.9	3.9	— 0.1	— 1.4	— 0.3	3.9	1951	16.5
1.8	— 1.5	— 2.0	— 0.1	4.6	3.5	1952	11.8
2.5	— 5.8	0.1	5.1	0.9	0.2	1953	— 6.6
5.7	— 3.4	8.3	— 1.9	8.1	5.1	1954	45.0
6.1	— 0.8	1.1	— 3.0	7.5	— 0.1	1955	26.4
5.2	— 3.8	— 4.5	0.5	— 1.1	3.5	1956	2.6
1.1	— 5.6	— 6.2	— 3.2	0.5	— 3.1	1957	—14.3
4.3	1.2	4.8	2.5	2.2	5.2	1958	38.1
3.5	— 1.5	— 4.6	1.1	1.3	2.8	1959	8.5
— 2.5	2.6	— 6.0	— 0.2	4.0	4.6	1960	— 3.0
3.3	2.0	— 2.0	2.8	3.9	0.3	1961	23.1
6.4	1.5	— 4.8	0.4	10.2	1.3	1962	—11.8
— 0.3	4.9	— 1.1	3.2	— 1.1	2.4	1963	18.9
1.8	— 1.6	2.9	0.8	— 0.5	0.4	1964	13.0
1.3	2.3	3.2	2.7	— 0.9	0.9	1965	9.1
— 1.3	— 7.8	— 0.7	4.8	0.3	— 0.1	1966	—13.1
4.5	— 1.2	3.3	— 2.9	0.1	2.6	1967	20.1
— 1.8	1.1	3.9	0.7	4.8	— 4.2	1968	7.7
— 6.0	4.0	— 2.5	4.4	— 3.5	— 1.9	1969	—11.4
7.3	4.4	3.3	— 1.1	4.7	5.7	1970	0.1
— 4.1	3.6	— 0.7	— 4.2	— 0.3	8.6	1971	10.8
0.2	3.4	— 0.5	0.9	4.6	1.2	1972	15.6
3.8	— 3.7	4.0	— 0.1	—11.4	1.7	1973	—17.4
— 7.8	— 9.0	—11.9	16.3	— 5.3	— 2.0	1974	—29.7
— 6.8	— 2.1	— 3.5	6.2	2.5	— 1.2	1975	31.5
— 0.8	— 0.5	2.3	— 2.2	— 0.8	5.2	1976	19.1
— 1.6	— 2.1	— 0.2	— 4.3	2.7	0.3	1977	—11.5
5.4	2.6	— 0.7	— 9.2	1.7	1.5	1978	1.1
0.9	5.3	0.0	— 6.9	4.3	1.7	1979	12.3
6.5	0.6	2.5	1.6	10.2	— 3.4	1980	25.8
— 0.2	— 6.2	— 5.4	4.9	3.7	— 3.0	1981	— 9.7
— 2.3	11.6	0.8	11.0	3.6	1.5	1982	14.8
— 3.3	1.1	1.0	— 1.5	1.7	— 0.9	1983	17.3
— 1.6	10.6	— 0.3	0.0	— 1.5	2.2	1984	1.4
— 0.5	— 1.2	— 3.5	4.3	6.5	4.5	1985	26.3
— 5.9	7.1	— 8.5	5.5	2.1	— 2.8	1986	14.6
4.8	3.5	— 2.4	—21.8	— 8.5	7.3	1987	2.0
— 0.5	— 3.9	4.0	2.6	— 1.9	1.5	1988	12.4
8.8	1.6	— 0.7	— 2.5	1.7	2.1	1989	27.3
— 0.5	— 9.4	— 5.1	— 0.7	6.0	2.5	1990	— 6.6
4.5	2.0	— 1.9	1.2	— 4.4	11.2	1991	26.3
3.9	— 2.4	0.9	0.2	3.0	1.0	1992	4.5
— 0.5	3.4	— 1.0	1.9	— 1.3	1.0	1993	7.1
3.1	3.8	— 2.7	2.1	— 4.0	1.2	1994	— 1.5
3.2	— 0.03	4.0	— 0.5	4.1	1.7	1995	34.1
— 4.6	1.9	5.4	2.6	7.3	— 2.2	1996	20.3
7.8	— 5.7	5.3	— 3.4	4.5	1.6	1997	31.0
						1998	

MONTHLY CLOSING PRICES
IN STANDARD & POOR'S 500

	JAN	FEB	MAR	APR	MAY	JUN
1950	17.05	17.22	17.29	18.07	18.78	17.69
1951	21.66	21.80	21.40	22.43	21.52	20.96
1952	24.14	23.26	24.37	23.32	23.86	24.96
1953	26.38	25.90	25.29	24.62	24.54	24.14
1954	26.08	26.15	26.94	28.26	29.19	29.21
1955	36.63	36.76	36.58	37.96	37.91	41.03
1956	43.82	45.34	48.48	48.38	45.20	46.97
1957	44.72	43.26	44.11	45.74	47.43	47.37
1958	41.70	40.84	42.10	43.44	44.09	45.24
1959	55.42	55.41	55.44	57.59	58.68	58.47
1960	55.61	56.12	55.34	54.37	55.83	56.92
1961	61.78	63.44	65.06	65.31	66.56	64.64
1962	68.84	69.96	69.55	65.24	59.63	54.75
1963	66.20	64.29	66.57	69.80	70.80	69.37
1964	77.04	77.80	78.98	79.46	80.37	81.69
1965	87.56	87.43	86.16	89.11	88.42	84.12
1966	92.88	91.22	89.23	91.06	86.13	84.74
1967	86.61	86.78	90.20	94.01	89.08	90.64
1968	92.24	89.36	90.20	97.59	98.68	99.58
1969	103.01	98.13	101.51	103.69	103.46	97.71
1970	85.02	89.50	89.63	81.52	76.55	72.72
1971	95.88	96.75	100.31	103.95	99.63	99.70
1972	103.94	106.57	107.20	107.67	109.53	107.14
1973	116.03	111.68	111.52	106.97	104.95	104.26
1974	96.57	96.22	93.98	90.31	87.28	86.00
1975	76.98	81.59	83.36	87.30	91.15	95.19
1976	100.86	99.71	102.77	101.64	100.18	104.28
1977	102.03	99.82	98.42	98.44	96.12	100.48
1978	89.25	87.04	89.21	96.83	97.29	95.53
1979	99.93	96.28	101.59	101.76	99.08	102.91
1980	114.16	113.66	102.09	106.29	111.24	114.24
1981	129.55	131.27	136.00	132.87	132.59	131.21
1982	120.40	113.11	111.96	116.44	111.88	109.61
1983	145.30	148.06	152.96	164.42	162.39	168.11
1984	163.41	157.06	159.18	160.05	150.55	153.18
1985	179.63	181.18	180.66	179.83	189.55	191.85
1986	211.78	226.92	238.90	235.52	247.35	250.84
1987	274.08	284.20	291.70	288.36	290.10	304.00
1988	257.07	267.82	258.89	261.33	262.16	273.50
1989	297.47	288.86	294.87	309.64	320.52	317.98
1990	329.08	331.89	339.94	330.80	361.23	358.02
1991	343.93	367.07	375.22	375.35	389.83	371.16
1992	408.79	412.70	403.69	414.95	415.35	408.14
1993	438.78	443.38	451.67	440.19	450.19	450.53
1994	481.61	467.14	445.77	450.91	456.50	444.27
1995	470.42	487.39	500.71	514.71	533.40	544.75
1996	636.02	640.43	645.50	654.17	669.12	670.63
1997	786.16	790.82	757.12	801.34	848.28	885.15
1998	980.28	1049.34	1101.76	1111.75	1090.82	1133.84

MONTHLY CLOSING PRICES
IN STANDARD & POOR'S 500

JUL	AUG	SEP	OCT	NOV	DEC	
17.84	18.42	19.45	19.53	19.51	20.41	**1950**
22.40	23.28	23.26	22.94	22.88	23.77	**1951**
25.40	25.03	24.54	24.52	25.66	26.57	**1952**
24.75	23.32	23.35	24.54	24.76	24.81	**1953**
30.88	29.83	32.31	31.68	34.24	35.98	**1954**
43.52	43.18	43.67	42.34	45.51	45.48	**1955**
49.39	47.51	45.35	45.58	45.08	46.67	**1956**
47.91	45.22	42.42	41.06	41.27	39.99	**1957**
47.19	47.75	50.06	51.33	52.48	55.21	**1958**
60.51	59.60	56.88	57.52	58.28	59.89	**1959**
55.51	56.96	53.52	53.39	55.54	58.11	**1960**
66.76	68.07	66.73	68.62	71.32	71.55	**1961**
58.23	59.12	56.27	56.52	62.26	63.10	**1962**
69.13	72.50	71.70	74.01	73.23	75.02	**1963**
83.18	81.83	84.18	84.86	84.42	84.75	**1964**
85.25	87.17	89.96	92.42	91.61	92.43	**1965**
83.60	77.10	76.56	80.20	80.45	80.33	**1966**
94.75	93.64	96.71	93.90	94.00	96.47	**1967**
97.74	98.86	102.67	103.41	108.37	103.86	**1968**
91.83	95.51	93.12	97.24	93.81	92.06	**1969**
78.05	81.52	84.21	83.25	87.20	92.15	**1970**
95.58	99.03	98.34	94.23	93.99	102.09	**1971**
107.39	111.09	110.55	111.58	116.67	118.05	**1972**
108.22	104.25	108.43	108.29	95.96	97.55	**1973**
79.31	72.15	63.54	73.90	69.97	68.56	**1974**
88.75	86.88	83.87	89.04	91.24	90.19	**1975**
103.44	102.91	105.24	102.90	102.10	107.46	**1976**
98.85	96.77	96.53	92.34	94.83	95.10	**1977**
100.68	103.29	102.54	93.15	94.70	96.11	**1978**
103.81	109.32	109.32	101.82	106.16	107.94	**1979**
121.67	122.38	125.46	127.47	140.52	135.76	**1980**
130.92	122.79	116.18	121.89	126.35	122.55	**1981**
107.09	119.51	120.42	133.71	138.54	140.64	**1982**
162.56	164.40	166.07	163.55	166.40	164.93	**1983**
150.66	166.68	166.10	166.09	163.58	167.24	**1984**
190.92	188.63	182.08	189.82	202.17	211.28	**1985**
236.12	252.93	231.32	243.98	249.22	242.17	**1986**
318.66	329.80	321.83	251.79	230.30	247.08	**1987**
272.01	261.52	271.91	278.97	273.70	277.72	**1988**
346.08	351.45	349.15	340.36	345.99	353.40	**1989**
356.15	322.56	306.05	304.00	322.22	330.22	**1990**
387.81	395.43	387.86	392.46	375.22	417.09	**1991**
424.21	414.03	417.80	418.68	431.35	435.71	**1992**
448.13	463.56	458.93	467.83	461.79	466.45	**1993**
458.26	475.49	462.69	472.35	453.69	459.27	**1994**
562.06	561.88	584.41	581.50	605.37	615.93	**1995**
639.95	651.99	687.33	705.27	757.02	740.74	**1996**
954.31	899.47	947.28	914.62	955.40	970.43	**1997**
						1998

DOW JONES INDUSTRIALS MONTHLY PERCENT CHANGES

	JAN	FEB	MAR	APR	MAY	JUN
1950	0.8%	0.8%	1.3%	4.0%	4.2%	— 6.4%
1951	5.7	1.3	— 1.6	4.5	— 3.7	— 2.8
1952	0.5	— 3.9	3.6	— 4.4	2.1	4.3
1953	— 0.7	— 1.9	— 1.5	— 1.8	— 0.9	— 1.5
1954	4.1	0.7	3.0	5.2	2.6	1.8
1955	1.1	0.7	— 0.5	3.9	— 0.2	6.2
1956	— 3.6	2.7	5.8	0.8	— 7.4	3.1
1957	— 4.1	— 3.0	2.2	4.1	2.1	— 0.3
1958	3.3	— 2.2	1.6	2.0	1.5	3.3
1959	1.8	1.6	— 0.3	3.7	3.2	0.0
1960	— 8.4	1.2	— 2.1	— 2.4	4.0	2.4
1961	5.2	2.1	2.2	0.3	2.7	— 1.8
1962	— 4.3	1.1	— 0.2	— 5.9	— 7.8	— 8.5
1963	4.7	— 2.9	3.0	5.2	1.3	— 2.8
1964	2.9	1.9	1.6	— 0.3	1.2	1.3
1965	3.3	0.1	— 1.6	3.7	— 0.5	— 5.4
1966	1.5	— 3.2	— 2.8	1.0	— 5.3	— 1.6
1967	8.2	— 1.2	3.2	3.6	— 5.0	0.9
1968	— 5.5	— 1.7	0.0	8.5	— 1.4	— 0.1
1969	0.2	— 4.3	3.3	1.6	— 1.3	— 6.9
1970	— 7.0	4.5	1.0	— 6.3	— 4.8	— 2.4
1971	3.5	1.2	2.9	4.1	— 3.6	— 1.8
1972	1.3	2.9	1.4	1.4	0.7	— 3.3
1973	— 2.1	— 4.4	— 0.4	— 3.1	— 2.2	— 1.1
1974	0.6	0.6	— 1.6	— 1.2	— 4.1	0.0
1975	14.2	5.0	3.9	6.9	1.3	5.6
1976	14.4	— 0.3	2.8	— 0.3	— 2.2	2.8
1977	— 5.0	— 1.9	— 1.8	0.8	— 3.0	2.0
1978	— 7.4	— 3.6	2.1	10.6	0.4	— 2.6
1979	4.2	— 3.6	6.6	— 0.8	— 3.8	2.4
1980	4.4	— 1.5	— 9.0	4.0	4.1	2.0
1981	— 1.7	2.9	3.0	— 0.6	— 0.6	— 1.5
1982	— 0.4	— 5.4	— 0.2	3.1	— 3.4	— 0.9
1983	2.8	3.4	1.6	8.5	— 2.1	1.8
1984	— 3.0	— 5.4	0.9	0.5	— 5.6	2.5
1985	6.2	— 0.2	— 1.3	— 0.7	4.6	1.5
1986	1.6	8.8	6.4	— 1.9	5.2	0.9
1987	13.8	3.1	3.6	— 0.8	0.2	5.5
1988	1.0	5.8	— 4.0	2.2	— 0.1	5.4
1989	8.0	— 3.6	1.6	5.5	2.5	— 1.6
1990	— 5.9	1.4	3.0	— 1.9	8.3	0.1
1991	3.9	5.3	1.1	— 0.9	4.8	— 4.0
1992	1.7	1.4	— 1.0	3.8	1.1	— 2.3
1993	0.3	1.8	1.9	— 0.2	2.9	— 0.3
1994	6.0	— 3.7	— 5.1	1.3	2.1	— 3.5
1995	0.2	4.3	3.7	3.9	3.3	2.0
1996	5.4	1.7	1.9	— 0.3	1.3	0.2
1997	5.7	0.9	— 4.3	6.5	4.6	4.7
1998	— 0.02	8.1	3.0	3.0	— 1.8	0.6

DOW JONES INDUSTRIALS MONTHLY PERCENT CHANGES

JUL	AUG	SEP	OCT	NOV	DEC		Year's Change
0.1%	3.6%	4.4%	— 0.6%	1.2%	3.4%	**1950**	17.6%
6.3	4.8	0.3	— 3.2	— 0.4	3.0	**1951**	14.4
1.9	— 1.6	— 1.6	— 0.5	5.4	2.9	**1952**	8.4
2.7	— 5.1	1.1	4.5	2.0	— 0.2	**1953**	— 3.8
4.3	— 3.5	7.3	— 2.3	9.8	4.6	**1954**	44.0
3.2	0.5	— 0.3	— 2.5	6.2	1.1	**1955**	20.8
5.1	— 3.0	— 5.3	1.0	— 1.5	5.6	**1956**	2.3
1.0	— 4.8	— 5.8	— 3.3	2.0	— 3.2	**1957**	—12.8
5.2	1.1	4.6	2.1	2.6	4.7	**1958**	34.0
4.9	— 1.6	— 4.9	2.4	1.9	3.1	**1959**	16.4
— 3.7	1.5	— 7.3	0.0	2.9	3.1	**1960**	— 9.3
3.1	2.1	— 2.6	0.4	2.5	1.3	**1961**	18.7
6.5	1.9	— 5.0	1.9	10.1	0.4	**1962**	—10.8
— 1.6	4.9	0.5	3.1	— 0.6	1.7	**1963**	17.0
1.2	— 0.3	4.4	— 0.3	0.3	— 0.1	**1964**	14.6
1.6	1.3	4.2	3.2	— 1.5	2.4	**1965**	10.9
— 2.6	— 7.0	— 1.8	4.2	— 1.9	— 0.7	**1966**	—18.9
5.1	— 0.3	2.8	— 5.1	— 0.4	3.3	**1967**	15.2
— 1.6	1.5	4.4	1.8	3.4	— 4.2	**1968**	4.3
— 6.6	2.6	— 2.8	5.3	— 5.1	— 1.5	**1969**	—15.2
7.4	4.1	— 0.5	— 0.7	5.1	5.6	**1970**	4.8
— 3.7	4.6	— 1.2	— 5.4	— 0.9	7.1	**1971**	6.1
— 0.5	4.2	— 1.1	0.2	6.6	0.2	**1972**	14.6
3.9	— 4.2	6.7	1.0	—14.0	3.5	**1973**	—16.6
— 5.6	—10.4	—10.4	9.5	— 7.0	— 0.4	**1974**	—27.6
— 5.4	0.5	— 5.0	5.3	2.9	— 1.0	**1975**	38.3
— 1.8	— 1.1	1.7	— 2.6	— 1.8	6.1	**1976**	17.9
— 2.9	— 3.2	— 1.7	— 3.4	1.4	0.2	**1977**	—17.3
5.3	1.7	— 1.3	— 8.5	0.8	0.7	**1978**	— 3.1
0.5	4.9	— 1.0	— 7.2	0.8	2.0	**1979**	4.2
7.8	— 0.3	0.0	— 0.9	7.4	— 3.0	**1980**	14.9
— 2.5	— 7.4	— 3.6	0.3	4.3	— 1.6	**1981**	— 9.2
— 0.4	11.5	— 0.6	10.7	4.8	0.7	**1982**	19.6
— 1.9	1.4	1.4	— 0.6	4.1	— 1.4	**1983**	20.3
— 1.5	9.8	— 1.4	0.1	— 1.5	1.9	**1984**	— 3.7
0.9	— 1.0	— 0.4	3.4	7.1	5.1	**1985**	27.7
— 6.2	6.9	— 6.9	6.2	1.9	— 1.0	**1986**	22.6
6.3	3.5	— 2.5	—23.2	— 8.0	5.7	**1987**	2.3
— 0.6	— 4.6	4.0	1.7	— 1.6	2.6	**1988**	11.8
9.0	2.9	— 1.6	— 1.8	2.3	1.7	**1989**	27.0
0.9	—10.0	— 6.2	— 0.4	4.8	2.9	**1990**	— 4.3
4.1	0.6	— 0.9	1.7	— 5.7	9.5	**1991**	20.3
2.3	— 4.0	0.4	— 1.4	2.4	— 0.1	**1992**	4.2
0.7	3.2	— 2.6	3.5	0.1	1.9	**1993**	13.7
3.8	4.0	— 1.8	1.7	— 4.3	2.5	**1994**	2.1
3.3	— 2.1	3.9	— 0.7	6.7	0.8	**1995**	33.5
— 2.2	1.6	4.7	2.5	8.2	— 1.1	**1996**	26.0
7.2	— 7.3	4.2	— 6.3	5.1	1.1	**1997**	22.6
						1998	

145

DOW JONES INDUSTRIALS POINT CHANGES

	JAN	FEB	MAR	APR	MAY	JUN
1950	1.66	1.65	2.61	8.28	9.09	— 14.31
1951	13.42	3.22	— 4.11	11.19	— 9.48	— 7.01
1952	1.46	— 10.61	9.38	— 11.83	5.31	11.32
1953	— 2.13	— 5.50	— 4.40	— 5.12	— 2.47	— 4.02
1954	11.49	2.15	8.97	15.82	8.16	6.04
1955	4.44	3.04	— 2.17	15.95	— 0.79	26.52
1956	— 17.66	12.91	28.14	4.33	— 38.07	14.73
1957	— 20.31	— 14.54	10.19	19.55	10.57	— 1.64
1958	14.33	— 10.10	6.84	9.10	6.84	15.48
1959	10.31	9.54	— 1.79	22.04	20.04	— 0.19
1960	— 56.74	7.50	— 13.53	— 14.89	23.80	15.12
1961	32.31	13.88	14.55	2.08	18.01	— 12.76
1962	— 31.14	8.05	— 1.10	— 41.62	— 51.97	— 52.08
1963	30.75	— 19.91	19.58	35.18	9.26	— 20.08
1964	22.39	14.80	13.15	— 2.52	9.79	10.94
1965	28.73	0.62	— 14.43	33.26	— 4.27	— 50.01
1966	14.25	— 31.62	— 27.12	8.91	— 49.61	— 13.97
1967	64.20	— 10.52	26.61	31.07	— 44.49	7.70
1968	— 49.64	— 14.97	0.17	71.55	— 13.22	— 1.20
1969	2.30	— 40.84	30.27	14.70	— 12.62	— 64.37
1970	— 56.30	33.53	7.98	— 49.50	— 35.63	— 16.91
1971	29.58	10.33	25.54	37.38	— 33.94	— 16.67
1972	11.97	25.96	12.57	13.47	6.55	— 31.69
1973	— 21.00	— 43.95	— 4.06	— 29.58	— 20.02	— 9.70
1974	4.69	4.98	— 13.85	— 9.93	— 34.58	0.24
1975	87.45	35.36	29.10	53.19	10.95	46.70
1976	122.87	— 2.67	26.84	— 2.60	— 21.62	27.55
1977	— 50.28	— 17.95	— 17.29	7.77	— 28.24	17.64
1978	— 61.25	— 27.80	15.24	79.96	3.29	— 21.66
1979	34.21	— 30.40	53.36	— 7.28	— 32.57	19.65
1980	37.11	— 12.71	— 77.39	31.31	33.79	17.07
1981	— 16.72	27.31	29.29	— 6.12	— 6.00	— 14.87
1982	— 3.90	— 46.71	— 1.62	25.59	— 28.82	— 7.61
1983	29.16	36.92	17.41	96.17	— 26.22	21.98
1984	— 38.06	— 65.95	10.26	5.86	— 65.90	27.55
1985	75.20	— 2.76	— 17.23	— 8.72	57.35	20.05
1986	24.32	138.07	109.55	— 34.63	92.73	16.01
1987	262.09	65.95	80.70	— 18.33	5.21	126.96
1988	19.39	113.40	— 83.56	44.27	— 1.21	110.59
1989	173.75	— 83.93	35.23	125.18	61.35	— 40.09
1990	—162.66	36.71	79.96	— 50.45	219.90	4.03
1991	102.73	145.79	31.68	— 25.99	139.63	— 120.75
1992	54.56	44.28	— 32.20	123.65	37.76	— 78.36
1993	8.92	60.78	64.30	— 7.56	99.88	— 11.35
1994	224.27	—146.34	—196.06	45.73	76.68	— 133.41
1995	9.42	167.19	146.64	163.58	143.87	90.96
1996	278.18	90.32	101.52	— 18.06	74.10	11.45
1997	364.82	64.65	—294.26	425.51	322.05	341.75
1998	— 1.75	639.22	254.09	263.56	—163.42*	52.07*
TOTALS	**1617.19**	**1178.33**	**495.55**	**1500.46**	**944.22**	**263.32**
UP	34	29	31	31	26	24
DOWN	15	20	18	18	22	24

*Not included in totals

146

DOW JONES INDUSTRIALS POINT CHANGES

JUL	AUG	SEP	OCT	NOV	DEC	Year's Close	
0.29	7.47	9.49	— 1.35	2.59	7.81	235.41	**1950**
15.22	12.39	0.91	— 8.81	— 1.08	7.96	269.23	**1951**
5.30	— 4.52	— 4.43	— 1.38	14.43	8.24	291.90	**1952**
7.12	— 14.16	2.82	11.77	5.56	— 0.47	280.90	**1953**
14.39	— 12.12	24.66	— 8.32	34.63	17.62	404.39	**1954**
14.47	2.33	— 1.56	— 11.75	28.39	5.14	488.40	**1955**
25.03	— 15.77	— 26.79	4.60	— 7.07	26.69	499.47	**1956**
5.23	— 24.17	— 28.05	— 15.26	8.83	— 14.18	435.69	**1957**
24.81	5.64	23.46	11.13	14.24	26.19	583.65	**1958**
31.28	— 10.47	— 32.73	14.92	12.58	20.18	679.36	**1959**
— 23.89	9.26	— 45.85	0.22	16.86	18.67	615.89	**1960**
21.41	14.57	— 18.73	2.71	17.68	9.54	731.14	**1961**
36.65	11.25	— 30.20	10.79	59.53	2.80	652.10	**1962**
— 11.45	33.89	3.47	22.44	— 4.71	12.43	762.95	**1963**
9.60	— 2.62	36.89	— 2.29	2.35	— 1.30	874.13	**1964**
13.71	11.36	37.48	30.24	— 14.11	22.55	969.26	**1965**
— 22.72	— 58.97	— 14.19	32.85	— 15.48	— 5.90	785.69	**1966**
43.98	— 2.95	25.37	— 46.92	— 3.93	29.30	905.11	**1967**
— 14.80	13.01	39.78	16.60	32.69	— 41.33	943.75	**1968**
— 57.72	21.25	— 23.63	42.90	— 43.69	— 11.94	800.36	**1969**
50.59	30.46	— 3.90	— 5.07	38.48	44.83	838.92	**1970**
— 32.71	39.64	— 10.88	— 48.19	— 7.66	58.86	890.20	**1971**
— 4.29	38.99	— 10.46	2.25	62.69	1.81	1020.02	**1972**
34.69	— 38.83	59.53	9.48	—134.33	28.61	850.86	**1973**
— 44.98	— 78.85	— 70.71	57.65	— 46.86	— 2.42	616.24	**1974**
— 47.48	3.83	— 41.46	42.16	24.63	— 8.26	852.41	**1975**
— 18.14	— 10.90	16.45	— 25.26	— 17.71	57.43	1004.65	**1976**
— 26.23	— 28.58	— 14.38	— 28.76	11.35	1.47	831.17	**1977**
43.32	14.55	— 11.00	— 73.37	6.58	5.98	805.01	**1978**
4.44	41.21	— 9.05	— 62.88	6.65	16.39	838.74	**1979**
67.40	— 2.73	— 0.17	— 7.93	68.85	— 29.35	963.99	**1980**
— 24.54	— 70.87	— 31.49	2.57	36.43	— 13.98	875.00	**1981**
— 3.33	92.71	— 5.06	95.47	47.56	7.26	1046.54	**1982**
— 22.74	16.94	16.97	— 7.93	50.82	— 17.38	1258.64	**1983**
— 17.12	109.10	— 17.67	0.67	— 18.44	22.63	1211.57	**1984**
11.99	— 13.44	— 5.38	45.68	97.82	74.54	1546.67	**1985**
—117.41	123.03	—130.76	110.23	36.42	— 18.28	1895.95	**1986**
153.54	90.88	— 66.67	—602.75	—159.98	105.28	1938.83	**1987**
— 12.98	— 97.08	81.26	35.74	— 34.14	54.06	2168.57	**1988**
220.60	76.61	— 44.45	— 47.74	61.19	46.93	2753.20	**1989**
24.51	—290.84	—161.88	— 10.15	117.32	74.01	2633.66	**1990**
118.07	18.78	— 26.83	52.33	—174.42	274.15	3168.83	**1991**
75.26	—136.43	14.31	— 45.38	78.88	— 4.05	3301.11	**1992**
23.39	111.78	— 96.13	125.47	3.36	70.14	3754.09	**1993**
139.54	148.92	— 70.23	64.93	—168.89	95.21	3834.44	**1994**
152.37	— 97.91	178.52	— 33.60	319.01	42.63	5117.12	**1995**
—125.72	87.30	265.96	147.21	492.32	— 73.43	6448.27	**1996**
549.82	—600.19	322.84	—502.46	380.33	85.12	7908.25	**1997**
							1998
1309.77	**— 425.25**	**105.45**	**— 604.54**	**1338.55**	**1140.19**		
30	27	18	26	32	34		
18	21	30	22	16	14		

DOW JONES INDUSTRIALS MONTHLY CLOSING PRICES

	JAN	FEB	MAR	APR	MAY	JUN
1950	201.79	203.44	206.05	214.33	223.42	209.11
1951	248.83	252.05	247.94	259.13	249.65	242.64
1952	270.69	260.08	269.46	257.63	262.94	274.26
1953	289.77	284.27	279.87	274.75	272.28	268.26
1954	292.39	294.54	303.51	319.33	327.49	333.53
1955	408.83	411.87	409.70	425.65	424.86	451.38
1956	470.74	483.65	511.79	516.12	478.05	492.78
1957	479.16	464.62	474.81	494.36	504.93	503.29
1958	450.02	439.92	446.76	455.86	462.70	478.18
1959	593.96	603.50	601.71	623.75	643.79	643.60
1960	622.62	630.12	616.59	601.70	625.50	640.62
1961	648.20	662.08	676.63	678.71	696.72	683.96
1962	700.00	708.05	706.95	665.33	613.36	561.28
1963	682.85	662.94	682.52	717.70	726.96	706.88
1964	785.34	800.14	813.29	810.77	820.56	831.50
1965	902.86	903.48	889.05	922.31	918.04	868.03
1966	983.51	951.89	924.77	933.68	884.07	870.10
1967	849.89	839.37	865.98	897.05	852.56	860.26
1968	855.47	840.50	840.67	912.22	899.00	897.80
1969	946.05	905.21	935.48	950.18	937.56	873.19
1970	744.06	777.59	785.57	736.07	700.44	683.53
1971	868.50	878.83	904.37	941.75	907.81	891.14
1972	902.17	928.13	940.70	954.17	960.72	929.03
1973	999.02	955.07	951.01	921.43	901.41	891.71
1974	855.55	860.53	846.68	836.75	802.17	802.41
1975	703.69	739.05	768.15	821.34	832.29	878.99
1976	975.28	972.61	999.45	996.85	975.23	1002.78
1977	954.37	936.42	919.13	926.90	898.66	916.30
1978	769.92	742.12	757.36	837.32	840.61	818.95
1979	839.22	808.82	862.18	854.90	822.33	841.98
1980	875.85	863.14	785.75	817.06	850.85	867.92
1981	947.27	974.58	1003.87	997.75	991.75	976.88
1982	871.10	824.39	822.77	848.36	819.54	811.93
1983	1075.70	1112.62	1130.03	1226.20	1199.98	1221.96
1984	1220.58	1154.63	1164.89	1170.75	1104.85	1132.40
1985	1286.77	1284.01	1266.78	1258.06	1315.41	1335.46
1986	1570.99	1709.06	1818.61	1783.98	1876.71	1892.72
1987	2158.04	2223.99	2304.69	2286.36	2291.57	2418.53
1988	1958.22	2071.62	1988.06	2032.33	2031.12	2141.71
1989	2342.32	2258.39	2293.62	2418.80	2480.15	2440.06
1990	2590.54	2627.25	2707.21	2656.76	2876.66	2880.69
1991	2736.39	2882.18	2913.86	2887.87	3027.50	2906.75
1992	3223.39	3267.67	3235.47	3359.12	3396.88	3318.52
1993	3310.03	3370.81	3435.11	3427.55	3527.43	3516.08
1994	3978.36	3832.02	3635.96	3681.69	3758.37	3624.96
1995	3843.86	4011.05	4157.69	4321.27	4465.14	4556.10
1996	5395.30	5485.62	5587.14	5569.08	5643.18	5654.63
1997	6813.09	6877.74	6583.48	7008.99	7331.04	7672.79
1998	7906.50	8545.72	8799.81	9063.37	8899.95	8952.02

DOW JONES INDUSTRIALS MONTHLY CLOSING PRICES

JUL	AUG	SEP	OCT	NOV	DEC	
209.40	216.87	226.36	225.01	227.60	235.41	**1950**
257.86	270.25	271.16	262.35	261.27	269.23	**1951**
279.56	275.04	270.61	269.23	283.66	291.90	**1952**
275.38	261.22	264.04	275.81	281.37	280.90	**1953**
347.92	335.80	360.46	352.14	386.77	404.39	**1954**
465.85	468.18	466.62	454.87	483.26	488.40	**1955**
517.81	502.04	475.25	479.85	472.78	499.47	**1956**
508.52	484.35	456.30	441.04	449.87	435.69	**1957**
502.99	508.63	532.09	543.22	557.46	583.65	**1958**
674.88	664.41	631.68	646.60	659.18	679.36	**1959**
616.73	625.99	580.14	580.36	597.22	615.89	**1960**
705.37	719.94	701.21	703.92	721.60	731.14	**1961**
597.93	609.18	578.98	589.77	649.30	652.10	**1962**
695.43	729.32	732.79	755.23	750.52	762.95	**1963**
841.10	838.48	875.37	873.08	875.43	874.13	**1964**
881.74	893.10	930.58	960.82	946.71	969.26	**1965**
847.38	788.41	774.22	807.07	791.59	785.69	**1966**
904.24	901.29	926.66	879.74	875.81	905.11	**1967**
883.00	896.01	935.79	952.39	985.08	943.75	**1968**
815.47	836.72	813.09	855.99	812.30	800.36	**1969**
734.12	764.58	760.68	755.61	794.09	838.92	**1970**
858.43	898.07	887.19	839.00	831.34	890.20	**1971**
924.74	963.73	953.27	955.52	1018.21	1020.02	**1972**
926.40	887.57	947.10	956.58	822.25	850.86	**1973**
757.43	678.58	607.87	665.52	618.66	616.24	**1974**
831.51	835.34	793.88	836.04	860.67	852.41	**1975**
984.64	973.74	990.19	964.93	947.22	1004.65	**1976**
890.07	861.49	847.11	818.35	829.70	831.17	**1977**
862.27	876.82	865.82	792.45	799.03	805.01	**1978**
846.42	887.63	878.58	815.70	822.35	838.74	**1979**
935.32	932.59	932.42	924.49	993.34	963.99	**1980**
952.34	881.47	849.98	852.55	888.98	875.00	**1981**
808.60	901.31	896.25	991.72	1039.28	1046.54	**1982**
1199.22	1216.16	1233.13	1225.20	1276.02	1258.64	**1983**
1115.28	1224.38	1206.71	1207.38	1188.94	1211.57	**1984**
1347.45	1334.01	1328.63	1374.31	1472.13	1546.67	**1985**
1775.31	1898.34	1767.58	1877.81	1914.23	1895.95	**1986**
2572.07	2662.95	2596.28	1993.53	1833.55	1938.83	**1987**
2128.73	2031.65	2112.91	2148.65	2114.51	2168.57	**1988**
2660.66	2737.27	2692.82	2645.08	2706.27	2753.20	**1989**
2905.20	2614.36	2452.48	2442.33	2559.65	2633.66	**1990**
3024.82	3043.60	3016.77	3069.10	2894.68	3168.83	**1991**
3393.78	3257.35	3271.66	3226.28	3305.16	3301.11	**1992**
3539.47	3651.25	3555.12	3680.59	3683.95	3754.09	**1993**
3764.50	3913.42	3843.19	3908.12	3739.23	3834.44	**1994**
4708.47	4610.56	4789.08	4755.48	5074.49	5117.12	**1995**
5528.91	5616.21	5882.17	6029.38	6521.70	6448.27	**1996**
8222.61	7622.42	7945.26	7442.80	7823.13	7908.25	**1997**
						1998

INDIVIDUAL RETIREMENT ACCOUNTS
MOST AWESOME INVESTMENT INCENTIVE EVER DEVISED

IRA INVESTMENTS OF $2,000 A YEAR
COMPOUNDING AT VARIOUS RATES OF RETURN
FOR DIFFERENT PERIODS

Annual Rate	5 Yrs	10 Yrs	15 Yrs	20 Yrs	25 Yrs
1%	$10,304	$21,134	$ 32,516	$ 44,478	$ 57,050
2%	10,616	22,337	35,279	49,567	65,342
3%	10,937	23,616	38,314	55,353	75,106
4%	11,266	24,973	41,649	61,938	86,623
5%	11,604	26,414	45,315	69,439	100,227
6%	11,951	27,943	49,345	77,985	116,313
7%	12,307	29,567	53,776	87,730	135,353
8%	12,672	31,291	58,649	98,846	157,909
9%	13,047	33,121	64,007	111,529	184,648
10%	13,431	35,062	69,899	126,005	216,364
11%	13,826	37,123	76,380	142,530	253,998
12%	14,230	39,309	83,507	161,397	298,668
13%	14,645	41,629	91,343	182,940	351,700
14%	15,071	44,089	99,961	207,537	414,665
15%	15,508	46,699	109,435	235,620	489,424
16%	15,955	49,466	119,850	267,681	578,177
17%	16,414	52,400	131,298	304,277	683,525
18%	16,884	55,510	143,878	346,042	808,544
19%	17,366	58,807	157,700	393,695	956,861
20%	17,860	62,301	172,884	448,051	1,132,755

IRA INVESTMENTS OF $2,000 A YEAR
COMPOUNDING AT VARIOUS RATES OF RETURN
FOR DIFFERENT PERIODS

Annual Rate	30 Yrs	35 Yrs	40 Yrs	45 Yrs	50 Yrs
1%	$ 70,265	$ 84,154	$ 98,750	$ 114,092	$ 130,216
2%	82,759	101,989	123,220	146,661	172,542
3%	98,005	124,552	155,327	191,003	232,362
4%	116,657	153,197	197,653	251,741	317,548
5%	139,522	189,673	253,680	335,370	439,631
6%	167,603	236,242	328,095	451,016	615,512
7%	202,146	295,827	427,219	611,504	869,972
8%	244,692	372,204	559,562	834,852	1,239,344
9%	297,150	470,249	736,584	1,146,372	1,776,882
10%	361,887	596,254	973,704	1,581,591	2,560,599
11%	441,826	758,329	1,291,654	2,190,338	3,704,672
12%	540,585	966,926	1,718,285	3,042,435	5,376,041
13%	662,630	1,235,499	2,290,972	4,235,612	7,818,486
14%	813,474	1,581,346	3,059,817	5,906,488	11,387,509
15%	999,914	2,026,691	4,091,908	8,245,795	16,600,747
16%	1,230,323	2,600,054	5,476,957	11,519,435	24,210,705
17%	1,515,008	3,337,989	7,334,781	16,097,540	35,309,434
18%	1,866,637	4,287,298	9,825,183	22,494,522	51,478,901
19%	2,300,775	5,507,829	13,160,993	31,424,150	75,006,500
20%	2,836,516	7,076,019	17,625,259	43,875,144	109,193,258

G.M. LOEB'S "BATTLE PLAN" FOR INVESTMENT SURVIVAL

LIFE IS CHANGE: Nothing can ever be the same a minute from now as it was a minute ago. Everything you own is changing in price and value. You can find that last price of an active security on the stock ticker, but you cannot find the *next* price anywhere. The value of your money is changing. Even the value of your home is changing, though no one walks in front of it with a sandwich board consistently posting the changes.

RECOGNIZE CHANGE: Your basic objective should be to profit from change. The art of investing is being able to recognize change and to adjust investment goals accordingly.

WRITE THINGS DOWN: You will score more investment success and avoid more investment failures if you write things down. Very few investors have the drive and inclination to do this.

KEEP A CHECKLIST: If you aim to improve your investment results, try to get into the habit of keeping a checklist on every issue you consider buying. Before making a commitment, it will pay you to write down the answers to at least some of the basic questions—How much am I investing in this company? How much do I think I can make? How much do I have to risk? How long do I expect to take to reach my goal?

HAVE A SINGLE RULING REASON: Above all, writing things down is the best way to find "the ruling reason." When all is said and done, there is invariably a single reason that stands out above all others why a particular security transaction can be expected to show a profit. All too often many relatively unimportant statistics are allowed to obscure this single important point.

Any one of a dozen factors may be the point of a particular purchase or sale. It could be a technical reason—a coming increase in earnings or dividend not yet discounted in the market price—a change of management—a promising new product—an expected improvement in the market's valuation of earnings—or many others. But, in any given case, one of these factors will almost certainly be more important than all the rest put together.

CLOSING OUT A COMMITMENT: If you have a loss in your stocks, the solution is automatic, provided you decide what to do at the time you buy. Otherwise, the question divides itself into two parts. Are we in a bull or bear market? Few of us really know until it is too late. For the sake of the record, if you think it is a bear market, just put that consideration first and sell as much as your conviction suggests and your nature allows.

If you think it is a bull market, or at least a market where some stocks move up, some mark time and only a few decline, do not sell unless:

✓ You see a bear market ahead.

✓ You see trouble for a particular company in which you own shares.

✓ Time and circumstances have turned up a new and seemingly far better buy than the issue you like least in your list.

✓ Your shares stop going up and start going down.

A subsidiary question is, which stock to sell first? Two further observations may help here:

✓ Do not sell solely because you think a stock is "overvalued."

✓ If you want to sell some of your stocks and not all, in most cases it is better to go against your emotional inclinations and sell first the issues with losses, small profits or none at all, the weakest, the most disappointing, etc.

Mr. Loeb is the author of *The Battle for Investment Survival,* Fraser Publishing, Box 494, Burlington VT 05402.

G.M. LOEB'S INVESTMENT SURVIVAL CHECKLIST

Objectives and Risks

Security		Price	Shares	Date

"Ruling reason" for commitment	Amount of commitment
	$ _____
	% of my investment capital
	_____%

Price objective	Est. time to achieve it	I will risk	Which would be
		_____points	$ _____

Technical Position

Price action of stock:

☐ hitting new highs ☐ in a trading range

☐ pausing in an uptrend ☐ moving up from low ground

☐ acting stronger than market ☐ _____

Dow Jones Industrial Average

Trend of Market

Selected Yardsticks

	Price Range		Earnings Per Share Actual or Projected	Price/Earnings Ratio Actual or Projected
	High	Low		
Current Year				
Previous Year				

Merger Possibilities	Years for earnings to double in past
Comment on Future	Years for market price to double in past

Periodic Re-checks

Date	Stock Price	D.J.I.A.	Comment	Action taken, if any

Completed Transactions

Date Closed	Period of time held	Profit or loss

Reason for profit or loss

153

LARGEST ONE-DAY DOW GAINS AND LOSSES SINCE OCTOBER 1928 BY POINTS AND PERCENT

Top Twenty Gains Since 1928 By Points			
Day	DJIA Close	Points Change	% Change
10/28/97	7498.32	337.17	4.7%
9/2/97	7879.78	257.36	3.4
11/3/97	7674.39	231.59	3.1
2/2/98	8107.78	201.28	2.5
12/1/97	8013.11	189.98	2.4
10/21/87	2027.85	186.84	10.1
4/29/97	6962.03	179.01	2.6
9/16/97	7895.92	174.78	2.3
6/5/98	9037.71	167.15	1.9
4/22/97	6833.59	173.38	2.6
6/17/98	8829.46	164.17	1.9
7/22/97	8061.65	154.93	2.0
6/24/97	7758.06	153.80	2.0
5/5/97	7214.49	143.29	2.0
10/21/97	8060.44	139.00	1.8
6/12/97	7711.47	135.64	1.8
4/15/97	6587.16	135.26	2.1
6/6/97	7435.78	130.49	1.8
12/19/96	6473.64	126.87	2.0
11/17/97	7698.22	125.74	1.7

Top Twenty Losses Since 1928 By Points			
Day	DJIA Close	Points Change	% Change
10/27/97	7161.15	−554.26	− 7.2%
10/19/87	1738.74	−508.00	−22.6
8/15/97	7694.66	−247.37	− 3.1
1/9/98	7580.42	−222.20	− 2.8
6/15/98	8627.93	−207.01	− 2.3
6/23/97	7604.26	−192.25	− 2.5
10/13/89	2569.26	−190.58	− 6.9
10/23/97	7847.77	−186.88	− 2.3
3/8/96	5470.45	−171.24	− 3.0
7/15/96	5349.51	−161.05	− 2.9
3/13/97	6878.89	−160.48	− 2.3
6/11/98	8811.77	−159.93	− 1.8
11/12/97	7401.32	−157.41	− 2.1
3/31/97	6583.48	−157.11	− 2.3
10/26/87	1793.93	−156.83	− 8.0
8/8/97	8031.22	−156.78	− 1.9
5/26/98	8963.73	−150.71	− 1.7
4/11/97	6391.69	−148.36	− 2.3
4/27/98	8917.64	−146.98	− 1.6
1/8/88	1911.31	−140.58	− 6.9

Top Twenty Gains Since 1950 By %			
Day	DJIA Close	Points Change	% Change
10/21/87	2027.85	186.84	10.1%
10/20/87	1841.01	102.27	5.9
5/27/70	663.20	32.04	5.1
10/29/87	1938.33	91.51	5.0
8/17/82	831.24	38.81	4.9
10/9/74	631.02	28.39	4.7
10/28/97	7498.32	337.17	4.7
5/29/62	603.96	27.03	4.7
1/17/91	2623.51	114.60	4.6
11/26/63	743.52	32.03	4.5
11/1/78	827.79	35.34	4.5
11/3/82	1065.49	43.41	4.2
10/23/57	437.13	17.34	4.1
10/6/82	944.26	37.07	4.1
4/22/80	789.85	30.72	4.0
10/29/74	659.34	25.50	4.0
1/4/88	2015.25	76.42	3.9
10/7/74	607.56	23.00	3.9
1/27/75	692.66	26.05	3.9
8/16/71	888.95	32.93	3.8

Top Twenty Losses Since 1950 By %			
Day	DJIA Close	Points Change	% Change
10/19/87	1738.74	−508.00	−22.6%
10/26/87	1793.93	−156.83	− 8.0
10/27/97	7161.15	−554.26	− 7.2
10/13/89	2569.26	−190.58	− 6.9
1/8/88	1911.31	−140.58	− 6.9
9/26/55	455.56	− 31.89	− 6.5
5/28/62	576.93	− 34.95	− 5.7
4/14/88	2005.64	−101.46	− 4.8
6/26/50	213.91	− 10.44	− 4.7
9/11/86	1792.89	− 86.61	− 4.6
10/16/87	2246.74	−108.35	− 4.6
11/30/87	1833.55	− 76.93	− 4.0
11/15/91	2943.20	−120.31	− 3.9
12/3/87	1776.53	− 72.44	− 3.9
10/22/87	1950.43	− 77.42	− 3.8
10/14/87	2412.70	− 95.46	− 3.8
6/29/50	206.72	− 7.96	− 3.7
10/25/82	995.13	− 36.33	− 3.5
11/18/74	624.92	− 22.69	− 3.5
10/6/87	2548.63	− 91.55	− 3.5

Top Ten Gains 1928–1950 By %			
Day	DJIA Close	Points Change	% Change
3/15/33	62.10	8.26	15.3%
10/6/31	99.34	12.86	14.9
10/30/29	258.47	28.40	12.3
6/22/31	145.82	15.51	11.9
9/21/32	75.16	7.67	11.4
8/3/32	58.22	5.06	9.5
9/5/39	148.12	12.87	9.5
2/11/32	78.60	6.80	9.5
11/14/29	217.28	18.59	9.4
12/18/31	80.69	6.90	9.4

Top Ten Losses 1928–1950 By %			
Day	DJIA Close	Points Change	% Change
10/28/29	260.64	−40.58	−13.5%
10/29/29	230.07	−30.57	−11.7
10/5/31	86.48	−10.40	−10.7
11/6/29	232.13	−25.55	− 9.9
8/12/32	63.11	− 5.79	− 8.4
1/4/32	71.59	− 6.31	− 8.1
6/16/30	230.05	−19.64	− 7.9
7/21/33	88.71	− 7.55	− 7.8
10/18/37	125.73	− 9.75	− 7.2
10/5/32	66.07	− 5.09	− 7.2

LARGEST WEEKLY DOW GAINS AND LOSSES SINCE OCTOBER 1928 BY POINTS AND PERCENT

Top Twenty Gains Since 1928 By Points				Top Twenty Losses Since 1928 By Points			
Week Ending	DJIA Close	Points Change	% Change	Week Ending	DJIA Close	Points Change	% Change
6/13/97	7782.04	346.26	4.7%	1/9/98	7580.42	−384.62	− 4.8%
5/2/97	7071.20	332.33	4.9	8/15/97	7694.66	−336.56	− 4.2
12/5/97	8149.13	326.00	4.2	12/12/97	7838.30	−310.83	− 3.8
4/18/97	6703.55	311.86	4.9	10/23/87	1950.76	−295.98	−13.2
11/21/97	7881.07	308.59	4.1	10/31/97	7442.80	−272.61	− 3.5
3/20/98	8906.43	303.91	3.5	8/29/97	7622.42	−265.49	− 3.4
1/2/98	7965.04	285.73	3.7	10/16/87	2246.74	−235.47	− 9.5
2/6/98	8189.49	282.99	3.6	10/13/89	2569.26	−216.26	− 7.8
6/26/98	8944.54	231.67	2.7	4/4/97	6526.07	−214.52	− 3.2
7/25/97	8113.44	222.98	2.8	5/29/98	8899.95	−214.49	− 2.4
7/3/97	7895.81	208.09	2.7	6/12/98	8834.94	−202.77	− 2.2
8/2/96	5679.83	206.77	3.8	10/17/97	7847.03	−198.18	− 2.5
1/30/98	7906.50	205.76	2.7	8/8/97	8031.22	−162.82	− 2.0
9/5/97	7822.41	199.99	2.6	10/9/87	2482.21	−158.78	− 6.0
11/8/96	6219.82	197.89	3.3	4/12/96	5532.59	−150.29	− 2.6
8/22/97	7887.91	193.25	2.5	12/4/87	1766.74	−143.74	− 7.5
4/3/98	8983.41	187.33	2.1	9/12/86	1758.72	−141.03	− 7.4
2/13/98	8370.10	180.61	2.2	6/24/94	3636.94	−139.84	− 3.7
12/20/96	6484.40	179.53	2.8	12/6/96	6381.94	−139.76	− 2.1
9/13/96	5838.52	178.66	3.2	3/31/94	3635.96	−138.77	− 3.7

Top Twenty Gains Since 1950 By %				Top Twenty Losses Since 1950 By %			
Week Ending	DJIA Close	Points Change	% Change	Week Ending	DJIA Close	Points Change	% Change
10/11/74	658.17	73.61	12.6%	10/23/87	1950.76	−295.98	−13.2%
8/20/82	869.29	81.24	10.3	10/16/87	2246.74	−235.47	− 9.5
10/8/82	986.85	79.11	8.7	10/13/89	2569.26	−216.26	− 7.8
8/3/84	1202.08	87.46	7.8	12/4/87	1766.74	−143.74	− 7.5
9/20/74	670.76	43.57	6.9	9/13/74	627.19	− 50.69	− 7.5
6/7/74	853.72	51.55	6.4	9/12/86	1758.72	−141.03	− 7.4
11/2/62	604.58	35.56	6.2	9/27/74	621.95	− 48.81	− 7.3
1/9/76	911.13	52.42	6.1	6/30/50	209.11	− 15.24	− 6.8
11/5/82	1051.78	60.06	6.1	6/22/62	539.19	− 38.99	− 6.7
6/3/88	2071.30	114.86	5.9	12/6/74	577.60	− 41.06	− 6.6
1/18/91	2646.78	145.29	5.8	10/20/78	838.01	− 59.08	− 6.6
12/18/87	1975.30	108.26	5.8	10/12/79	838.99	− 58.62	− 6.5
11/14/80	986.35	53.93	5.8	8/23/74	686.80	− 44.74	− 6.1
5/29/70	700.44	38.27	5.8	10/9/87	2482.21	−158.78	− 6.0
12/27/91	3101.52	167.04	5.7	10/4/74	584.56	− 37.39	− 6.0
12/11/87	1867.04	100.30	5.7	5/25/62	611.88	− 38.82	− 6.0
4/11/75	789.50	42.24	5.7	8/16/74	731.54	− 45.76	− 5.9
1/31/75	703.69	37.08	5.6	5/22/70	662.17	− 40.05	− 5.7
11/29/63	750.52	39.03	5.5	11/2/73	935.28	− 51.78	− 5.2
3/14/86	1792.74	92.91	5.5	3/25/88	1978.95	−108.42	− 5.2

Top Ten Gains 1928–1950 By %				Top Ten Losses 1928–1950 By %			
Week Ending	DJIA Close	Points Change	% Change	Week Ending	DJIA Close	Points Change	% Change
6/26/31	154.04	23.73	18.2%	7/21/33	88.71	−16.33	−15.5
8/5/32	62.60	8.71	16.2	5/17/40	124.20	−20.57	−14.2
6/24/38	129.06	16.00	14.2	11/8/29	236.53	−36.98	−13.5
7/29/32	53.89	6.20	13.0	4/8/32	62.90	− 9.28	−12.9
3/17/33	60.73	6.89	12.8	10/7/32	62.67	− 8.89	−12.4
8/26/32	74.43	7.59	11.4	9/16/32	67.10	− 9.09	−11.9
4/21/33	69.78	7.09	11.3	10/2/31	96.88	−12.98	−11.8
9/8/39	150.04	14.79	10.9	11/19/37	118.13	−14.96	−11.2
11/11/32	68.03	6.50	10.6	6/20/30	221.92	−27.77	−11.1
7/15/32	45.47	4.25	10.3	5/27/32	47.47	− 5.84	−11.0

LARGEST MONTHLY DOW GAINS AND LOSSES SINCE OCTOBER 1928 BY POINTS AND PERCENT

Top Twenty Gains Since 1928 By Points

Month	DJIA Close	Points Change	% Change
Feb 98	8545.72	639.22	8.1%
Jul 97	8222.61	549.82	7.2
Nov 96	6521.70	492.32	8.2
Apr 97	7008.99	425.51	6.5
Nov 97	7823.13	380.33	5.1
Jan 97	6813.09	364.82	5.7
Jun 97	7672.79	341.75	4.7
Sep 97	7945.26	322.84	4.2
May 97	7331.04	322.05	4.6
Nov 95	5074.49	319.01	6.7
Jan 96	5395.30	278.18	5.4
Dec 91	3168.83	274.15	9.5
Sep 96	5882.17	265.96	4.7
Apr 98	9063.37	263.56	3.0
Jan 87	2158.04	262.09	13.8
Mar 98	8799.81	254.09	3.0
Jan 94	3978.36	224.27	6.0
Jul 89	2660.66	220.60	9.0
May 90	2876.66	219.90	8.3
Sep 95	4789.08	178.52	3.9

Top Twenty Losses Since 1928 By Points

Month	DJIA Close	Points Change	% Change
Oct 87	1993.53	−602.75	−23.2%
Aug 97	7622.42	−600.19	− 7.3
Oct 97	7442.80	−502.46	− 6.3
Mar 97	6583.48	−294.26	− 4.3
Aug 90	2614.36	−290.84	−10.0
Mar 94	3635.96	−196.06	− 5.1
Nov 91	2894.68	−174.42	− 5.7
Nov 94	3739.23	−168.89	− 4.3
May 98	8899.95	−163.42	− 1.8
Jan 90	2590.54	−162.66	− 5.9
Sep 90	2452.48	−161.88	− 6.2
Nov 87	1833.55	−159.98	− 8.0
Feb 94	3832.02	−146.34	− 3.7
Aug 92	3257.35	−136.43	− 4.0
Nov 73	822.25	−134.33	−14.0
Jun 94	3624.96	−133.41	− 3.5
Sep 86	1767.58	−130.76	− 6.9
Jul 96	5528.91	−125.72	− 2.2
Jun 91	2906.75	−120.75	− 4.0
Jul 86	1775.31	−117.41	− 6.2

Top Twenty Gains Since 1950 By %

Month	DJIA Close	Points Change	% Change
Jan 76	975.28	122.87	14.4%
Jan 75	703.69	87.45	14.2
Jan 87	2158.04	262.09	13.8
Aug 82	901.31	92.71	11.5
Oct 82	991.72	95.47	10.7
Apr 78	837.32	79.96	10.6
Nov 62	649.30	59.53	10.1
Nov 54	386.77	34.63	9.8
Aug 84	1224.38	109.10	9.8
Oct 74	665.52	57.65	9.5
Dec 91	3168.83	274.15	9.5
Jul 89	2660.66	220.60	9.0
Feb 86	1709.06	138.07	8.8
Apr 68	912.22	71.55	8.5
Apr 83	1226.20	96.17	8.5
May 90	2876.66	219.90	8.3
Jan 67	849.89	64.20	8.2
Nov 96	6521.70	492.32	8.2
Feb 98	8545.72	639.22	8.1
Jan 89	2342.32	173.75	8.0

Top Twenty Losses Since 1950 By %

Month	DJIA Close	Points Change	% Change
Oct 87	1993.53	−602.75	−23.2%
Nov 73	822.25	−134.33	−14.0
Sep 74	607.87	− 70.71	−10.4
Aug 74	678.58	− 78.85	−10.4
Aug 90	2614.36	−290.84	−10.0
Mar 80	785.75	− 77.39	− 9.0
Jun 62	561.28	− 52.08	− 8.5
Oct 78	792.45	− 73.37	− 8.5
Jan 60	622.62	− 56.74	− 8.4
Nov 87	1833.55	−159.98	− 8.0
May 62	613.36	− 51.97	− 7.8
Aug 81	881.47	− 70.87	− 7.4
May 56	478.05	− 38.07	− 7.4
Jan 78	769.92	− 61.25	− 7.4
Sep 60	580.14	− 45.85	− 7.3
Aug 97	7622.42	−600.19	− 7.3
Oct 79	815.70	− 62.88	− 7.2
Nov 74	618.66	− 46.86	− 7.0
Jan 70	744.06	− 56.30	− 7.0
Aug 66	788.41	− 58.97	− 7.0

Top Ten Gains 1928–1950 By %

Month	DJIA Close	Points Change	% Change
Apr 33	77.66	22.26	40.2%
Aug 32	73.16	18.90	34.8
Jul 32	54.26	11.42	26.7
Jun 38	133.88	26.14	24.3
Jun 31	150.18	21.72	16.9
Nov 28	293.38	41.22	16.3
Sep 39	152.54	18.13	13.5
May 33	88.11	10.45	13.5
Feb 31	189.66	22.11	13.2
Aug 33	102.41	11.64	12.8

Top Ten Losses 1928–1950 By %

Month	DJIA Close	Points Change	% Change
Sep 31	96.61	−42.80	−30.7%
Mar 38	98.95	−30.69	−23.7
Apr 32	56.11	−17.17	−23.4
May 40	116.22	−32.21	−21.7
Oct 29	273.51	−69.94	−20.4
May 32	44.74	−11.37	−20.3
Jun 30	226.34	−48.73	−17.7
Dec 31	77.90	−15.97	−17.0
Feb 33	51.39	− 9.51	−15.6
May 31	128.46	−22.73	−15.0

LARGEST YEARLY DOW GAINS AND LOSSES
SINCE 1928 RANKED BY POINTS AND PERCENT

Best Twenty Years Since 1928 By Points

Year	DJIA Close	Points Change	% Change
1997	7908.25	1459.98	22.6%
1996	6448.27	1331.15	26.0
1995	5117.12	1282.68	33.5
1989	2753.20	584.63	27.0
1991	3168.83	535.17	20.3
1993	3754.09	452.98	13.7
1986	1895.95	349.28	22.6
1985	1546.67	335.10	27.7
1975	852.41	236.17	38.3
1988	2168.57	229.74	11.8
1983	1258.64	212.10	20.3
1982	1046.54	171.54	19.6
1976	1004.65	152.24	17.9
1958	583.65	147.96	34.0
1992	3301.11	132.28	4.2
1972	1020.02	129.82	14.6
1980	963.99	125.25	14.9
1954	404.39	123.49	44.0
1967	905.11	119.42	15.2
1961	731.14	115.25	18.7

Worst Twenty Years Since 1928 By Points

Year	DJIA Close	Points Change	% Change
1974	616.24	−234.62	−27.6%
1966	785.69	−183.57	−18.9
1977	831.17	−173.48	−17.3
1973	850.86	−169.16	−16.6
1969	800.36	−143.39	−15.2
1990	2633.66	−119.54	− 4.3
1981	875.00	− 88.99	− 9.2
1962	652.10	− 79.04	−10.8
1957	435.69	− 63.78	−12.8
1960	615.89	− 63.47	− 9.3
1984	1211.57	− 47.07	− 3.7
1978	805.01	− 26.16	− 3.1
1953	280.90	− 11.00	− 3.8
1956	499.47	11.07	2.3
1952	291.90	22.67	8.4
1979	838.74	33.73	4.2
1951	269.23	33.82	14.4
1950	235.41	35.28	17.6
1970	838.92	38.56	4.8
1968	943.75	38.64	4.3

Best Twenty Years Since 1950 By %

Year	DJIA Close	Points Change	% Change
1954	404.39	123.49	44.0%
1975	852.41	236.17	38.3
1958	583.65	147.96	34.0
1995	5117.12	1282.68	33.5
1985	1546.67	335.10	27.7
1989	2753.20	584.63	27.0
1996	6448.27	1331.15	26.0
1997	7908.25	1459.98	22.6
1986	1895.95	349.28	22.6
1955	488.40	84.01	20.8
1991	3168.83	535.17	20.3
1983	1258.64	212.10	20.3
1982	1046.54	171.54	19.6
1961	731.14	115.25	18.7
1976	1004.65	152.24	17.9
1950	235.41	35.28	17.6
1963	762.95	110.85	17.0
1959	679.36	95.71	16.4
1967	905.11	119.42	15.2
1980	963.99	125.25	14.9

Worst Twenty Years Since 1950 By %

Year	DJIA Close	Points Change	% Change
1974	616.24	−234.62	−27.6%
1966	785.69	−183.57	−18.9
1977	831.17	−173.48	−17.3
1973	850.86	−169.16	−16.6
1969	800.36	−143.39	−15.2
1957	435.69	− 63.78	−12.8
1962	652.10	− 79.04	−10.8
1960	615.89	− 63.47	− 9.3
1981	875.00	− 88.99	− 9.2
1990	2633.66	−119.54	− 4.3
1953	280.90	− 11.00	− 3.8
1984	1211.57	− 47.07	− 3.7
1978	805.01	− 26.16	− 3.1
1994	3834.44	80.35	2.1
1987	1938.83	42.88	2.3
1956	499.47	11.07	2.3
1992	3301.11	132.28	4.2
1979	838.74	33.73	4.2
1968	943.75	38.64	4.3
1970	838.92	38.56	4.8

Best Ten Years 1928–1950 By %

Year	DJIA Close	Points Change	% Change
1933	99.90	39.97	66.7%
1928	300.00	97.60	48.2
1935	144.13	40.09	38.5
1938	154.76	33.91	28.1
1945	192.91	40.59	26.6
1936	179.90	35.77	24.8
1943	135.89	16.49	13.8
1949	200.13	22.83	12.9
1944	152.32	16.43	12.1
1942	119.40	8.44	7.6

Worst Ten Years 1928–1950 By %

Year	DJIA Close	Points Change	% Change
1931	77.90	−86.68	−52.7%
1930	164.58	−83.90	−33.8
1937	120.85	−59.05	−32.8
1932	59.93	−17.97	−23.1
1929	248.48	−51.52	−17.2
1941	110.96	−20.17	−15.4
1940	131.13	−19.11	−12.7
1946	177.20	−15.71	− 8.1
1939	150.24	− 4.52	− 2.9
1948	177.30	− 3.86	− 2.1

WEB-VESTING—GET FREE QUOTES, COMPANY DATA, RESEARCH, AND MORE THROUGH THE INTERNET

Your computer can be used to perform sophisticated financial analysis or simply to retrieve stock quotes and basic company information. (We suggest signing up with one of the services that provides unlimited Internet access.) There are millions of pages of information available on the Internet. We've selected some of the most useful sites for investors. But remember that the World Wide Web is in its infancy and new sites are being added every day. Many web sites will link you to other sites with related information at the touch of a mouse. Here are some of the best sites for a variety of market information.

Wall Street City   www.wallstreetcity.com
Complete one-stop source for research and state-of-the-art analytical tools on the Internet. Provides everything you need to make profitable investment decisions. Quotes, charts and company snapshots are available on all domestic and foreign stocks—plus, options, futures and mutual funds. Screen stocks as the professionals do using the Prosearch database of all listed stocks, choose from any of the 700 criteria relevant to your search. Backtest any combination of criteria to see what has worked in the past, or else, let *wallstreetcity.com* tell you what's working now. Provides over 50 of the most popular screens for stocks designed by the experts at Telescan. Maintain one portfolio of up to 150 stocks for free, or subscribe and maintain up to seven portfolios.

Quote.com   www.quote.com
One of the premiere sources for financial market information on the Internet. Innovative new technology lets *Quote.com* users receive free financial market information, quotes, news, and charts—just like Wall Street professionals. See all the stocks in an industry at a glance with last price, change and volume. *Quote.com* offers many free services, like mutual fund screening. Subscription services are available on a 30-day free-trial basis.

Hoover's Online   www.hoovers.com
Profiles from a database of over 3,200 companies. $9.95 per month but some data free. Other useful Web links, plus a 12,600 company directory. Free stock screening.

Zacks Analyst Watch   www.zacks.com
Free company reports, earnings surprises, market analysis. For a fee, the famous earnings estimate service, email alerts on earnings surprises, access to 2,200 brokerage analysts.

Yahoo Finance   quote.yahoo.com
The popular search site also has quotes, short and long term charts and news for each company at a single stroke. Set up multiple portfolios with ease for free.

Briefing.com   www.briefing.com
Quotes, charts, news, and your own portfolio of 25 stocks. Lots more on 8,300 companies for $6.95 a month.

Big Charts   www.bigcharts.com
Free charts, quotes, reports, indicators on over 50,000 stocks, funds and indexes.

Market Guide   www.marketguide.com
Company snapshots, quotes, charts, news, projections and more on 10,000 companies in any sector or industry. Stock screening too, all free.

Microsoft Investor   www.investor.com
Getting into the Internet act with many free interesting features. Just $9.95 a month for additional services such as screening 16,000 stocks.

Stocksmart   www.stocksmart.com
Quotes, charts on 30,000 stocks, bonds, and funds US and worldwide. Comprehenisive additional services for a fee.

Morningstar   www.morningstar.net
Has a free simple stock screening site of 8,000 stocks. A much more advanced screener for $9.95 a month.

Market Technicians Association   www.mta-usa.org
Everything you ever wanted to know about technical analysis, technical indicators and software is provided by this non-profit organization. Links to over 150 sites with access to

portfolio and stock Internet resources and on-line trading and market discussion groups. See graphs on all commodities, connect to top analysts such as John Murphy, Ralph Acompora, John Bollinger, and others.

Goldsheet   www.goldsheet.simplenet.com
Goldbugs will be delighted to find spreadsheets on 250 mining companies including symbol, exchange, proven and probable reserves. Has links to 6,000 mining-related sites which include 875 mining company home pages and 70 gold newsletters.

Westergaard Online   www.westergaard.com
Research and commentary on small companies.

Securities and Exchange Commission   www.sec.gov
The EDGAR data base makes available every corporate document filed with the SEC.

EDGAR Online   www.edgar-online.com
Gives you, for a modest fee, what the SEC offers for free. But their searching software is easier to use, they manage to get new filings on line quicker than the government, and they have a notification service that will send you an e-mail message any time a company on your "WatchList" list makes a filing.

CoveredCall.com   www.coveredcall.com
Various attractive option strategies for option writers. Free trial. See article on page 82.

Federal Reserve Bank St. Louis   www.stls.frb.org
Access to the FRED database which can also be downloaded. Get the Consumers Price Index monthly figures since 1946 or all the Discount Rate changes since 1934 and 30 other interest rate categories. Help yourself to similar data on employment, gross domestic product, population, exchange rates, plus most monetary and business indicators. Direct links are provided to all Federal Reserve branch banks and most US Government sites.

Global Financial Data   www.globalfindata.com
The most extensive, long-term data (back many centuries) on stock market indexes (especially foreign markets), interest rates, inflation available anywhere. Some of it is free.

Dorsey, Wright & Associates   www.dorseywright.com
A site for professionals and point & figure aficionados. Tom Dorsey is the author of last year's Best Investment Book. Several thousand brokers case this site to find breakouts, shakeouts, double tops and bottoms, catapults, reversals and other patterns being formed by stocks. You can see the NYSE bullish percent chart and sector bullish percent charts. Monthly fees are charged but there's a two-week free trial.

Horsesmouth   www.horsesmouth.com
Brokers only. Commentaries and analysis by the foremost independent financial experts.

Pinnacle Data Corp.   www.pinnacledata.com
Order any financial, stock market, commodity, economic or monetary database here.

Technical Tools   www.techtool.com
Order data on all indexes, futures, mutual funds, cash prices, foreign exchanges, individual contract history. Graphing capability and conversion into Metastock and Super Charts.

Upside   www.upside.com
A site for technology and Internet buffs. Charts Bill Gates' daily worth.

Ziff-Davis   www.zdnet.com
Information on high-tech Internet companies.

Wall Street Research Net   www.wsrn.com
Over 250,000 links and stock screening.

Investor Guide   www.investorguide.com
Free comprehensive site, many links.

Silicon Investor   www.techstocks.com
All about tech stocks. The largest discussion community on the web.

CNN*fn* The Financial Network   www.cnnfn.com
Many of the major news organizations are now on line. This site has current market and other developments, "hot stories," opinion and more.

Wall Street Journal   interactive.wsj.com
Value Line   www.valueline.com
Finance Wise   www.financewise.com
Excellent search site for financial research.

THE IDEAL BUSINESS

1) Sells the world, rather than a single neighborhood or even a single city or state. In other words, it has an unlimited global market (and today this is more important than ever, since world markets have now opened up to an extent unparalleled in my lifetime). By the way, how many times have you seen a retail store that has been doing well for years, then another bigger and better store moves nearby, and it's kaput for the first store.

2) Offers a product which enjoys an **"inelastic" demand**. Inelastic refers to a product that people need or desire—almost regardless of price.

3) Markets a product which **cannot be easily copied**. This means that the product is an original or at least it's something that can be copyrighted or patented.

4) Has **minimal labor** requirements (the fewer personnel, the better). Today's example of this is the much talked about "virtual corporation." The virtual corporation may consist of an office with three executives, where literally all manufacturing and services are farmed out to other companies.

5) Operates on **low overhead**. It does not need an expensive location; it does not need large amounts of electricity, advertising, legal advice, high-priced employees, large inventory, etc.

6) Does not require big cash outlays or major investments in equipment. In other words, it does not tie up your capital (incidentally, one of the major reasons for new-business failure is under-capitalization).

7) Enjoys cash billings. In other words, it does not tie up your capital with lengthy or complex credit terms.

8) Is **relatively free of all kinds of government regulations** and strictures (and if you're now in your own business, you most definitely know what I mean with this one).

9) Is **portable or easily moveable**. This means that you can take your business (and yourself) anywhere you want—Nevada, Florida, Texas, Washington, South Dakota (none have state income taxes) or hey, maybe even Monte Carlo or Switzerland or the south of France.

10) Satisfies your intellectual needs. There's nothing like being fascinated with what you're doing. When that happens, you're not working, you're having fun.

11) Leaves you with **free time**. In other words, it doesn't require your labor and attention 12, 16 or 18 hours a day (my lawyer wife, who leaves the house at 6:30 AM and comes home at 6:30 PM and often later, has been well aware of this one).

12) Is one in which your **income is not limited by your personal output** (lawyers and doctors have this problem). No, in the ideal business you can sell 10,000 customers as easily as you sell one (publishing is an example).

That's it. If you use this list it may help you cut through a lot of nonsense and hypocrisy and wishes and dreams regarding what you are looking for in life and in your work.

The above was written by Richard Russell, publisher of Dow Theory Letters, PO Box 1759, La Jolla CA 92038. Incidentally, many points listed above should be taken into consideration when you are looking for great stock investments.

STRATEGY PLANNING & RECORD SECTION

CONTENTS

PORTFOLIO AT START OF 1999

DATE ACQUIRED	NO. OF SHARES	SECURITY	PRICE	TOTAL COST	PAPER PROFITS	PAPER LOSSES

PORTFOLIO AT START OF 1999

DATE ACQUIRED	NO. OF SHARES	SECURITY	PRICE	TOTAL COST	PAPER PROFITS	PAPER LOSSES

ADDITIONAL PURCHASES

DATE ACQUIRED	NO. OF SHARES	SECURITY	PRICE	TOTAL COST	REASON FOR PURCHASE PRICE OBJECTIVE, ETC.

ADDITIONAL PURCHASES

DATE ACQUIRED	NO. OF SHARES	SECURITY	PRICE	TOTAL COST	REASON FOR PURCHASE PRICE OBJECTIVE, ETC.

ADDITIONAL PURCHASES

DATE ACQUIRED	NO. OF SHARES	SECURITY	PRICE	TOTAL COST	REASON FOR PURCHASE PRICE OBJECTIVE, ETC.

SHORT-TERM TRANSACTIONS

Pages 169-176 can accompany next year's income tax return (Schedule D). Enter transactions as completed to avoid last minute pressures

NO. OF SHARES	SECURITY	DATE ACQUIRED	DATE SOLD	SALES PRICE	COST	LOSS	GAIN

TOTALS: Carry over to next page

169

SHORT-TERM TRANSACTIONS (continued)

NO. OF SHARES	SECURITY	DATE ACQUIRED	DATE SOLD	SALES PRICE	COST	LOSS	GAIN

TOTALS:
Carry over to next page

SHORT-TERM TRANSACTIONS (continued)

NO. OF SHARES	SECURITY	DATE ACQUIRED	DATE SOLD	SALES PRICE	COST	LOSS	GAIN

TOTALS:
Carry over to next page

SHORT-TERM TRANSACTIONS (continued)

NO. OF SHARES	SECURITY	DATE ACQUIRED	DATE SOLD	SALES PRICE	COST	LOSS	GAIN

TOTALS:
Carry over to next page

172

LONG-TERM TRANSACTIONS

Pages 169-176 can accompany next year's income tax return (Schedule D). Enter transactions as completed to avoid last minute pressures

NO. OF SHARES	SECURITY	DATE ACQUIRED	DATE SOLD	SALES PRICE	COST	LOSS	GAIN

TOTALS: Carry over to next page

173

LONG-TERM TRANSACTIONS (continued)

NO. OF SHARES	SECURITY	DATE ACQUIRED	DATE SOLD	SALES PRICE	COST	LOSS	GAIN

TOTALS:

LONG-TERM TRANSACTIONS (continued)

NO. OF SHARES	SECURITY	DATE ACQUIRED	DATE SOLD	SALES PRICE	COST	LOSS	GAIN

TOTALS:
Carry over to next page

LONG-TERM TRANSACTIONS (continued)

NO. OF SHARES	SECURITY	DATE ACQUIRED	DATE SOLD	SALES PRICE	COST	LOSS	GAIN

TOTALS:

176

BROKERAGE ACCOUNT DATA 1999

	MARGIN INTEREST	TRANSFER TAXES	CAPITAL ADDED	CAPITAL WITHDRAWN
JAN				
FEB				
MAR				
APR				
MAY				
JUN				
JUL				
AUG				
SEP				
OCT				
NOV				
DEC				

INTEREST/DIVIDENDS RECEIVED DURING 1999

AMOUNT	STOCK/BOND	FIRST QUARTER	SECOND QUARTER	THIRD QUARTER	FOURTH QUARTER
		$	$	$	$

INTEREST/DIVIDENDS RECEIVED DURING 1999

AMOUNT	STOCK/BOND	FIRST QUARTER	SECOND QUARTER	THIRD QUARTER	FOURTH QUARTER
		$	$	$	$

PORTFOLIO AT END OF 1999

DATE ACQUIRED	NO. OF SHARES	SECURITY	PRICE	TOTAL COST	PAPER PROFITS	PAPER LOSSES

PORTFOLIO AT END OF 1999

DATE ACQUIRED	NO. OF SHARES	SECURITY	PRICE	TOTAL COST	PAPER PROFITS	PAPER LOSSES

PORTFOLIO PRICE RECORD 1999 (First Half)

Place original purchase price above stock name

Week Ending	1	2	3	4	5	6	7	8	Dow Jones Industrial Average	Net Change For Week
JANUARY 8										
15										
22										
29										
FEBRUARY 5										
12										
19										
26										
MARCH 5										
12										
19										
26										
APRIL 2										
9										
16										
23										
30										
MAY 7										
14										
21										
28										
JUNE 4										
11										
18										
25										

Enter weekly closing prices for stocks in your portfolio

STOCKS / Week Ending	9	10	11	12	13	14	15	16	17	18
JANUARY 8										
15										
22										
29										
FEBRUARY 5										
12										
19										
26										
MARCH 5										
12										
19										
26										
APRIL 2										
9										
16										
23										
30										
MAY 7										
14										
21										
28										
JUNE 4										
11										
18										
25										

PORTFOLIO PRICE RECORD 1999 (Second Half)

Place original purchase price above stock name

STOCKS / Week Ending	1	2	3	4	5	6	7	8	Dow Jones Industrial Average	Net Change For Week
JULY										
2										
9										
16										
23										
30										
AUGUST										
6										
13										
20										
27										
SEPTEMBER										
3										
10										
17										
24										
OCTOBER										
1										
8										
15										
22										
29										
NOVEMBER										
5										
12										
19										
26										
DECEMBER										
3										
10										
17										
24										
31										

Enter weekly closing prices for stocks in your portfolio

STOCKS / Week Ending	9	10	11	12	13	14	15	16	17	18
JULY										
2										
9										
16										
23										
30										
AUGUST										
6										
13										
20										
27										
SEPTEMBER										
3										
10										
17										
24										
OCTOBER										
1										
8										
15										
22										
29										
NOVEMBER										
5										
12										
19										
26										
DECEMBER										
3										
10										
17										
24										
31										

WEEKLY INDICATOR DATA 1999 (First Half)

Week Ending	Dow Jones Industrial Average	Net Change For Week	Net Change On Friday	Net Change Next Monday	S & P Or NYSE Comp.	NYSE Advances	NYSE Declines	New Highs	New Lows		90-Day Treas. Rate	30-Year AAA Rate
JANUARY 8												
15												
22												
29												
FEBRUARY 5												
12												
19												
26												
MARCH 5												
12												
19												
26												
APRIL 2												
9												
16												
23												
30												
MAY 7												
14												
21												
28												
JUNE 4												
11												
18												
25												

See instructions on page 188

WEEKLY INDICATOR DATA 1999 (Second Half)

Week Ending	Dow Jones Industrial Average	Net Change For Week	Net Change On Friday	Net Change Next Monday	S & P Or NYSE Comp.	NYSE Ad- vances	NYSE De- clines	New Highs	New Lows		90- Day Treas. Rate	30- Year AAA Rate
JULY												
2												
9												
16												
23												
30												
AUGUST												
6												
13												
20												
27												
SEPTEMBER												
3												
10												
17												
24												
OCTOBER												
1												
8												
15												
22												
29												
NOVEMBER												
5												
12												
19												
26												
DECEMBER												
3												
10												
17												
24												
31												

See instructions on page 188

MONTHLY INDICATOR DATA 1999

MONTH	DJIA 4th from Last Day Prev. Mo.	DJIA 2nd Trading Day	Point Change These 6 Days	Point Change Rest Of Mo.	% Change Whole Period	% Change Your Stocks	Prime Rate	Trade Deficit $ Bil.	CPI % Change	% Unemployment Rate
JAN										
FEB										
MAR										
APR										
MAY										
JUN										
JUL										
AUG										
SEP										
OCT										
NOV										
DEC										

INSTRUCTIONS:

Weekly Indicator Data (page 186-187). Keeping data on several indicators may give you a better feel of the market. In addition to the closing DJIA and its net change for the week, post the net change for Friday's Dow and also the following Monday's. Watching their performance vis-à-vis each other is fascinating (see pages 56, 132 and 133). Tracking either of the S&P or NYSE composites, and advances and declines, will help prevent the Dow from misleading you. New highs and lows are also useful indicators. All these weekly figures appear in weekend papers or *Barron's*. Data for 90-day Treasury Rate and 30-year AAA Bond Rate are quite important to track short- and long-term interest rates. These figures are available from:

Weekly U.S. Financial Data
Federal Reserve Bank of St. Louis
P.O. Box 442
St. Louis, MO 63166
http://www.stls.frb.org

Monthly Indicator Data. The purpose of the first four columns is to enable you to track (and possibly take advantage of) the market's bullish bias near the end of the month (see page 134). Prime Rate, Trade Deficit, Consumers Price Index, and Unemployment Rate are worthwhile indicators to follow. Or, readers may wish to use those columns for other data.

IF YOU DON'T PROFIT FROM YOUR INVESTMENT MISTAKES—SOMEONE ELSE WILL

No matter how much we may deny it, almost every successful person in Wall Street pays a great deal of attention to trading suggestions—especially when they come from "the right sources."

One of the hardest things to learn is to distinguish between good tips and bad ones. Usually the best tips have a logical reason in back of them, which accompanies the tip. Poor tips usually have no reason to support them.

The important thing to remember is that the market discounts. It does not review, it does not reflect. The Street's real interest in "tips," inside information, buying and selling suggestions, and everything else of this kind, emanates from a desire to find out just what the market has on hand to discount. The process of finding out involves separating the wheat from the chaff—and there is plenty of chaff.

How to Make Use of Stock "Tips"

1 The source should be **reliable**. (By listing all "tips" and suggestions on a Performance Record of Recommendations, such as below, and then periodically evaluating the outcomes, you will soon know the "batting average" of your sources.)

2 The story should make sense. Would the merger violate anti-trust laws? Are there too many computers on the market already? How many years will it take to become profitable?

3 The stock should not have had a recent sharp run-up. Otherwise, the story may already be discounted and confirmation or denial in the press would most likely be accompanied by a sell-off in the stock.

PERFORMANCE RECORD OF RECOMMENDATIONS

STOCK RECOMMENDED	BY WHOM	DATE	PRICE	REASON FOR RECOMMENDATION	SUBSEQUENT ACTION OF STOCK

(continued on next page)

PERFORMANCE RECORD OF RECOMMENDATIONS

STOCK RECOMMENDED	BY WHOM	DATE	PRICE	REASON FOR RECOMMENDATION	SUBSEQUENT ACTION OF STOCK

FINANCIAL DIRECTORY

Broker, Lawyer, Accountant, Banker etc.

NAME AND ADDRESS	AREA CODE	NUMBER

(over)

FINANCIAL DIRECTORY

Broker, Lawyer, Accountant, Banker etc.

NAME AND ADDRESS	AREA CODE	NUMBER